What People Are Saying About James Tan and *Seeing the Spirit*...

In his book *Seeing the Spirit*, author James Tan gives us a view from a great height as he lays out what the Word of God says about the multifaceted workings of the Holy Spirit among men. James carries a depth of spiritual insight that gleans the gold from Scripture when he teaches, and that gift shines through in this book in a way that's wonderful to behold. In a sense, James serves as a guide, ushering the reader through every book of the Bible, staying just long enough in each book to weave a new truth into a revelatory tapestry that I call "God's mighty Spirit at work on the earth"! Well done, James!

—*Roberts Liardon*
Author, God's Generals Series

Rev. James Tan's book *Seeing the Spirit* is an insightful, power-packed volume that helps us see the realities of the Holy Spirit in every book of the Bible, and what they mean to us today. This is a must-read for those who are hungry to see all that God has for them. Expect your life to change as you embrace the truth within these pages.

—*Rev. Marvin Yoder*
Professor, Bible teacher, and author
Marvin Yoder Ministries, Broken Arrow, OK
Dean (2006–2008), Rhema Bible Training College, Broken Arrow

As the world stands on the precipice of a new level of uncertainty, and the body of Christ at the entrance of the next great move of God, this book comes right on time with revelation necessary to navigate what lies ahead. Through deep research and study commingled with stories of encounters from his own life, Dr. James Tan's latest book invites you into a new understanding of the dual working of the Word of God and the power of the Holy Spirit. The truths within these pages will ignite a fire within you and position you powerfully for what lies ahead.

—*Rev. Jen Tringale*
Author and speaker

It was my privilege to work directly with Oral Roberts while I was the chaplain of Oral Roberts University. During that time, I heard him preach a message called "The Fourth Man," in which he showed Jesus in every book of the Bible. In *Seeing the Spirit*, my newfound friend Dr. James Tan has done the same thing with the Holy Spirit: he shows you the Holy Spirit in every book of the Bible. Somehow, in our day, we have lost sight of the revelation of the Holy Spirit. Even in the Spirit-filled movement, we rarely hear the essential message of the baptism with the Holy Spirit and of our partnership with the third person of the Trinity. James Tan has given us a poignant and revealing look at the person and power of the Holy Spirit. Your life will be blessed and equipped with new power and meaning as you read this monumental work.

—*Ron McIntosh*
President, Ron McIntosh Ministries
Chaplain (1985–1992), Oral Roberts University, Tulsa, OK
Executive Director (2004–2021), Victory Bible College, Tulsa
Author, *The Quest for Revival, The Missing Ingredient, The Greatest Secret,* and other books

Today, many people are in great need of the healing and transforming power of the Holy Spirit in their body, soul, and spirit, and in all aspects of their everyday life. In *Seeing the Spirit*, James Tan opens our eyes to the multifaceted ways in which the Spirit worked in the lives of biblical figures from Genesis to Revelation. In doing so, he reveals what the Spirit wants to do for us as individual believers and as the body of Christ amid the challenges of our day. This book will build your faith in the ever-present and all-powerful Holy Spirit and deepen your personal relationship with Him as One who will never leave you or forsake you.

—*Joan Hunter*
Author and evangelist
Host, *Miracles Happen* TV program

James Tan's *Seeing the Spirit: Revealing the Holy Spirit in Every Book of the Bible* gives a fresh perspective of how transcendent the Word of God really is! James masterfully shows us how the Word and the Spirit work together to ignite our hearts and lead us into God's abundance—spiritually, physically, and economically. With every page, you'll discover how a deep knowledge of Scripture, paired with a vibrant relationship with the Holy Spirit, brings guidance, wisdom, and power for daily living. Prepare for a journey through the Bible where the Holy Spirit's presence leaps off the page and transforms your life. This book isn't just a study—it's an invitation to experience God's fullness and live out His purposes with fresh passion and power.

—*Jason Avanzini*
Jason Avanzini Ministries

As someone who has taught a lot about the person and work of the Holy Spirit over the years, I am always interested in resources dealing with that subject. In *Seeing the Spirit: Revealing the Holy Spirit in Every Book of the Bible,* Dr. James Tan goes beyond the usual obvious references to the Holy Spirit in the Old Testament, pulling back the veil to see His hand at work throughout the Scriptures—connecting the dots of familiar stories in the Bible to show the involvement of the Spirit of God in each situation. Dr. Tan continues through the pages of the New Testament. Throughout his book, he shows us how these truths apply to our lives as we walk with the Lord on our journeys. *Seeing the Spirit* is a good read for those who want to grow in their relationship with the Holy Spirit.

—*Dr. Kirk A. DuBois*
Harvest International Ministries
Professor, Rhema Bible Training College, Broken Arrow, OK

Dr. James Tan's *Seeing the Spirit: Revealing the Holy Spirit in Every Book of the Bible* offers a rich and important journey through Scripture, showcasing the person and work of the Holy Spirit in each book of the Bible. At a time when many believers may compartmentalize the Spirit's ministry as a New Testament phenomenon, Dr. Tan reminds us that the work of the Spirit is woven into the fabric of the entire canon. Using personal experience and profound scriptural reflection, he presents a balanced theology essential to Christian maturity. This work is more than a theological survey: it is an invitation to cultivate intimacy with the Spirit, who illuminates Scripture (see John 14:26) and empowers every believer for life and ministry (see Acts 1:8). With pastoral insight and scholarly clarity, Dr. Tan demonstrates how the Spirit inspires, convicts, leads, and transforms—from Genesis's brooding Creator to Revelation's eschatological Revealer. His repeated emphasis on the interplay between the Word and the Spirit calls the church to a holistic discipleship that avoids the extremes of sterile intellectualism and unscriptural spiritual experiences. Accessible yet profound, *Seeing the Spirit* is an invaluable resource for pastors, teachers, and Spirit-filled believers who long to walk in step with the Spirit and accurately divide the Word of Truth. I wholeheartedly commend this work as foundational for anyone who seeks to understand and live by the Spirit's power from Genesis to Revelation.

—Matt Hattabaugh
Pastor, GoChurch, Beirut, Lebanon
National Director, RHEMA Bible Training College, Beirut

Seeing the Spirit by Dr. James Tan combines both revelation and biblical teaching concerning the workings of the Holy Spirit in the life of a believer. These workings will touch something deep within every believer who desires transformation and change. Once you begin to engage the truths in this book, you will be inspired and strengthened as you journey through its pages. As James writes, "Both the Word and the Spirit are required to grasp what God is doing and saying," and "The Word and the Spirit can set the altar of our heart on fire from heaven and keep the fire of God lit in us." Increase your spirit-knowledge of the nature and work of the Holy Spirit through each of the 66 biblical reflections in this book—and gain new insights into the extraordinary ways He desires to work in your life and in the lives of those around you. It's been said that God cannot always be explained, but He can be experienced. Prepare to encounter the living God as you begin *Seeing the Spirit* in new and life-changing ways.

—*Apostle Les Bowling*
Founder and Senior Pastor, Eagle Rock Church, Pickerington, OH
Founder, Eagle Rock Covenant Network

The great faithfulness and love of God toward us is demonstrated by His gift of the Holy Spirit—an incalculable blessing at all times, and especially when we are going through difficulties. He has the answers to our every need. How well do you know this priceless Gift? In *Seeing the Spirit* by Dr. James Tan, you will take a fascinating and spirit-strengthening journey through each book of the Bible, discovering potent truths about who Holy Spirit is and how He desires to work in our lives to bring hope, empowerment, and victory. Let James introduce you anew to the Spirit through the Word, and enter into the fullness of God's purposes for your life.

—*Karen Jensen Salisbury*
Author and speaker
Host, *Elevate the Day* podcast

In *Seeing the Spirit,* Dr. James Tan uncovers what many people miss: the Holy Spirit's presence and power woven through every book of the Bible. This isn't just a study—it's a divine unveiling. Each page invites you into deeper intimacy with the Spirit, revealing His movement, voice, and purpose in places you've likely overlooked. It's bold, prophetic, and profoundly needed for today's church. A dear friend and a man I deeply respect, Dr. Tan writes with authority and humility. I trust his voice on this subject, and this book will open your eyes, stir your spirit, and reawaken your walk with God.

—*Mondo De La Vega*
Host, *The Mondo Show*
Author, *My Crazy Life: The Moments That Brought a Gangster to Grace*

Seeing the SPIRIT

Revealing the Holy Spirit in Every Book of the Bible

JAMES TAN

WHITAKER
HOUSE

Boldface type in the Scripture quotations indicates the author's emphasis.

SEEING THE SPIRIT:
Revealing the Holy Spirit in Every Book of the Bible

ISBN: 979-8-88769-376-7
eBook ISBN: 979-8-88769-377-4
Printed in the United States of America

Whitaker House
1030 Hunt Valley Circle
New Kensington, PA 15068
www.whitakerhouse.com

Library of Congress Cataloging-in-Publication Data has been applied for.

1 2 3 4 5 6 7 8 9 10 11 32 31 30 29 28 27 26 25

For Bon and Boots

And Kenei

CONTENTS

NEW TESTAMENT

PART ONE: THE HOLY SPIRIT IN THE GOSPELS AND ACTS

PART TWO: THE HOLY SPIRIT IN THE PAULINE EPISTLES

PREFACE

In the same measure that I seek to love and appreciate my Bible, I seek to love and appreciate the Holy Spirit! Jesus specifically said that the ministry of the Holy Spirit is a necessity in the life of a believer. (See John 16:7.) It is the Spirit who illuminates the Word of God for us. (See John 14:26.) The Word and the Spirit are forever intertwined in the plans of God for our lives. We need the Word because it is *"a lamp to* [our] *feet and a light to* [our] *path"* (Psalm 119:105), and we need the Holy Spirit to open up the Word to us. God would not entrust His Word to be comprehended by our mental faculties alone. The things of God must be spiritually discerned. (See 1 Corinthians 2:14.)

We live in a season when there is much talk and expectation in the church about the Holy Spirit. Many people in the body of Christ accept the idea that signs and wonders and the empowerment of the believer through the nine manifestations of the Spirit (see 1 Corinthians 12:4–11) are available to us today. Yet, like the Bereans before us (see Acts 17:10–11), we need to allow the Word to define for us both the person and the ministry of the Spirit. Just as God does not trust our intellect alone to understand His

Word, He does not trust our experiences alone to enable us to comprehend the ministry of His Spirit. God intends that His own Spirit will illuminate His Word to us and that His Word will define His Spirit for us.

The Word and the Spirit are the two legs upon which God purposes a believer to stand—and the enemy would not mind if we chose either one. Too many believers are attempting to hop through life on one leg! As the old adage goes, "If we have the Word only, we will dry up. If we have the Spirit only, we will blow up. If we have the Word and the Spirit, we will grow up!"

Although the Holy Spirit is unseen in physical form, His tangible influence, character, and personhood may be seen throughout the Scriptures. And, as we will discover in our study together, He may actually be found in every book of the Bible. The Holy Spirit is the Author of the Book, the Instigator of the plot, the Facilitator of the characters, and the Divine Empowerment for every miraculous act recorded. As the One who inspired the Word, the Holy Spirit is the only One who is uniquely qualified to open the Word to us. Since the Spirit is so vital in this way, it should be no surprise that He is woven into the very fabric of the Word.

Another reason we need the Spirit to illuminate the Word for us is that the Word is alive (see Hebrews 4:12) and therefore can speak to our specific needs at different stages of our lives and maturity *from the same verses and passages*. There will never be a time when we *completely* comprehend *all* of God's Word and wisdom. Yet His Word is as magnificent in the way it unfolds to us as God is as He progressively reveals Himself to us! It is the Spirit who spoons out the amount of knowledge and understanding of God that we require and are able to receive at a given time as we grow.

We need a working, scriptural grasp of the Spirit for another reason as well: so that the flames of revival and awakening that have been ignited today can continue to burn strong in the generation yet to come. It is my sincere prayer that this book will add to that fire!

One of the things the Lord has tasked me to do in ministry is to teach about the Holy Spirit by both the precept of the Word and the example of the Spirit's demonstrations of the miraculous today. I have seen many supernatural acts of the Spirit in services that I have led, as well as in services where others have ministered—from physical healings and deliverances to prophetic utterances that opened the hearts of those attending the services. Yet I have also been in ministry long enough to have personally seen that exposing people to the ministry of the Spirit without establishing them in the Word can soon lead to their embracing a form of mystical fanaticism.

I believe this is part of the reason why the Spirit led me to make my thoughts and notes, developed from my personal reading, study, and meditations on the Holy Spirit, available in this single volume. My research and study have brought me through a journey that has illuminated the Spirit's activity in the lives of the men and women we read about in the Bible. The chapters of this book vary in length depending on the length of the corresponding book of the Bible and the type of manifestations of the Spirit expressed in it. There will also be a natural overlap of some themes and concepts as each book unfolds its spiritual riches.

My research and study have made me appreciate the truth that, just as the Holy Spirit moved in ways both seen and unseen in the lives of these biblical figures, He moves in my life in ways that I can clearly see, as well as in ways that are beyond my sight or knowledge. What I see and know of the Holy Spirit is in no way all that He is and does! The Holy Spirit's ministry toward us is in both the seen and the unseen realms. The Spirit gives us insight into the things of God, but He Himself is not confined to what we can see or comprehend.

We all have felt the wind blow, and, at times, we have seen the effects of that wind—but none of us has ever seen the wind itself. Wind can be as gentle as a cool, refreshing breeze or as forceful as a tornado. In some ways, you could say that the Holy Spirit is the wind of God. Of course, unlike the impersonal wind, the Holy Spirit is not just an energy source. The Holy Spirit is God Himself, a divine Person with all the traits and characteristics of personhood and personality. This means that we can know Him. We cannot have a personal relationship with the wind, but we can personally know the Holy Spirit. As in any relationship, purposeful time and attention are needed to nurture and cultivate intimacy with Him. Thus, sensitivity to the Holy Spirit is the key to our success in life as believers. Learning about someone—their likes, dislikes, and mannerisms—is part of the development of every good relationship. And through His imprint in nature and in Scripture, the Holy Spirit invites us to know Him.

With each passing day, as I grow in the things of the Lord, it becomes clearer to me that I desperately need both the Word and the Spirit working concurrently in my life. The ideas in this book are among the truths that I have sought to hide in my heart. (See Psalm 119:19.) I have been spiritually strengthened and stabilized by them, and I pray that the same will be true for you.

OLD TESTAMENT

PART ONE

THE HOLY SPIRIT IN THE PENTATEUCH

GENESIS

Bringing Light into Darkness

From the very start of human history, we see that the Holy Spirit was active on earth:

> *The earth was without form, and void; and darkness was on the face of the deep. And the Spirit of God was hovering over the face of the waters.* (Genesis 1:2 NKJV)

The Spirit was not passively waiting, but He was "*hovering*." The Hebrew word translated as "*hovering*," *rachaph* (*Strong's*, H7363), means "to brood," "to flutter," "to move," or "to shake." Although the Holy Spirit was active, He chose not to act independently of the Father and the Son, but, as I will shortly describe, He moved according to the word of God. This is something we notice very quickly about the Trinity: Father, Son, and Holy Spirit act in divine unity and in unison with each other.

THE SPIRIT STILL HOVERS

There is an *active stillness* to the Holy Spirit's hovering or brooding.

Birds brood over eggs to hatch them. Even though it might seem as if nothing is happening in the eggs during this time, the incubation period is crucial to the embryos' development. There is a protective aspect to brooding. Similarly, the Holy Spirit broods over our lives, incubating us until our callings, anointings, giftings, and destinies are ready to be hatched.

When I was a young teenager and a new believer, before I ever even thought that I would or could be in ministry, there was many a night when I would stay awake praying in tongues and listening to cassette tapes of Bible teachings. I did this because I was hungry for God, and that was all I knew to do. I was the first in my family to be born again, and I didn't know many Spirit-filled believers back then. I had started attending a Spirit-filled church, but the people there didn't seem as hungry for God as I was. When I told them about my late nights of praying and studying, they said I was so zealous only because I was young and a new believer! I had many experiences with God during those lonely late nights. I look back now and see that some of the experiences I had and insights the Lord showed me are things that God has developed in me and are part of what I teach and preach worldwide today. I recognize that the Holy Spirit was brooding over my life during those nights as I was praying and studying. He was incubating the embryo of the call and anointing on my life.

Hold steady in the quiet places and seasons of life! Even when it looks like nothing is happening or moving, the Holy Spirit is still hovering over you to hatch your calling and anointing at a later but appointed time.

THE WORD AND THE SPIRIT

Even though the Spirit was hovering over the formless earth, the earth was still dark until God spoke these words: "*Let there be light*" (Genesis 1:3 NKJV). This tells us that while the Spirit may be hovering over something or someone, and desirous of bringing light to it, that thing or person might still be dark because it is only after God's word is spoken that He causes that word to manifest!

We know that Jesus is the Word personified (see John 1:14) and that "*by Him all things were created that are in heaven and that are on earth, visible and invisible, whether thrones or dominions or principalities or powers. All things were created through Him and for Him*" (Colossians 1:16 NKJV).

So, creation was a result of the Word and the Spirit working together.

This is still true with regard to the Spirit today. He hastens to perform the spoken Word. (See Jeremiah 1:12 KJV.) The power of the Spirit is released when we speak God's Word!

As has often been said, the Word and the Spirit agree because the Word and the Spirit are one.

Throughout the first chapter of Genesis, the Holy Spirit is the Agent of creation, acting on God's spoken words to separate day and night, and the heavens above from the waters below; acting to bring forth fruit and herb-yielding seed; animals, both on the land and in the waters; and then mankind.

Not only does the Holy Spirit brood over darkness, waiting for a word from God to be spoken to bring light, but He also inspires words so they can be spoken. *"All Scripture is given* ***by inspiration*** *of God, and is profitable for doctrine, for reproof, for correction, for instruction in righteousness"* (2 Timothy 3:16 NKJV). The Holy Spirit is the breath that inspired God's Word. By inspiring the written Word, the Holy Spirit once again brought light to darkness. (See Psalm 119:105.)

The Holy Spirit breathed the written Word so the Holy Spirit could manifest the spoken Word!

THE SPIRIT STILL BRINGS LIGHT AND ORDER

The same Spirit—with the same power that dispelled darkness with light and brought divine order to utter chaos in creation—is available today! We are not just talking about some historical record of the creation but about the Creator Himself. The Holy Spirit, as God, transcends time. He is timeless because He is outside of time. He is outside of time because He created time. What He did then, He can do now.

The Holy Spirit was not just involved in creation one time but is still the Agent of divine creation. This same Spirit lives in the believer, and all His creative power is still accessible. Any area of your life that is formless, void, barren, and in darkness can be changed by the power of the Holy Spirit!

The Holy Spirit is the Creator of new beginnings. The Spirit of creation can be seen and activated in the following:

- The healing of bodies and minds
- The restoration of families and relationships
- The birthing of ideas and opportunities
- The providence of needs and wants
- The deliverance of lives and destinies

THE HOLY SPIRIT WORKS WITH MANKIND

As we move along in the creation account in Genesis, we see mankind sinning by rebelling against God, so that that they could no longer remain in Eden, the garden that God had prepared for them in which to live and thrive. (See Genesis 3.) However, after Adam and Eve left Eden, God indicated that the Holy Spirit would continue working on human beings as long as they were on the earth.

> *And the LORD said, "**My Spirit shall not strive with man forever**, for he is indeed flesh; yet his days shall be one hundred and twenty years."*
> (Genesis 6:3 NKJV)

I believe this means that the Holy Spirit actively works with those who don't know God to steer them toward a relationship with Him!

> *And when He has come, **He will convict the world of sin...**.*
> (John 16:8 NKJV)

The Holy Spirit is not out convicting the world of worldliness. As far as the world is concerned, the Spirit is working on only one issue: the singular thing that the Holy Spirit convicts the world of is sin in the form of unbelief. (See verse 9). In other words, He convicts people of their need for Jesus!

I am always cautious when I see the church complain about or get flustered by the worldliness of the world. My attitude has always been this: dogs bark, cats meow, and the world is worldly! Again, the Holy Spirit is not trying to get the world to simply quit sin. The Holy Spirit is working on the world to accept God's remedy for the sin nature—Jesus.

As believers, we must work with and trust the Holy Spirit to present Jesus to those around us who do not yet know Him. Great power is available when we place in His care those whom we are concerned about.

POWER TO CONCEIVE THE PROPHETIC PROMISES OF GOD

Later on in Genesis, we see the Holy Spirit at work in the lives of Abraham and Sarah to bring about God's prophetic promises. God had promised Abraham that He would make him into a great nation (see, for example, Genesis 12:2) and that Abraham's wife, Sarah, who had been barren, would give birth to their son (see Genesis 18:10).

Not only did God pronounce this prophetic promise and inspire Abraham and Sarah's faith to believe for a child, but, also, the Holy Spirit gave Sarah the strength to conceive Isaac:

> *And the LORD visited Sarah as He had said, and the LORD did for Sarah as He had spoken. For Sarah conceived and bore Abraham a son in his old age, at the set time of which God had spoken to him.*
> (Genesis 21:1–2 NKJV)

> *By faith Sarah herself also received strength to conceive seed, and she bore a child when she was past the age, because she judged Him faithful who had promised.* (Hebrews 11:11 NKJV)

The Greek word translated *"strength"* in verse 11 is *dunamis,* which is "often used in the New Testament to describe the power of God, the power of the Holy Spirit, and the miraculous power evident in Jesus' ministry."[1] Every prophetic promise requires supernatural strength to conceive!

The Holy Spirit is both the Inspirer of prophetic promises and the Performer of those promises.

Whatever promise of God you are standing on, know that the strength to stand on that promise to be fulfilled also comes from Him! He is both the Giver of the seed and the Provider of the harvest.

1. Strong's Lexicon, "1411, Dunamis," https://biblehub.com/greek/1411.htm.

THE SPIRIT CALLS YOU BY A DIFFERENT NAME

We see another truth from the life of Abraham and his grandson Jacob that has to do with our identity in God—which the Holy Spirit is directly involved in providing for us and helping us to understand.

> *No longer shall your name be called Abram, but your name shall be Abraham; for I have made you a father of many nations.*
>
> (Genesis 17:5 NKJV)

> *Your name shall no longer be called Jacob, but Israel; for you have struggled with God and with men, and have prevailed.*
>
> (Genesis 32:28 NKJV)

Any time God speaks to man, in any form, the Holy Spirit is involved—directly or indirectly. The Holy Spirit is the breath of God, and breath is needed for speech!

Abraham's natural name was Abram, which means "exalted father"; Israel's natural name was Jacob, meaning "deceiver/supplanter." The original names were what Abram and Jacob were known as based on how other people viewed them. But God saw them differently.

God saw Abram as Abraham, "father of multitudes/nations"—and He called him so!

God saw Jacob as Israel, "prince of God"—and He called him so!

God changed what Abram and Jacob (and others) called themselves to reflect what He called them instead. This was a prophetic act of the highest order because neither of these men was what God called them to be when He gave them the new names. A recurring theme in Scripture is that, as we saw with creation, *manifestation is always and only a result of utterance.*

God needed them to call themselves something different for His plans to be fulfilled in their lives.

God may not visit you, as He did with Abram and Jacob, and change your name, but there are many things He calls you in His Word that may not yet be true in your life. Go to His Word, see what He says about you, and start calling yourself that. You can prophesy your future with the Word of God.

Right now, it might look like there are inabilities in your life, but God says you can do *"all things through Christ who strengthens* [you]" (Philippians 4:13 NKJV).

It might seem like finances are a challenge to you, but God says He will *"supply all your need according to His riches in glory by Christ Jesus"* (Philippians 4:19 NKJV).

Your medical report may not paint a picture of health, but God says that, by Jesus's stripes, you are healed. (See 1 Peter 2:24.)

It might seem like there are areas in your life or in the lives of people you care about that are bound by the enemy, but God says that Jesus was manifested to destroy the works of the enemy. (See 1 John 3:8.)

It might look like you'll never get ahead in life, but God says you are more than a conqueror through Him who loves you. (See Romans 8:37.)

There may be more than one area of your life in which you are experiencing lack, but God says Jesus came so that you might have life, and have it more abundantly. (See John 10:10.)

Let the Holy Spirit change what you call yourself. Prophesy!

DREAMERS AND DISCERNMENT

In Genesis, the Bible depicts the Holy Spirit as One who can communicate through dreams and who also gives the interpretation of those dreams.

Joseph—the son of Jacob and great-grandson of Abraham—started having prophetic dreams as a teenager but lacked the maturity and wisdom to process them. He quickly got into trouble with his family, and the situation became so intense that his brothers sold him into slavery to the Egyptians. (See Genesis 37.)

Years later, after experiencing a series of high and low points in which God continued to show him favor and work out His purposes for him, Joseph found himself in a position to give spiritual and practical guidance to the pharaoh of Egypt himself.

> *And Pharaoh said to his servants, "Can we find such a one as this, a man in whom is the Spirit of God?" Then Pharaoh said to Joseph, "Inasmuch as God has shown you all this, there is no one as discerning and wise as you."* (Genesis 41:38–39 NKJV)

We see that Joseph could interpret dreams by the inspiration of the Spirit and that he had grown in maturity so that the pagan pharaoh recognized God's Spirit on him! The example of Joseph's life shows us that our exercise of spiritual manifestations must be balanced with our growth in spiritual maturity.

One is the operation of spiritual gifts, and the other is the manifestation of spiritual fruit.

Gifts are freely given by grace. Fruit takes time to mature and ripen.

The same Spirit who allows us entrance into experiences in the spiritual realm can also endue us with wisdom for processing these experiences so that they might benefit those in the physical realm.

Excellence and maturity will get us into places that spiritual manifestations alone often will not.

Thus, in Genesis, we see the Spirit hovering, creating, and bringing light into darkness. We see Him continually working with the Word to fulfill God's prophetic purposes and to enable people to enter into supernatural encounters and ministries—empowering them to reflect the very character of God.

EXODUS

Liberating Us from Bondage

Throughout the book of Exodus, we can see the Holy Spirit manifest in various forms. He is seen as fire, cloud, and wind, but He is also present as the anointing, which endows individuals with the ability to do what God has ordained for them to do. In this book, we see that all the manifestations of God are for the purpose of liberating people so that His plan for their lives can be fulfilled. And we again see the Holy Spirit hovering—this time over the people of Israel to incubate them for entering their promised land.

THE FLAME OF FREEDOM AND PURPOSE

> *And the Angel of the LORD appeared to* [Moses] *in a flame of fire from the midst of a bush. So he looked, and behold, the bush was burning with fire, but the bush was not consumed.... And the LORD said: "I have surely seen the oppression of My people who are in Egypt, and have heard their cry because of their taskmasters, for I know their sorrows. So I have come down to deliver them out of the hand of the Egyptians, and to bring them up from that land to a good and large land, to a*

> *land flowing with milk and honey, to the place of the Canaanites and the Hittites and the Amorites and the Perizzites and the Hivites and the Jebusites. Now therefore, behold, the cry of the children of Israel has come to Me, and I have also seen the oppression with which the Egyptians oppress them. Come now, therefore, and I will send you to Pharaoh that you may bring My people, the children of Israel, out of Egypt."* (Exodus 3:2, 7–10 NKJV)

The Holy Spirit was the flame burning in the bush. Not only was the flame instrumental in calling Moses to his true purpose, but it also burned to set the people of God free. The Holy Spirit is a spirit of liberty, and evangelism is the initial sounding of liberty to all the world! (See, for example, Luke 4:18.) Evangelism is an invitation to the journey of discipleship. The Holy Spirit wants to set us on fire so we can bring light to the darkness of the world. This is the primary calling of all believers.

Moses could not have been the only one who saw the injustice against the people of God. He could not have been the only one who wanted something to be done. But the fire of God called Moses, and it empowered him. The Spirit of God still calls people today to free the captives.

In the spirit of service and love, it is good and right to "See a need; meet a need." It's important to recognize, though, that we are not called by needs *alone* but, rather, by the will of God. The world is full of needs and needy people, but where would we start if we were moved *only* by needs? If needs alone were what moved us, the enemy would happily keep throwing needy situations across our paths so we would spend our lives chasing needs instead of getting before God and asking for our place in His plan.

Again, serving and volunteering are always right. Doing these things builds character and helps to keep a generous spirit within us. Yet in our volunteering and serving, we should keep our hearts open for God to show us some specifics to which we can give ourselves wholly.

I liken it to being part of a church or partnering with a ministry. There are probably any number of good churches and ministries right where you live that you could visit or whom you could support as a financial partner. But it is only when you commit to the ones that God plants in you that you gain traction and start building in both the natural and in the spirit. There is nothing wrong with visiting churches while you are looking for a home church, but if all you do is routinely visit whichever church has the newest programs or the worship team with the catchiest songs, then you are not allowing yourself to be planted by God.

Similarly, sending an offering to a ministry or other organization because you are shown pictures of starving orphans is not wrong, because God's Word tells us to help orphans. (See, for example, James 1:27.) But there is a higher way to give. Ask the Holy Spirit to lead you to the organizations or ministries that He wants you to support and to show you how to help.

I have many opportunities to speak to ministers, and I always tell them that it's not enough to say they are called by God. To be effective, they must press in to God to hear where and to whom they are called and what they are called to say. *I do this!* My ministry would be too broad otherwise. We couldn't build a house with just a general blueprint. Similarly, God is the God of details and specifics. We can start with a general sense of a call, but that's when we must allow the Spirit's incubation to bring form to the embryo of our life.

Rest in this: the Holy Spirit has a specific plan for you!

THE PILLARS OF FIRE AND CLOUD: PROVISION IN TIMES OF NEED

Once the Israelites were freed from slavery in Egypt, they needed to learn to depend on God's leading through His Holy Spirit.

> *And the LORD went before them by day in a pillar of cloud to lead the way, and by night in a pillar of fire to give them light, so as to go by day and night. He did not take away the pillar of cloud by day or the pillar of fire by night from before the people.* (Exodus 13:21–22 NKJV)

> *Then the cloud covered the tabernacle of meeting, and the glory of the LORD filled the tabernacle. And Moses was not able to enter the tabernacle of meeting. because the cloud rested above it, and the glory of the LORD filled the tabernacle. Whenever the cloud was taken up from above the tabernacle, the children of Israel would go onward in all their journeys. But if the cloud was not taken up, then they did not journey*

> *till the day that it was taken up. For the cloud of the* L*ORD* *was above the tabernacle by day, and fire was over it by night, in the sight of all the house of Israel, throughout all their journeys.*
>
> (Exodus 40:34–38 NKJV)

At the point when they departed from Egypt, the children of Israel had been slaves for four hundred years. This means that all who were a part of the exodus had no memory of being free. At times, it must have seemed harsher living in the desolate wilderness than it had been living under slavery. Perhaps that was why they complained about Moses and wanted to return to Egypt. In this setting of disillusionment, the Spirit manifested as a pillar of cloud by day and a pillar of fire by night. He manifested prominently enough for all to see that He was with them. Similarly, when it seems as if we are the most alone, we can count on the Holy Spirit to show up in the most prominent ways! Jesus promised that the Holy Spirit would never leave us. (See John 14:16.)

Consider further how the Holy Spirit manifested as a pillar of cloud during the day and a pillar of fire at night. He appeared to the children of Israel in visible forms regardless of the circumstances of their environment. In the day, when they could see clearly in the sunlight, He appeared in a distinctly visible form. At night, when they could not see in the darkness, he appeared in a form that illuminated the darkness surrounding them. The Holy Spirit is determined to be noticed by you, and He knows how to get your attention!

In our times of "day," when we have light, and we think we can see what's ahead of us, He wants to lead us. In our times of "night," when we cannot see in the darkness, He wants to provide us with clarity. When we think it's "day" and know our way ahead, we need to learn to pause from what our physical senses tell us and seek Him to see if He has a preferred route. When it's "night," and we can't see our way out of the darkness, we need to look to the Light that can dispel the darkness.

God's provision of the pillars of cloud and fire for the Israelites shows us that He yearns to be *among* His people to lead them. God was not just a booming voice from heaven; He was *in the midst of* the people. Likewise, we do not have a Holy Spirit who yells instructions at us from heaven—we have the Holy Spirit who dwells inside us! The Greater One lives within us and will lead and guide us.

WIND, BILLOWING SMOKE, AND INDWELLING PRESENCE

> *Then Moses stretched out his hand over the sea; and the* Lord *caused the sea to go back by a strong east* ***wind*** *all that night, and made the sea into dry land, and the waters were divided.* (Exodus 14:21 NKJV)

In addition to the above verse, we see the Holy Spirit manifested as, or compared to, wind in various parts of the Bible. (See, for example, Ezekiel 37:7–10; John 3:8; Acts 2:2.) The Holy Spirit is the "power aspect" of God. Every time you are on the shore of your Red Sea, the Holy Spirit is the wind that parts the waters so that you can cross over.

Exodus has additional beautiful images of the Holy Spirit. On Mount Sinai, the Holy Spirit manifested as the fire and billowing smoke (Exodus 19:18–19) in which God descended and spoke to the children of Israel through Moses. Again, this event points to the Holy Spirit's desire to speak to His people. If this was the case for the Israelites in Exodus, how much more is it true for us today who have been born again as God's children?

In another image, the Holy Spirit is the Indwelling Presence in the tabernacle. And He desires to indwell the believer today. (See, for example, Exodus 25:8–9; 40:34; John 14:17; 1 Corinthians 3:16.)

THE ANOINTER FOR SERVICE

> *See, I have called by name* ***Bezalel*** *the son of Uri, the son of Hur, of the tribe of Judah. And I have filled him with the Spirit of God, in wisdom, in understanding, in knowledge, and in all manner of workmanship, to design artistic works, to work in gold, in silver, in bronze, in cutting jewels for setting, in carving wood, and to work in all manner of [artistic] workmanship.* (Exodus 31:2–5 NKJV)

> *And Moses said to the children of Israel, "See, the* Lord *has called by name* ***Bezalel*** *the son of Uri, the son of Hur, of the tribe of Judah; and He has filled him with the Spirit of God, in wisdom and understanding,*

> *in knowledge and all manner of workmanship, to design artistic works, to work in gold and silver and bronze, in cutting jewels for setting, in carving wood, and to work in all manner of artistic workmanship. And He has put in his heart the ability to teach, in him and Aholiab, the son of Ahisamach, of the tribe of Dan. He has filled them with skill to do all manner of work of the engraver and the designer and the tapestry maker, in blue, purple, and scarlet thread, and fine linen, and of the weaver—those who do every work and those who design artistic works."* (Exodus 35:30–35 NKJV)

Not many people have heard of Bezalel, but he is an important figure for understanding the Holy Spirit and the anointing. Bezalel is the first person the Bible records as having the Spirit of God upon him who wasn't a traditional priest or prophet. He was an artisan tradesman. He worked with his hands and crafted pieces of wood and precious material. Yet he had the anointing of the Spirit upon him. This tells me that the anointing is not just for "preachers"—God intended it for all His people from all walks of life!

The anointing may manifest on those who serve in the fivefold ministry offices (see Ephesians 4:11–12) differently from, for example, a believer who is a schoolteacher or a police officer. Still, an anointing is available for all believers to function in all areas of life. The anointing can make you stand out in your profession. The anointing causes you to rise to the top of your field.

The anointing is the coating that makes all of our life's work bear minimal friction; it eases our moving forward and onward in life as we grow in our relationship with and service to God. God intends there to be divine ease in your life. The anointing doesn't do away with the mountains or Goliaths in the land, but it does position you to have supernatural victory over them.

As a believer, choose to do life with the anointing! You can receive God's anointing by seeking the infilling of His Spirit, surrendering your life to Him, and being open to enter into all that He desires for you. Seek to have and maintain an awareness of the Spirit's presence in and with you throughout the day.

THE PRESENCE THAT ACCOMPANIES

> *Then Moses said to the* Lord, *"...Now therefore, I pray, if I have found grace in Your sight, show me now Your way, that I may know You and that I may find grace in Your sight. And consider that this nation is Your people." And He said, "My* **Presence** *will go with you, and I will give you rest." Then he said to Him, "If Your* **Presence** *does not go with us, do not bring us up from here. For how then will it be known that Your people and I have found grace in Your sight, except You go with us? So we shall be separate, Your people and I, from all the people who are upon the face of the earth." So the* Lord *said to Moses, "I will also do this thing that you have spoken; for you have found grace in My sight, and I know you by name."* (Exodus 33:12–17 NKJV)

The Holy Spirit is the presence of God that continually accompanies us. It is this presence that administers the ministry of God through our lives. We enter into this level of presence by prayer—that is how God led Moses to the level that he obtained. Moses was a man of prayer. We could say it in this way: living in the presence is a result of prayer, which is an expression of communion with God—something God always wanted with us from the beginning! Being led by the Spirit is simple because prayer is simple. Prayer is simple because God wants to talk to us. Knowing this, let us "pray always." (See Ephesians 6:18; 1 Thessalonians 5:17.)

Just as He desired to be present with the Israelites so He could personally lead them in their journey though the wilderness to the promised land, God's heart in wanting communion with us has always been so He could lead us day by day in fulfillment of His kingdom purposes.

LEVITICUS

Setting Us Apart for God

The holiness of God reflected in the holiness of the believer's life is a prominent theme in Leviticus. The Holy Spirit's nature and presence are interwoven throughout the standards and practices that God established for the Israelites as recorded in this book.

CONSECRATED UNTO HOLINESS

> *Take Aaron and his sons with him, and the garments, the anointing oil, a bull as the sin offering, two rams, and a basket of unleavened bread.... Also Moses took the anointing oil, and anointed the tabernacle and all that was in it, and consecrated them.... Then Moses took some of the anointing oil and some of the blood which was on the altar, and sprinkled it on Aaron, on his garments, on his sons, and on the garments of his sons with him; and he consecrated Aaron, his garments, his sons, and the garments of his sons with him.*
>
> (Leviticus 8:2–3, 10, 30 NKJV)

In Leviticus, we see the Holy Spirit as the One who consecrates those who are called to the priesthood, as well as the institutions related to the priesthood. Their holiness was not based on their efforts alone; it began with the Spirit's consecration, which enabled them to live the holy life that was required.

As New Testament believers, we are *"a royal priesthood"* (1 Peter 2:9), and we, too, have been consecrated to a holy lifestyle. Our holiness is not to be based on our own strength because if we could accomplish the level of holiness acceptable to God in our strength, then Jesus's sacrifice would not have been necessary. *You could say that God's plan for having a holy people was that the blood of Jesus would cleanse us so the Holy Spirit could fill us!*

As we go further in our study of the Holy Spirit in every book of the Bible, I want to emphasize one thing that has always struck me: how gently and firmly, but progressively, the Holy Spirit reveals Himself. The Holy Spirit is not just holy; He is also gentle! Through my exercise of the gifts of private tongues and the interpretation of tongues, the Spirit once told me, "I couldn't be holy if I were not also gentle." There is comfort in knowing that He is gentle!

In the same way that the tabernacle was to be consecrated to holiness, today, we are the tabernacle, the dwelling place of God, and we are to be holy. (See 1 Corinthians 6:19–20.) The Holy Spirit marked us to set us apart so that He could indwell us.

The presence of God in the tabernacle was also where the power of God was located. This is still true today. The presence of God in the believer is where the power of God may be found. We are both the storage units and the dispensers of the presence and power of God!

A CONSUMING FIRE

In the book of Exodus, the Holy Spirit manifests as fire, and it's no different in Leviticus. In Exodus, we first saw the Holy Spirit revealed in the burning bush—experienced only by Moses, and calling him to ministry. Then we saw the Spirit as a pillar of fire, which extended high enough for all to see, leading the people. In Leviticus, we see Him as a consuming fire. It seems as if the further the people walked with God, the hotter the fire of God became!

What a picture this is of walking with the Holy Spirit today. First, He woos us to the cross at Calvary, and then He leads us to the resurrection. Finally, He lifts us to the ascension to be seated in heavenly places with Christ. (See Ephesians 2:6.)

> *And fire came out from before the Lord and consumed the burnt offering and the fat on the altar. When all the people saw it, they shouted and fell on their faces.* (Leviticus 9:24 NKJV)

The first time the Holy Spirit's fire is mentioned in Leviticus is when it comes to receive the people's sacrificial offerings. By God's acceptance of the offerings by fire, the people were symbolically made holy. It was a fire that brought joy to the people because they knew, by this heavenly fire, that God was pleased with them.

Just as the people brought their offerings, which the holy fire consumed, we can prepare for the revival fire of God by bringing our offerings of prayer, faith, and consecration. The fire of God never falls on an empty altar; there has to be something on the altar for the fire to consume.

In the era in which we live, I believe with all my heart that we, the church, need to fill the altars again so that revival fires can fall from heaven! There is yet a harvest for and from our generation. Fill the altars, and God will be faithful to send the fire!

> *Then Nadab and Abihu, the sons of Aaron, each took his censer and put fire in it, put incense on it, and offered profane fire before the Lord, which He had not commanded them. So fire went out from the Lord and devoured them, and they died before the Lord.*
> (Leviticus 10:1–2 NKJV)

The second time the fire of the Spirit appears in Leviticus, it is to keep the people holy from the profane fire that two rogue priests, Nadab and Abihu, tried to offer.

As New Testament believers, we need not be concerned about being engulfed by the wrath of God's fire today, but we must see that not only does the Spirit's fire make us holy, but it can keep us holy.

The same flame that purified them, preserved them.

The lesson for us is to rest in the flame of the Spirit!

PURE OIL

The church is given pure oil in order for it to have pure fire.

> *Command the children of Israel that they bring to you pure oil of pressed olives for the light, to make the lamps burn continually.*
>
> (Leviticus 24:2 NKJV)

Another way to see the Holy Spirit is to see Him as the Pure Spirit. The Holy Spirit in us is the Source of the pure oil that fuels the pure fire, which is always graciously supplied to and for us.

Like most Old Testament types, the pure oil and the lamps in Leviticus 24:2 point to Jesus—and to His sacrifice. The olives had to be pressed to create oil, and the gold had to be beaten to be shaped into lampstands. What a picture of the cross! How like the Holy Spirit to always point us to Jesus. This is an important aspect of the Holy Spirit's mission: the revealing of Jesus.

NUMBERS

Providing Guidance for Daily Living

Numbers is a historical record of Israel's initial experience under a theocracy. As a people, the Israelites had a painful past; now, for the first time in a long while, they were no longer under an oppressive human government but were directly under God Himself.

In the book of Numbers, the Holy Spirit starts getting deeply involved in the daily life and activities of the Israelites. In chapters 1–4 alone, warriors, worshippers, and workers are preemptively prepared by the leading of the Spirit.

As we saw in Exodus, the Holy Spirit was slowly but surely shifting from leading His people from a distance to leading them day by day so they could learn to trust and follow Him.

OUR GUIDE

> *At the command of the LORD the children of Israel would journey, and at the command of the LORD they would camp; as long as the cloud stayed above the tabernacle they remained encamped.... At the*

> *command of the* Lord *they remained encamped, and at the command of the* Lord *they journeyed; they kept the charge of the* Lord*, at the command of the* Lord *by the hand of Moses.*
>
> (Numbers 9:18, 23 NKJV)

The Israelites were being discipled by the Holy Spirit to be led by Him. This was vital because victories result from our obedience to the leading of the Holy Spirit. But securing victories also required overcoming giants and conquering lands. The Holy Spirit would lead the people into both the battlefield and the victory. The children of Israel would walk into all that God had for them as long as they let the Holy Spirit lead them.

Jesus told His disciples that the Holy Spirit wanted to guide them. (See John 16:13.) In this account of the Israelites, we see that the Holy Spirit was already showing God's people that He would lead them into all truth. Like God the Father and God the Son, the Holy Spirit does not change!

The leading of the Spirit is something we can be schooled into. Like everything else in our spiritual life, our understanding of how God's Spirit leads us is gradual and requires intention. But it is God's will for us to be led by Him. This was so for Israel, and it is even more so for us New Testament believers.

We may not always see external manifestations of the Spirit, as the children of Israel did, but that is because the Holy Spirit now lives within us; He no longer dwells in man-made temples. (See, for example, Acts 17:24.) *The Holy Spirit leads by His presence, and He dwells inside us.*

THE SPIRIT CAN BE TRANSFERRED!

> [The Lord said,] *"Then I will come down and talk with you* [Moses] *there. I will take of the Spirit that is upon you and will put the same upon them; and they shall bear the burden of the people with you, that you may not bear it yourself alone."... Then the* Lord *came down in the cloud, and spoke to him, and took of the Spirit that was upon him, and placed the same upon the seventy elders; and it happened, when the Spirit rested upon them, that they prophesied, although they never did so again.* (Numbers 11:17, 25 NKJV)

For all of the miraculous events that Moses had witnessed and been instrumental in, it is only here in Numbers 11 that the Holy Spirit is first directly mentioned in connection with him. Before this pronouncement from heaven, Moses and the people knew that it was God's hand on Moses that had worked the miraculous, so this tells us that the Holy Spirit is and can be the Unseen Hand on us as well. However, it was only after this announcement that Moses's anointing could be imparted to the seventy and the ministry could be multiplied. This speaks of a higher flow of the anointing. *Multiplication is always the goal of the anointing.*

Many years ago, a powerful, seasoned prayer minister visited me in Asia before I did much ministry in America. During her visit to some of the churches and outreaches I had started, she grabbed my hand and said, "James, there is an apostolic anointing on you to raise ministers and build!" Back then, I shied away from using terms like *apostle* or *prophet*—not because I didn't believe in these ministry offices but because it seemed that people I knew who used those titles had no fruit to back up what they called themselves and had questionable lives and ministries. A few years later, while I was in prayer, the Spirit of God brought up the words that the prayer general had said to me. Then, through tongues and the interpretation of tongues, the Spirit of God said, "The anointing requires recognition because the anointing requires cooperation, and you cannot cooperate with what you do not recognize!"

We are to recognize what God has *already* spoken about us and done in us; *it will bear fruit* after we have recognized what God has done in us.

When I did start to personally acknowledge the grace God had given me to gather, lay foundations, and build up other ministers and ministries, I saw an increase in the anointing in and through me. This is similar to what happened to Jesus at the start of His ministry when He announced that the Spirit of the Lord had come upon Him. (See Luke 4:16–19; 31–41.)

When we acknowledge the works of God in our lives, those works increase!

I have also seen the opposite play out when individuals "decide" that they are apostles or prophets. Without the acknowledgment of other qualified leaders and elders, they self-announce their title and try to market and gather others around their "gift." In most such situations that I have seen, there was usually very little fruit to prove such a call. These individuals may have been eloquent in their self-promotion—but they did not exhibit much actual fruit that accompanies the anointing. It might be that they were called, but their announcement was premature; their gift had not been given the time needed to develop and grow.

Obviously, I don't mean to imply that a person cannot be called unless others approve of them and their ministry, but why would God anoint someone without making that anointing recognizable to other mature ministers? It is not the approval of man but the recognition of the anointing that qualities a minister. The apostle Paul was definitely called, but it took a while for the church to recognize this. They eventually did. What proved his calling was his humility and willingness to let God validate his call to the other leaders. He did not flaunt his call and try to force it on others.

Gifts can be received quietly, but fruit is always seen openly!

> *So the LORD said to Moses: "Gather to Me seventy men of the elders of Israel,* ***whom you know to be the elders of the people and officers over them****; bring them to the tabernacle of meeting, that they may stand there with you."* (Numbers 11:16 NKJV)

Impartations are most often the results of a partnership. True spiritual partnership should involve resources, but it always includes a shared vision and purpose.

The ministries that influence you will also impart to you. Associations matter!

DESIRE EARNESTLY TO PROPHESY

> *And a young man ran and told Moses, and said, "Eldad and Medad are prophesying in the camp." So Joshua the son of Nun, Moses' assistant, one of his choice men, answered and said, "Moses my lord, forbid them!" Then Moses said to him, "Are you zealous for my sake? Oh, that all the LORD's people were prophets and that the LORD would put His Spirit upon them!"* (Numbers 11:27–29 NKJV)

The result of Moses's anointing being transferred to others was that they started to prophesy. It was the first sign they had of the Spirit being upon them. This mirrors what happened to the church on the day of Pentecost. After the fresh wind of the Spirit blew into the upper room, Peter quoted Joel, saying, *"And it shall come to pass in the last days, says God, that I will pour out My Spirit on all flesh;* ***your sons and your daughters shall prophesy****, your young men shall see visions, your old men shall dream dreams"* (Acts 2:17 NKJV).

The Holy Spirit has a way of overflowing through our mouths!

Prophesying, speaking by divine inspiration, is not just foretelling but also *forth*-telling. Some inspired utterance always accompanies the presence of the Spirit. Prophesying occurred in the Old Testament, and it also occurred in the New Testament.

Joshua zealously, but not maliciously, asked Moses to command the two men to stop prophesying; it seems like, even today, some people want prophesying stopped.

Moses's response matches this later command of Paul: *"Therefore, brethren, desire earnestly to prophesy, and do not forbid to speak with tongues"* (1 Corinthians 14:39 NKJV; see also 1 Thessalonians 5:20). We see the same Spirit, in two different eras, say almost the same thing—first through Moses, and then through Paul. When the Spirit comes upon people, He inspires prophetic utterances that we are not to stop but rather to expect and encourage!

DISCIPLESHIP THAT DUPLICATES

> *And the LORD said to Moses: "Take Joshua the son of Nun with you, a man in whom is the Spirit, and lay your hand on him.... And you shall give some of your authority to him, that all the congregation of the children of Israel may be obedient."* (Numbers 27:18–20 NKJV)

> *Now Joshua the son of Nun was full of the spirit of wisdom, for Moses had laid his hands on him; so the children of Israel heeded him, and did as the LORD had commanded Moses.* (Deuteronomy 34:9 NKJV)

We should not limit the Holy Spirit's workings to the realm of signs and wonders. One result of Moses laying his hands on Joshua was that

Joshua was *"full of the spirit of wisdom."* This would explain why Jesus later referred to the Holy Spirit as *Parakletos*: Counselor and Guide. We should look for demonstrations of the Spirit, but we shouldn't forget that the Holy Spirit is not just empowerment but endowment. As God, He endows us with all the qualities inherent in God.

While the seventy received the "same Spirit" (see Numbers 11:17, 25) after being given a portion of Moses's anointing, Joshua received some of Moses's authority. Clearly, God intended Moses's laying hands on Joshua to be publicly and spiritually symbolic to the people that a portion of Moses's spiritual strength was being transferred to Joshua to continue governing and leading God's people.

This is a true picture of the procedure and the result of discipleship. Joshua, who had served and been mentored by Moses, was now the recipient of Moses's "strength"—his leadership anointing, which enabled him to fulfill his call and vision.

The purpose of discipleship is duplication. Duplication does not mean cloning—Joshua wasn't a "little Moses"—but it does mean a duplication of valor, vision, and values. Impartations through discipleship are God's path for the spiritual succession of ministries and anointing. Please note that impartations are a spiritual transaction; they are not biologically hereditary.

Impartation is a popular word today, and people get excited when they think that their favorite minister will anoint them with oil and lay hands on them in order to impart to them, because they think they will receive the minister's anointing. You don't receive someone else's anointing just because they slap oil on your forehead! *You receive the most from the anointings of those with whom you are in relationship.*

THE SPIRIT IS THE DIFFERENCE

> *But My servant Caleb, because he has a different spirit in him and has followed Me fully, I will bring into the land where he went, and his descendants shall inherit it.* (Numbers 14:24 NKJV)

What differentiates the church from the world is that we have "a different spirit." This doesn't just mean we have a different worldview or attitude from the world; it means we are vessels filled with a different substance. The Holy Spirit is the difference! We have the Christ Spirit, and the world has an antichrist spirit. (See, for example, 1 John 4:2–3.) Since He is from the kingdom of God, the Spirit in us exhibits the kingdom's languages, culture, and characteristics through us and will ultimately bring us back to the kingdom—our promised land.

If Caleb had not had *"a different spirit,"* he would not have been able to follow God *"fully."* Similarly, our ability to fully live as believers rests upon our dependence on the Holy Spirit. As has often been said, "It's not difficult to be a follower of Jesus without the Holy Spirit—it's impossible!" We need the power of God to live the life of God. That's why being filled with the Spirit is nonnegotiable for living a successful Christian life.

Having a different Spirit is what lifts us above the world system.

Having a different Spirit is tangibly noticeable. The believer living the Spirit-filled life will always stand out in a crowd. I have taught this in countries with restrictions against sharing the gospel and some prejudices against believers. I have seen that having a different Spirit from what the world has, when it is allowed to manifest through one's life, can bring promotion in the workplace and be a powerful witness in the family. Tune in and trust the Holy Spirit within you to bring you to your inheritance.

THE HOLY SPIRIT AVENGES US

> *Then Miriam and Aaron spoke against Moses because of the Ethiopian woman whom he had married; for he had married an Ethiopian woman.... **Then the Lord came down in the pillar of cloud** and stood in the door of the tabernacle, and called Aaron and Miriam. And they both went forward.... So the anger of the Lord was aroused against them, and He departed. And when the cloud departed from above the tabernacle, suddenly Miriam became leprous, as white as snow. Then Aaron turned toward Miriam, and there she was, a leper.*
>
> (Numbers 12:1, 5, 9–10 NKJV)

The Holy Spirit can vindicate you for words spoken against you publicly and in secret. He is both the protector and the restorer of your reputation.

The same manifestation of the cloud that led and guided the children of Israel now appeared to protect Moses and avenge him. (In verses 11–15, we see that Miriam was later healed of the leprosy after Moses prayed for her and Aaron.) The Holy Spirit raises standards for and around us against enemy attacks. Just as He hovered over the unformed earth, He is a protective covering over us as He broods or hovers over our lives.

"SPRING UP, O WELL"

> *From there they went to Beer, which is the well where the LORD said to Moses, "Gather the people together, and I will give them water." Then Israel sang this song: "Spring up, O well! All of you sing to it."*
> (Numbers 21:16–17 NKJV)

Both the water and the well are symbolic of the Holy Spirit.

A prophetic element is released when we sing or speak the promises of God. In the desert wilderness, Israel sang *after* the promise of water was given but *before* the manifestation was realized. That is faith and prophesying in action! Any promise from God must be spoken before it is manifested. Sing your promises. The waters in the deep well—God's gifts, callings, and anointings inside you—are stirred and bubble up when you prophesy to them. Prophesy to your well!

THE GIVER OF BLESSINGS

> *Now when Balaam saw that it pleased the LORD to bless Israel, he did not go as at other times, to seek to use sorcery, but he set his face toward the wilderness. And Balaam raised his eyes, and saw Israel encamped according to their tribes; and the Spirit of God came upon him. Then he took up his oracle and said....* (Numbers 24:1–3 NKJV)

Balaam is proof that having a knowledge of spiritual things is not the same thing as having a relationship with the Holy Spirit. Balaam had a reputation for making prophetic utterances of blessings and curses (see Numbers 22:6), so Balak, a Moabite king, tried employing Balaam to curse Israel. Balaam knew the Lord well enough to understand that He had the power to do this, but he did not know God well enough to understand that He would not curse Israel, His people.

Finally, the Lord allowed Balaam to return with Balak's messengers because, even though He had already told Balaam not to go ahead with cursing Israel when he was offered more money for the job, Balaam had gone back to ask God about it again. Since God is a gentle Spirit, He allows us our desires to an extent, even when those desires are outside His will. This doesn't mean God endorses or blesses those desires, but He allows us to make decisions of our will. In this case, God eventually allowed Balaam to go to Balak but did everything He could to warn him against it—even to the point of opening the eyes of Balaam's donkey to see the Angel of the Lord standing against Balaam, and then loosing the donkey's tongue so it could tell Balaam what it saw! Even this event did not stop Balaam from ultimately making his way toward the children of Israel in an attempt to curse them for material gain.

In the end, despite numerous sacrifices and repeated petitioning, Balaam could not get God to change His mind to curse Israel. God is not a God of confusion, and He will not contradict Himself. (See 1 Corinthians 14:33.) Earlier, God had said to Balaam, *"Only the word which I speak to you—that you shall do"* (Numbers 22:20). God turned what Balak and Balaam intended to be a curse into a blessing as the true spirit of prophecy overtook Balaam, and he spoke words of blessing from God over Israel. (See Numbers 22:21–24:25.)

The Spirit of God is well able to cause even those who mean to harm us to bless us instead. When people plot against us in secret, the Holy Spirit can change their plans!

DEUTERONOMY

Bestowing Fresh Revelation

Deuteronomy means "second law"; the name is taken from the title of the book in the Septuagint, an early translation of the Old Testament into Greek, also known as LXX. In Deuteronomy, Moses gives his last words to a new generation. The previous stubborn, unbelieving generation had passed away. Moses restates the Law for the benefit of this new generation of Israelites. Many of these people had likely been in their early twenties when Israel failed to possess the promised land. (See Numbers 10–14.)

Once, in my prayer time, through tongues and interpretation, the Lord said, "Revelation only lives one generation! Every generation must have a fresh voice!" I immediately knew what that meant: every generation must know God for themselves, and every generation must have a voice that will proclaim God to them. This does not do away with what previous generations have received from God and established, but it does mean that we are not made to live off the last generation's manna. There is a generation arising that will know the Holy Spirit for themselves!

REMEMBER WHAT THE LORD HAS DONE FOR YOU

> *Yet, for all that, you did not believe the* Lord *your God, who went in the way before you to search out a place for you to pitch your tents, to show you the way you should go, in the fire by night and in the cloud by day.* (Deuteronomy 1:32–33 NKJV)

One of the Holy Spirit's functions is to show us all truth, including reminding us of things God has said and done for us. (See John 16:13–15.) When we are reminded of what God has done for us, it strengthens us; and, as in this case with the Israelites, it provides us with an opportunity to reconsider our responses to the Spirit. The Holy Spirit, through Moses, reminded the children of Israel that they did not need to be concerned because, if He led them in the past, He intended to lead them again.

The Holy Spirit intends to be an ongoing influence in our lives. Some people, after they have had an encounter with Jesus and receive salvation (which is the result of the Spirit's ministry, who is the One who convicts the world of their need for Jesus), forget that the same Spirit who led them to meet Christ at Calvary also purposes to lead them to their seat in the heavenly places in Christ Jesus. (See Ephesians 2:4–6.)

The Holy Spirit leads us from death to life, from victory to victory!

THE SPIRIT OF SIGNS AND WONDERS

> *Or did God ever try to go and take for Himself a nation from the midst of another nation, by trials, by signs, by wonders, by war, by a mighty hand and an outstretched arm, and by great terrors, according to all that the* Lord *your God did for you, in Egypt before your eyes? To you it was shown, that you might know that the* Lord *Himself is God; there is none other besides Him.* (Deuteronomy 4:34–35 NKJV)

> *And the* Lord *showed signs and wonders before our eyes, great and severe, against Egypt, Pharaoh, and all his household.*
> (Deuteronomy 6:22 NKJV)

> *So the* L*ORD* *brought us out of Egypt with a mighty hand and with an outstretched arm, with great terror and with signs and wonders.*
> (Deuteronomy 26:8 NKJV)

> *...in all the signs and wonders which the* L*ORD* *sent him* [Moses] *to do in the land of Egypt, before Pharaoh, before all his servants, and in all his land, and by all that mighty power and all that great terror which Moses performed in the sight of all Israel.* (Deuteronomy 34:11–12 NKJV)

Continuing to remind the Israelites (and us) about what God had done, Deuteronomy records the miraculous works the Lord did in Egypt. Stirring our remembrance is a powerful tool against the enemy. The enemy "steals, kills, and destroys" (see John 10:10) by robbing us of the memory of God's previous interventions in our lives. When we forget what God has done, we weaken our faith in what He will do. Psalm 103, in its entirety, exhorts us to "*forget not all His benefits*" (verse 2). The book of Deuteronomy contains Moses's final words to the Israelites, and Moses carefully called the people to remember what they had seen God do because he knew God wanted to do so much more for them!

Signs and wonders are like both a finger that points and the fingerprint of God.

They are a pointing finger because they point to God's personhood.

They are the fingerprint of God because they are a lasting testament to His willingness and ability to work on our behalf, to His glory.

THE OIL OF BLESSING AND PROSPERITY

> *And of Asher he said: "Asher is most blessed of sons; let him be favored by his brothers, and let him dip his foot in oil."*
> (Deuteronomy 33:24 NKJV)

The name *Asher* means "blessed," and oil is a type of the Holy Spirit. To have his foot dipped in oil implies that Asher did not have just a trickle of the Spirit in his life, but he had access to a pool deep enough to dip his feet in. This speaks of the fullness of the Spirit available to us. We can have more than a mere trickle of the Spirit in our lives.

Oil is also a symbol of abundance, prosperity, and provision. Thus, the Word of God, inspired by the Holy Spirit, portrays oil as a type of both the Holy Spirit and prosperity, which means that prosperity is not something we need to be deprived of.

In the same way that God supplies His Spirit for our empowerment to live the God-kind of life in the earthly realm, God has material provision available for us. We need both natural and spiritual provision to function in this world, and heavenly oil is available to give us both. Expect to dip your feet in the oil of prosperity in the same way you expect to dip your feet in the oil of the Holy Spirit!

FULL OF WISDOM, FULL OF THE SPIRIT

> *Now Joshua the son of Nun was full of the spirit of wisdom, for Moses had laid his hands on him; so the children of Israel heeded him, and did as the Lord had commanded Moses.* (Deuteronomy 34:9 NKJV)

In our study of the book of Numbers, we read that Moses laid his hands on Joshua for an impartation of anointing and authority (see Numbers 27:18–20), and we saw the manifestation of that spiritual transaction. Joshua was now "*full of the spirit of wisdom.*" This would mean that Joshua either had relatively little wisdom before Moses laid hands on him, or he had some measure of wisdom, but now, after Moses had laid hands on him, he was "*full.*" Since Joshua had had a distinguished career of leading the children of Israel in military endeavors, starting with the battle against the Amalekites (see Exodus 17:13), he couldn't have been devoid of wisdom. He was also one of only two of Moses's twelve spies to the promised land who believed that God could give the Israelites victory. (See Numbers 13:1–14:9.) So Joshua possessed a keen mind in both natural and spiritual matters. Yet, for all his great capabilities, he was *filled* with wisdom only after Moses laid hands on him.

There are deeper degrees of fullness we can enter into with the Holy Spirit. There are ministries and ministers that God will lead us to both serve with and receive from to move us into deeper realms of the Spirit. This is the essence of discipleship: Spirit-fed and Spirit-led!

PART TWO

THE HOLY SPIRIT IN THE HISTORICAL BOOKS

JOSHUA

Revealer of Breakthrough Strategies

The book of Joshua records Joshua's leadership abilities and military exploits as he sought to further fulfill what God had told Moses about possessing the promised land. Just as we see the work and person of the Holy Spirit demonstrated through the lives of the disciples in the New Testament, we see the Holy Spirit performing through the actions and advancements of Joshua.

DIRECTOR OF OUR SIGHT

> *The* L*ORD said to Joshua, "***See***, I have given Jericho into your hand, with its king and the valiant warriors. You shall march around the city, all the men of war circling the city once. You shall do so for six days. Also seven priests shall carry seven trumpets of rams' horns before the ark; then on the seventh day you shall march around the city seven times, and the priests shall blow the trumpets. It shall be that when they make a long blast with the ram's horn, and when you hear the sound of the trumpet, all the people shall shout with a great shout; and the*

wall of the city will fall down flat, and the people will go up every man straight ahead." (Joshua 6:2–5 NASB95)

The Lord speaks through the voice of His Spirit. And, when the Spirit speaks, He often does this so that we can *see* something. God made us visually responsive. This is particularly true with regard to our inner vision: the way in which we see ourselves or our situations on the inside is exactly how we act in response to them. We act out in real life the "movie" we see within. That is why the Lord's immediate command to Joshua was to "see" that Jericho had been given to him before the rest of the instructions were delivered.

God did the same thing for Abraham when He led him to ponder the stars (see Genesis 15:5) and the sand (see Genesis 22:17). Through the means of Abraham's visualization and meditation, God painted a picture in Abraham's spirit of multitudes of offspring.

Visualization is simply the process of holding and nurturing an inner image of what the Lord has spoken or promised to you. This is what meditation does: it ponders a promise.

When we meditate on and visualize God's promises, we invite the Spirit of God to hover and brood over any part of our lives that is *"without form, and void"* and in *"darkness,"* just as He did at the creation of the earth. (See Genesis 1:2 NKJV.)

From the position of meditation and visualization, the vision you see and hold as a result of God's promise is God's will and plan for you!

The Spirit will always cause you to *see* before He leads you to *do* because you will not do until you see.

This is why, as believers, we are told to *"walk by faith, not by sight"* (2 Corinthians 5:7, various translations). We are to be moved by what we see in faith, not by what we see with our physical senses. There is no such thing as "blind faith" because faith always sees what God has promised before it is manifested!

Jesus also operated on this principle: *"Truly, truly, I say to you, the Son can do nothing of Himself, unless it is something He sees the Father doing; for whatever the Father does, these things the Son also does in like manner"* (John

5:19 NASB95). Jesus was led by what the Scripture had prophesied about Him, but He was also led by spiritual inner vision. For example, since there was no prior example in Scripture of the use of spittle and clay in relation to healing, Jesus must have had an inner leading to use this type of action to help a blind man be made whole! (See John 9:1–7.)

BREAKTHROUGH STRATEGIES

After Joshua could see the victory, God gave him a most unusual strategy. I have noticed that while God can and does provide simple solutions to complex challenges, He also often provides strategies that, in the natural, seem far-fetched. I've seen God give me both.

Years ago, there was a family in my church whose members had been believers long before they joined the church. In their earlier days, as newer believers, they had attended a meeting where the guest minister preached a strong message on giving and prosperity. They were very inspired, and, at the end of the message, when the altar call was given, they, like many others in the congregation, went forward and pledged their house to the church. They delivered the deed to their house to the church the very next morning. I firmly believe in the principles of giving, seedtime, harvest, and abundance. I also believe that faith grows over time and that sometimes people get in trouble when they act out of presumption in their excitement instead of in true faith. This was the case with this couple. I cannot speak about the message that was preached or the guest minister because I was not present, but it was clear that this couple had acted prematurely out of presumption, regardless of what had been preached.

They repeatedly said that they had felt pressured and manipulated into giving up their house. They were not giving a gift of that magnitude in faith, nor had they been led by God to do so. Not only did they not get "a hundredfold" of houses (see, for example, Matthew 13:23), as they had been promised they would, but, professionally and financially, they started declining fast. By the time they became members of my church, over fifteen years later, they had lived hand to mouth and were constantly afraid they would be evicted and homeless if their previous church decided to take possession of the house. They were still living in the home because, legally, the church had not yet officially removed the couple's names from the house deed due to the legal costs needed for each such transaction.

One afternoon, the Spirit suddenly told me, "Tell them to go take the deed back." I didn't know if that was legally possible, but I knew that, socially, in that culture, it was unacceptable to ask for a fifteen-year-old gift to a church to be returned. I also thought that to even consider that request would put the church in a difficult position because, if they returned this couple's deed, it might open them up to a flood of other requests. But I knew I had heard from God, so I arranged for the couple to come to see me. I told them what the Spirit had said, and, although they were hesitant about it, I explained that there was an urgency in my heart that they obey quickly. I advised them to be firm and to apologize to their previous pastor.

The next week, they let me know that they were miraculously able to get an appointment to see the pastor, and even though he was taken aback and a little displeased by their request, he agreed to it.

Three months later, unexpectedly, this pastor, who was only in his early sixties, had a massive heart attack and passed away. Within a month, the board that took over the church initiated a process of changing the names on all the house deeds to that of the ministry. Had the Spirit not intervened with that seemingly simple but unusual instruction, the couple would have been without a home.

I have found that most of God's instructions for our receiving a breakthrough in any area of life are exactly just that—simple but unusual.

- *"Give, and it will be given to you"* (Luke 6:38, various translations).
- Believe, and nothing will be impossible. (See, for example, Matthew 17:19–20.)
- Bless the Lord, and your youth will be renewed like the eagle's. (See Psalm 103:1–5.)

Simple but doable instructions, each with a promise that far outweighs what we are asked to do.

In faith and obedience, when we do what God asks of us, no matter how insignificant or unusual, He, in turn, does for us what we could not do for ourselves.

This is what breakthrough is. A breakthrough is when we break through the natural, or what we can do, and go over into another realm that we could not otherwise get ourselves into.

Breakthrough is always the result of our determinedly following a simple instruction from God that allows Him entry into our circumstances.

In Joshua 6, why didn't God give Joshua a more practical military strategy? Because God intended to move on the Israelites' behalf, and it wasn't their military might, but their obedience, that He needed.

PRAISE LEADS THE WAY

Perhaps even more unusual than God's instruction to march around the walls of Jericho was His instruction to place the priests, with their praise instruments, at the front of the march. It was already strange to have people marching around the walls, but now the praisers were leading them. What a sight that must have been!

Praise takes our eyes off ourselves and our circumstances and puts our focus on God. As the children of Israel marched around Jericho, they could have focused on how impregnable the walls seemed, but because the priests were leading the way and leading them in praise, their minds shifted heavenward instead of toward the walls.

You might have a wall of Jericho in front of you. It might be a financial Jericho. It might be a physical Jericho. It might be a marriage Jericho. But if you let praise lead the way, pointing you to God, those walls won't seem so impregnable and will soon come down!

Imagine what the priests must have thought when Joshua placed them out in front! They weren't trained for military conquest. That wasn't their main function. Yet they had to lead the march and praise by faith. *Faith has a sound of praise!*

Praise is the language of faith because faith causes you to praise and give glory to God *before* the walls fall down. Hebrews 11:30 (NLT) states, *"It was by faith that the people of Israel marched around Jericho for seven days, and the walls came crashing down."*

God instructed the Israelites to lift up praise for six days *before* they shouted at the walls on the seventh day. The Lord inhabits the praises of

His people. (See Psalm 22:3 KJV.) So, by praising for six days, the Israelites were inviting the presence of God to inhabit their praises and be among them.

Seven is God's number of completion and perfection. Praise brings you to the seventh day!

YIELD TO THE SPIRIT'S PROMPTINGS

> *Joshua said, "Alas, O Lord GOD, why did You ever bring this people over the Jordan, only to deliver us into the hand of the Amorites, to destroy us? If only we had been willing to dwell beyond the Jordan!..." So the LORD said to Joshua: "...Israel has sinned, and they have also transgressed My covenant which I commanded them. And they have even taken some of the things under the ban and have both stolen and deceived. Moreover, they have also put them among their own things."*
>
> (Joshua 7:7, 10–11 NASB95)

Defeat in any area of life is not God's plan for His people. Defeat results from our ignorance of the enemy's devices or our willful, continual resistance to God's wooing.

The remedy for the former is to let the Spirit lead us to truth.

The remedy for the latter is to yield to the promptings of the Spirit.

Either way, the Spirit can illuminate our blind spots for us. He only does so to offer us a way of escape upward. The Holy Spirit never exposes wrong thinking or wrong actions for the purpose of shaming or ridicule. He could not be the *Holy* Spirit if He did because nothing about shame or ridicule is holy. But the Holy Spirit, as our Guide and Teacher, does help us to discern right from wrong. He can even help us to discern *who and what* are right and wrong!

It should come as no surprise that the Holy Spirit leads us into holy living. Holy living is not the result of adhering to a set of rules and regulations. Holy living is the result of being led by the Holy Spirit.

Thus, in the book of Joshua, we discover that the Spirit leads us to see God's will and ways, to receive breakthrough strategies, to praise Him until we see the victory, and to continually yield to His loving promptings.

JUDGES

Supplier of Supernatural Strength

Picking up after the death of Joshua, Judges is a book about men who did right in their own eyes. (See Judges 21:25.) Those of Joshua's generation who had a "different spirit" had died, and now a new generation had arisen that had not yet personally witnessed the power of God. This post-Joshua generation had only secondhand knowledge of God's power. That is always a dangerous position to be in. No generation can live off the previous generations' exploits with God. Because this was the case with the generations recorded in the book of Judges, it wasn't long before they forsook God altogether and started following after idols.

The book of Judges lists thirteen judges and their attempts to govern during a particularly troubled time in Israel's history. The idolatry that had overrun the land resulted in Israel's falling into the hands of various oppressors. Yet God, in His mercy and faithfulness, raised up a judge each time Israel cried out for deliverance. These judges were anointed to be military and civic leaders and to bring deliverance to Israel.

Five judges were specifically noted as being Spirit-filled: Othniel, Deborah, Gideon, Jephthah, and Samson.

THE SPIRIT UPON OTHNIEL

> *When the sons of Israel cried to the* Lord, *the* Lord *raised up a deliverer for the sons of Israel to deliver them, Othniel the son of Kenaz, Caleb's younger brother. The Spirit of the* Lord ***came upon him,*** *and he judged Israel. When he went out to war, the* Lord *gave Cushan-rishathaim king of Mesopotamia into his hand, so that he prevailed over Cushan-rishathaim. Then the land had rest forty years. And Othniel the son of Kenaz died.* (Judges 3:9–11 NASB95)

The phrase *"came upon him"* means that the Spirit was actively present upon Othniel. It implies a sudden, unannounced coming of the power of God on him. This sudden "coming" was similar to what happened to the one hundred and twenty disciples on the day of Pentecost.

Othniel was the nephew and son-in-law of Caleb and had stood out because of his faith and obedience ever since Caleb's challenge to capture Kiriath-sepher. (See Joshua 15:16–17; Judges 1:12–13.) Othniel was accustomed to having "splashes" of God's Spirit on him, but, at this moment, the Spirit came upon him again suddenly. This is a picture of the gift of faith (see 1 Corinthians 12:9) available to all believers. We should expect God's Spirit to come upon us suddenly in times of need.

As with Othniel, the Spirit of God can empower you with leadership and with plans to usher in peace in your times of turmoil.

THE SPIRIT UPON DEBORAH

> *Village life ceased, it ceased in Israel, until I, Deborah, arose, arose a mother in Israel.* (Judges 5:7 NKJV)

Deborah was a prophetess; like the other judges, she was a civic and military leader. The Spirit's coming upon Deborah was a foretaste of what would happen in the book of Acts when the Spirit was poured out on all flesh—male and female.

Many scholars consider Deborah to be one of the more spiritual judges because she needed no external promptings like fleeces (as did Gideon) to boost her faith. She was also the only publicly acknowledged judge who did not personally engage in or win any military conquest. Thus, our faith should not *just* be that "God promotes me *after* a battle." Of course, if there is a battle of any kind for us to fight, we should believe we will win and receive promotion afterward; but to set our faith in that way might position us to have battles even in times of peace! Our attitude should be that the Spirit of God can bring us to a place of prominence even without our directly engaging in a fight.

THE SPIRIT UPON GIDEON

> *The angel of the LORD appeared to him and said to him, "The LORD is with you, O valiant warrior." Then Gideon said to him, "O my lord,* ***if the LORD is with us, why then has all this happened to us? And where are all His miracles which our fathers told us about****, saying, 'Did not the LORD bring us up from Egypt?' But now the LORD has abandoned us and given us into the hand of Midian." The LORD looked at him and said, "Go in this your strength and deliver Israel from the hand of Midian. Have I not sent you?" He said to Him, "O Lord, how shall I deliver Israel?* ***Behold, my family is the least in Manasseh, and I am the youngest in my father's house.****" But the LORD said to him, "Surely I will be with you, and you shall defeat Midian as one man." So Gideon said to Him, "If now I have found favor in Your sight, then* ***show me a sign*** *that it is You who speak with me."*
>
> (Judges 6:12–17 NASB95)

SIGNS AND WONDERS FOR OUR GENERATION

Revival is often the result of unrest in the natural and spiritual status quo among the people of God. This unrest comes from our natural observations of our environment and circumstances and also a stirring from the Spirit of God Himself. The Spirit stirs us so we can ask Him to cause His rain to fall upon us. It is a divine cycle that the Spirit initiates and orchestrates.

Just as Gideon asked for a supernatural manifestation to meet the lack of physical evidence that God was present among the people, I see a generation rising up that is unsatisfied with a signless religion. May we have a generation that will rise up and ask God for signs and wonders for and in their generation!

Gideon came from a small tribe, and he saw himself as such. His humble circumstances had ingrained in him a small vision and small expectations. He wondered if God could move through him, and, because of this, God replied that because *He* was on Gideon's side, Gideon could defeat the Midianites. The same reality is true for us today. Paul echoes this thought in Romans 8:31 (NLT): *"If God is for us, who can ever be against us?"* Our circumstances do not determine what God can do for us and through us. A move of the Spirit is not limited by our situations but by our hunger; you can be hungry for God regardless of your circumstances!

> *Then the angel of the LORD put out the end of the staff that was in his hand and touched the meat and the unleavened bread; and fire sprang up from the rock and consumed the meat and the unleavened bread. Then the angel of the LORD vanished from his sight.*
> (Judges 6:21 NASB95)

The sign that the angel of the Lord gave Gideon was one of prophetic fire. Jesus is the Rock, and the fire coming from the rock is a picture of Jesus baptizing us in the fire of the Holy Spirit. Whenever an individual or generation cries out for God, God's response is always a baptism of the Holy Spirit's fire—because nothing else will do!

TO FLEECE OR NOT TO FLEECE

> *Then Gideon said to God, "If You will deliver Israel through me, as You have spoken, behold, I will put a fleece of wool on the threshing floor. If there is dew on the fleece only, and it is dry on all the ground, then I will know that You will deliver Israel through me, as You have spoken."* (Judges 6:36–37 NASB95)

Even after his encounter with God and the fire from the rock, Gideon questioned whether God could move through him. So, he asked God for another sign. This time, rather than asking for a spiritually significant sign and wonder, he asked God to give him a natural sign of a dew-soaked, wet fleece on dry ground. After God answered this request, Gideon immediately asked for yet another sign involving the fleece: he asked for the ground to be wet and the fleece to be dry. (See verses 38–40.)

Although Gideon had the Spirit of God *on* him to be victorious against the Midianites, under the Old Testament, Gideon did not have the Spirit *in* him as we do today. Gideon had to look for external signs. Because we have the Holy Spirit inside us, the Spirit primarily leads us by an inward witness. If we seek "fleeces" for guidance, we open ourselves up to influences from the physical realm. As new creations, we have direct access to God through the Spirit, where the enemy has no access. Again, when we seek our primary guidance from the physical realm, it opens us up to possible deception because that's the realm where the devil has easy access. Any external guidance we seek and receive, including personal prophecies, dreams, and fleece-like experiences, should only confirm (or be *after*) a "green light" from our spirit-man.

THE SPIRIT UPON JEPHTHAH

> *Now Jephthah the Gileadite was a valiant warrior, but he was the son of a harlot. And Gilead was the father of Jephthah. Gilead's wife bore him sons; and when his wife's sons grew up, they drove Jephthah out and said to him, "You shall not have an inheritance in our father's house, for you are the son of another woman." So Jephthah fled from his brothers and lived in the land of Tob; and worthless fellows gathered themselves about Jephthah, and they went out with him.... Then Jephthah said to the elders of Gilead, "Did you not hate me and drive me from my father's house? So why have you come to me now when you are in trouble?"... Now the Spirit of the* LORD ***came upon*** *Jephthah, so that he passed through Gilead and Manasseh; then he passed through Mizpah of Gilead, and from Mizpah of Gilead he went on to the sons of Ammon.* (Judges 11:1–3, 7, 29 NASB95)

Jephthah is a wonderful example of how God can take anyone from a painfully broken family and then bless and increase them. He was born of a prostitute and later driven out and deprived of his inheritance by his half-brothers; he then banded together with other broken men—and still the Spirit came upon him. Your history does not have to be a prophecy of your future. The Spirit of God on Jephthah, and in you, is the Great Equalizer! The same phrase, *"came upon,"* that was used to describe the Spirit upon Othniel is used here with Jephthah. This again means that

Jephthah would experience an occasional burst of the Spirit upon him, but, at an appointed time, the Spirit would come upon him strongly. Maintain a relationship with the Holy Spirit, and He will suddenly show up for you at necessary, appointed times in your life as well!

THE SPIRIT UPON SAMSON

Perhaps the judge that is the most well-known to us is Samson. His life story is often retold in Sunday school classes around the world.

STIRRED UP

Two specific phrases are used to describe the Holy Spirit's activity in Samson's life. We see the first in Judges 13:25 (NKJV): *"And the Spirit of the LORD began to **move upon him** at Mahaneh Dan between Zorah and Eshtaol."*

Many other Bible translations, including the NASB95, render the phrase *"began to move upon him"* as *"began to stir him."* This means that the Spirit agitated or troubled Samson's spirit. The same Hebrew word is used to describe the troubled spirits of Pharaoh (see Genesis 41:8), Asaph the psalmist (see Psalm 77:4), and Nebuchadnezzar (Daniel 2:1).

God *"began to move upon"* Samson to stir him to action. A stirring of dissatisfaction from God is a spiritual call to arms, a call to press for more. This is a way that God raises up leaders. God's leaders are often those who are no longer content with the spiritual state of society. *God stirs a hunger for more so that He can send more!*

The Lord once told me that I could not crave something I had never tasted. When we hunger for more of anything in God, that desire, that craving, originates with Him so it can come *to* us and then flow *through* us. As we pray and get into His Word, God transmits His desires to us as our spiritual senses are heightened.

YIELDING TO GOD'S "SUDDENLIES"

The other phrase regarding the Holy Spirit's activity in Samson's life is in Judges 14:6 (NASB95): *"The Spirit of the LORD **came upon him mightily**...."*

This phrase is repeated in verse 19 and in Judges 15:14. This means that the Spirit *"rushed upon"* Samson. (See verse 6 ESV.) Again, as with Othniel and Jephthah, this was a type of a "suddenly" from the Holy Spirit.

When yielded to, this suddenly was the secret to Samson's strength and mighty exploits. Yielding to the Spirit is the key to the miraculous! The Spirit may nudge you to pray, give, lay hands on an individual, or even reach out to someone with a call or text; whatever the Spirit nudges you to do will produce the power of God if it is yielded to.

THE SPIRIT SUPPLIES SUPERNATURAL STRENGTH

> *The Spirit of the LORD came upon him mightily, so that he tore him as one tears a young goat though he had nothing in his hand; but he did not tell his father or mother what he had done.* (Judges 14:6 NASB95)

> *When he came to Lehi, the Philistines shouted as they met him. And the Spirit of the LORD came upon him mightily so that the ropes that were on his arms were as flax that is burned with fire, and his bonds dropped from his hands.* (Judges 15:14 NASB95)

There are two sources of strength that we can choose to operate from. They each have a different cost, and each bears different fruit.

Operating in our own strength costs us toil to achieve and toil to maintain. To operate in our own strength is to live a life of never-ending striving, plotting, and unrest. Peace is never available when we live according to our own strength because, when we do so, we put our fallible, finite selves in charge.

Operating in life from God's strength allows for the all-knowing, all-powerful, ever-present Spirit of God to supply us with His resources. That is what supernatural strength is: the Spirit of God exercising the might of God through us.

THE GENTLE SPIRIT

> *She* [Delilah] *said, "The Philistines are upon you, Samson!" And he awoke from his sleep and said, "I will go out as at other times and shake myself free." But he did not know that the LORD had departed from him.* (Judges 16:20 NASB95)

It has been said that the Holy Spirit arrives loudly but departs quietly.

A better way to say it would be that the Holy Spirit manifests roaringly but retreats quietly. As blood-washed, new-creation believers, we know that the Holy Spirit never departs from us in the sense of abandoning us or exiting from us; but, if we ignore Him, His presence in and through our lives can be dull and distant.

This happens in degrees, as it did in the life of Samson. While most people think of that pivotal moment when Samson had his hair cut and lost his anointing (see Judges 16:18–20), they forget that his slide from the presence of God began long before that. We see in Judges 14 that he was already breaking the Nazirite law, which he had been promised to since birth, of not touching anything unclean or dead (see Judges 13; Numbers 6:1–8), when he took honey from the lion's carcass.

He had also married a Philistine woman. To celebrate his illicit marriage, he hosted a wedding feast. (See Judges 14:1–11.) In Hebrew, the term translated as "*feast*" (verse 10) refers to a drinking party. As a Nazirite, Samson was supposed to have stayed away from alcohol as well. So we see that his slide from God was gradual.

Watch the small things in your life because they are what constitute the major things!

The same is true of faith. Some people live daily without exercising their faith or developing an awareness of God—but when something major, like a sickness, comes along, they expect to immediately "speak to the mountain." Faith, for anything, is developed in our daily life and not just when mountains arise!

Be intentional and consistent to daily develop your spiritual life.

THE FAITHFUL SPIRIT

> *Then Samson called to the* Lord *and said, "O Lord* God*, please remember me and please strengthen me...."* (Judges 16:28 NASB95)

At his lowest, most desperate moment, Samson cried out to God, and the Spirit empowered him again. Even when it seemed as if the presence of God had departed from Samson, the Holy Spirit was still near enough to hear and reply to him. The Holy Spirit is a faithful Spirit. The Lord once showed me that the Spirit always hovers over lives in darkness so that He can bring light to them.

Call on the Holy Spirit, and you will see His faithfulness!

RUTH

Doorkeeper to the Kinsman-Redeemer

The book of Ruth starts tragically with the death of a father, Elimelech, followed by the deaths of his two sons. Naomi, originally from Israel, is the widow of Elimelech, and Ruth and Orpah, who are from the land of Moab where the family is living, are the widows of the sons Mahlon and Chilion.

After the death of her sons, Naomi decides to make her way back to Israel. Since her daughters-in-law are from Moab, and seeing no benefit for them in traveling back with her, Naomi tries to dissuade them from joining her. Orpah agrees and leaves Naomi, but Ruth persists in staying with her mother-in-law and decides to accompany her to Israel.

Back in Bethlehem, tired and poor, Naomi and Ruth try to make a living. Ruth takes advantage of a law that allows the poor and destitute to glean leftover crops from harvested fields. (See Leviticus 23:22.)

At these fields, the prophetic drama in the book of Ruth takes off.

This book paints us a picture of the sovereignty of God through the heavy use of Hebrew symbolism. The Holy Spirit moves through some of the words and ways of Naomi but is otherwise hidden in the external story.

As we saw with the symbolism of Eliezer, the unnamed servant of Abraham in Genesis 24, aspects of Naomi's role exemplify the role of the Holy Spirit in the life of Ruth. The book of Ruth also includes an unnamed servant. Again, similar to Eliezer's role, as we will see, this unnamed servant brings Ruth to Boaz.

With Naomi as a representative type of the Holy Spirit, Ruth's faithfulness to Naomi is honored, and her social and financial standing are restored. Ruth moves from being a foreigner (see, for example, Ruth 2:10) to less than a lower servant (see verse 13) to a maidservant (see Ruth 3:9) to a wife (see Ruth 4:13).

Eliezer and the unnamed servant in the book of Ruth prophetically speak of the Holy Spirit's role in introducing and uniting Jesus and His bride, the church.

THE SPIRIT WEAVES RUTH INTO ADOPTION

> *Then Boaz said to his servant who was in charge of the reapers, "Whose young woman is this?" The servant in charge of the reapers replied, "She is the young Moabite woman who returned with Naomi from the land of Moab...." Then Boaz said to Ruth, "Listen carefully, my daughter. Do not go to glean in another field; furthermore, do not go on from this one, but stay here with my maids. Let your eyes be on the field which they reap, and go after them. Indeed, I have commanded the servants not to touch you. When you are thirsty, go to the water jars and drink from what the servants draw."* (Ruth 2:5–6, 8–9 NASB95)

The unnamed servant introduces Ruth, a Moabite foreigner, to Boaz, a kinsman. (See Ruth 2:1.) This is a beautiful picture of the spirit of adoption, an aspect of the work of the Holy Spirit. Romans 8:16 teaches us that the Holy Spirit enables us to call God our Abba Father.

Naomi later identifies Boaz as *goel*, a Hebrew word meaning kinsman-redeemer. (See Ruth 2:20.) This was important because of the law of Levirate marriage (see Deuteronomy 25:5–10), which allowed for a widow without children to go to the husband's next of kin and put a claim on him to marry her to raise children for the family. The kinsman-redeemer had to be a near kinsman, be able to fulfill his duties, and be willing.

Technically, using this law, Naomi could have claimed Boaz for herself, but she decided to forsake her claim in favor of Ruth. This speaks again of the favor with which the Holy Spirit showers us in introducing us to our Kinsman-Redeemer, Jesus!

If Naomi had claimed Boaz for herself, she would have come into immediate wealth. Yet since she was no longer of childbearing age (see Ruth 1:11–12), no offspring would have come from that union. This would then have affected the messianic line that Jesus ultimately came from because Ruth would go on to be the great-grandmother of David. Naomi's tender selflessness and sensitivity to the Holy Spirit positioned Ruth in the plans of God. The Holy Spirit does not guide only us into God's will but, through us, also aids others to enter into God's will!

Naomi and Ruth had some property that they had inherited from Elimelech, Mahlon, and Chilion. The man Ruth married would also have claim to that property. But there was another kinsman who was the first in line to marry Ruth since he was a closer relative. This meant that Boaz had to offer this other man the right to refuse to marry Ruth so that Boaz could buy the land and thus earn himself the right to marry her. This speaks of how Jesus, our Kinsman-Redeemer, purchased His right to His bride!

DRINKING LIVING WATER

> *Let your eyes be on the field which they reap, and go after them. Indeed, I have commanded the servants not to touch you. When you are thirsty, go to the water jars and drink from what the servants draw.*
>
> (Ruth 2:9 NASB95)

Just as Boaz offers Ruth water, Jesus offers us living water. To drink the water Jesus offers is to drink the Spirit Himself.

> *But those who drink the water I give will never be thirsty again. It becomes a fresh, bubbling spring within them, giving them eternal life.*
>
> (John 4:14 NLT)

> *Anyone who believes in me may come and drink! For the Scriptures declare, "Rivers of living water will flow from his heart."*
>
> (John 7:38 NLT)

SHAVUOT

> *Then Ruth the Moabitess said, "Furthermore, he said to me, 'You should stay close to my servants until they have finished all my harvest.'"*
> (Ruth 2:21 NASB95)

Boaz wanted Ruth to stay until the grain harvest. The Jewish people would celebrate the end of the harvest during Shavuot.

Later, Shavuot would not only be a harvest celebration but also a commemoration of the giving of the law (on Mount Sinai), also known as the Torah, which signified the legal marriage relationship between Jehovah and Israel.

Shavuot is also known as Pentecost, as it comes fifty days after the first day of Passover.

And, in Acts 2, on the day of Pentecost, there was a divine marriage between the Holy Spirit and the church.

On Shavuot, Jehovah and Israel were united.

On Pentecost, the Holy Spirit and the church were united.

The Holy Spirit works with Christ in the redemption and unification of the family of God!

We are not weary foreigners trying to eke out an existence. We, the redeemed, are part of the family of God—here on earth and there in heaven.

CLEANSED, ANOINTED, AND CLOTHED

> [Naomi told Ruth,] "*Wash yourself therefore, and anoint yourself and put on your best clothes, and go down to the threshing floor; but do not make yourself known to the man until he has finished eating and drinking.*"
> (Ruth 3:3 NASB95)

Ruth presents herself to Boaz only *after* washing, anointing herself, and wearing new garments. That's exactly what happens to the church! The Spirit washes us, anoints us, and then gives us robes of righteousness as the bride of Christ.

Again, remember that the spiritual types in the Old Testament speak of the divine Author's overall goal in His dealings with mankind: to bring forth the plan of redemption and restoration for human beings. Since that was His end goal, it would make sense that He would weave this plot into the preceding chapters of the grand finale of Calvary! Modern-day authors follow the same pattern when writing series of books. Hints of the main plot are scattered throughout the earlier books, which are tied together only in the series' final book.

THE SPIRIT GIVES LIFE

> *So Boaz took Ruth, and she became his wife, and he went in to her. And the* Lord *enabled her to conceive* [literally, "gave her conception"[2]], *and she gave birth to a son.* (Ruth 4:13 NASB95)

We don't know if Ruth was barren in her previous marriage, but we can see that the Spirit orchestrated this conception. The Holy Spirit "gave"; in Hebrew, this word can mean "to put" or "to make" (*Strong's*, H5414). The Holy Spirit is the One who gives life.

Boaz and Ruth named their son Obed. Obed fathered Jesse, who fathered David, from whose line the Messiah was born. Boaz himself was the son of Rahab, the former harlot from Jericho who had protected the Israelite spies. (See Joshua 6:17–25; Matthew 1:5.) The Holy Spirit had His hand on Ruth in bringing her to Boaz!

As in Ruth's situation, from your brokenness, the Spirit of God can move you toward your destiny in the Son.

---

2. NASB95, verse 13, footnote a.

1 SAMUEL

Appointer of the Anointed

Under the governance of the judges, Israel had degenerated even further spiritually and politically; even the priesthood was corrupt. This opened the door to the successful attacks of the Philistines. With this backdrop, the faithfulness of God miraculously raised up the prophet Samuel. In his later years, Samuel grew weary of the request of his sons and the people for a king. Saul was chosen to be king but quickly revealed his true colors by his disobedience and lack of faithfulness toward God. Saul's old age was sadly consumed by his paranoia and jealousy over David, the young shepherd. But David acted with godly reverence and wisdom and was responsive to the Lord.

THE SPIRIT CALLS YOUNG SAMUEL

> *Now the boy Samuel was ministering to the LORD before Eli. And word from the LORD was rare in those days, visions were infrequent.... The LORD called Samuel; and he said, "Here I am."*
>
> (1 Samuel 3:1, 4 NASB95)

Traditionally, Samuel is believed to have been twelve years old at this time. Because of his praying mother, Hannah, and his miraculous birth (see 1 Samuel 1), he grew up around the things of God.

These were spiritually dark times in Israel; words from the Lord were all but nonexistent on the earth, largely because of the priesthood's corruption. Society is always a reflection of the house of God, never the other way around. Rather than complain about how dark the world is, we in the church need to turn up the light in God's house!

First Samuel 3:1, which records, "*Word from the Lord was rare in those days,*" tells us that words from the Lord are supposed to be abundant in the land. Their rarity was so unusual that it had to be stated! God intends for His written and spoken word to be declared across the land. This will require hungry hearts and anointed lips.

God's speaking to twelve-year-old Samuel about the corrupt priesthood (under which Samuel was mentoring) indicated the rise of a prophetic generation that would bring advancement and correction to the previous generation's errors. This did not mean that Samuel did not respect Eli the priest. He honored and served the office Eli occupied. Samuel faithfully delivered the word of the Lord to Eli (see 1 Samuel 3) but did not seek to correct Eli himself. He set a higher standard of the prophetic for his generation.

The Holy Spirit is always seeking to raise up a new generation that will be a voice for the Lord. He does this in His mercy because He doesn't want a generation to grow up without hearing words from the Lord (from both the written Word and spoken rhema words). The proper role of the Eli generation would have been to groom the Samuel generation for hearing and proclaiming the voice of the Spirit. Ironically, Eli did provide proper instructions to Samuel on how to respond to the Spirit's voice, but his heart was so cold that he agreed with, but didn't heed, the word that came through Samuel about his impending judgment.

THE SPIRIT APPOINTS, AND THE SPIRIT ANOINTS

The Holy Spirit raises up companies of prophets and uses oil as a symbol of His anointing; this symbol is used extensively in the book of 1 Samuel.

Then Samuel took the flask of oil, poured it on his [Saul's] *head, kissed him and said, "Has not the* Lord *anointed you a ruler over His inheritance?... And it shall be as soon as you have come there to the city, that you will meet a group of prophets coming down from the high place with harp, tambourine, flute, and a lyre before them, and they will be prophesying. Then the Spirit of the* Lord *will come upon you mightily, and you shall prophesy with them and be changed into another man. It shall be when these signs come to you, do for yourself what the occasion requires, for God is with you...." Then it happened when he turned his back to leave Samuel, God changed his heart; and all those signs came about on that day.* (1 Samuel 10:1, 5–7, 9 NASB95)

The anointing, symbolized by the oil, was necessary to set Saul apart as king.

We need God's anointing to extend kingdom rule over His inheritance. The anointing is the strength-giver and the difference-maker!

The anointing on the company of prophets was amplified by their praise and worship. Spirit-led worship enhances the anointing. Music can charge the atmosphere and set the stage for the moving of the Spirit!

When the anointing oil was applied, the Spirit came upon Saul, cloaking him in the presence of God, and he started to prophesy. (See verses 10–13.) Prophesying in some form is always the result of the Spirit coming upon anyone. Not only that, but Saul was also *"changed into another man"* (verse 6).

The anointing empowers us to manifest the workings of the Spirit, and it transforms us so that this empowerment can be sustained. This shows us that the anointing *upon* is for service, and the anointing *within* is for our personal life and relationship with God.

It takes the anointing of the Spirit to be able to "do what the occasion requires." In other words, it takes an anointing to do what God requires at the moment.

The anointing is God's response to situations through us.

Like Saul's, our hearts are changed by the anointing, since it is the anointing that breaks the yoke (see Isaiah 10:27), and it is the anointing that sets our hearts free to obey God.

MY UMBRELLA AND I...

A longtime pastor friend of mine, who has taken many trips with me to Southeast Asia, often talks about a specific memory from one of our early trips there.

Once, I brought the mission team out to a village on an island where we had done a lot of humanitarian work and church planting. My friend had walked alone deeper into the village, and he noticed a group of brutish-looking men whispering to themselves, glaring at him, and seemingly sizing him up. He thought they were going to rob or attack him. Just as it seemed like they were going to move toward him, they suddenly looked scared and backed away. He turned around to see what had caused them to scatter, and, to his surprise, he saw me slowly walking toward him, totally oblivious to what was happening, with my blue umbrella opened over me. I always had an umbrella on those islands because the sun would beat down on us relentlessly. Since it wasn't my umbrella that scared them off, and I wasn't even specifically looking in their direction, my friend quickly recognized that the men sensed the call and anointing that I walked in as I went into these regions, which caused the evil they had planned to dissipate! The anointing is like a heavenly cloak that is tangibly on us, is visible by manifestation, and can even be spiritually sensed by those around us.

Just as Saul was changed into another man by the anointing and could do what the occasion required, so will you as you walk in the anointing!

A TALE OF TWO KINGS

> *Now the* Lord *said to Samuel, "How long will you grieve over Saul, since I have rejected him from being king over Israel? Fill your horn with oil and go; I will send you to Jesse the Bethlehemite, for I have selected a king for Myself among his sons."... Then Samuel took the horn of oil and anointed him* [David] *in the midst of his brothers; and the Spirit of the* Lord *came mightily upon David from that day forward. And Samuel arose and went to Ramah.*
>
> (1 Samuel 16:1, 13 NASB95)

The anointing changed Saul and moved through him; however, the Holy Spirit won't move outside of what we allow Him to do in our life.

Saul made some very bad decisions in his reign as king, ultimately leading to God's raising up David to take his place.

Again, we see a principle of the anointing: what made David king in the eyes of God was the anointing, not David's current status or position. It wasn't until about fifteen years later that David assumed the throne. Likewise, it may take the anointing a while to get you to where you are supposed to be, but the anointing will get you to where you are supposed to be! Between the time of his anointing and his enthronement, David's tender heart toward the Lord and obedience to the Spirit kept him safe. The anointing doesn't just empower you; it can also preserve you.

After David was anointed as king by Samuel, he was later anointed two more times—once as king of Judah (see 2 Samuel 2:4) and once by the full twelve tribes when he was crowned king of Israel as well (see 2 Samuel 5:3; 1 Chronicles 11:3).

The anointing on David enabled him to kill the lion, the bear, and Goliath. (See 1 Samuel 17:20–51.)

The anointing on David was transmitted to Saul when David played the harp. (See 1 Samuel 16:23.)

The anointing on David brought Saul's son Jonathan to him for friendship and drew the four hundred desperate men together in the cave of Adullam to support him. (See 1 Samuel 18:1–4; 22:1–2.)

All of these events drew out aspects of the call of God on David that were necessary to bring him to his anointed place.

Anointings are *singular* in purpose but *plural* in manifestation.

DON'T GO ON WITHOUT THE SPIRIT!

> *But the Spirit of the Lord departed from Saul, and a distressing spirit from the Lord troubled him.* (1 Samuel 16:14 NKJV)

It is important to remember that before the blood of Jesus was shed, no one was righteous enough for the Spirit to dwell in. The Spirit would come upon a prophet, a king, or a priest, but it was an anointing *on* them, not *in* them. This is why the Spirit departed from Saul: the Spirit couldn't be *on*

Saul while he was walking in the direction he was—away from obedience to God.

As a result of Saul's continued wrong choices, the Spirit of God lifted from him, but Saul still forged ahead in his own willful strength. At this point, Saul either did not know that the Spirit had lifted from him, meaning he was no longer sensitive to the Spirit, or he knew it but did not care, meaning he was in rebellion against God. Either of these positions is spiritually dangerous.

The *"distressing spirit"* (or *"evil spirit,"* various translations; see also 18:10; 19:9) that came on Saul would be better understood as one that was allowed or permitted by God. God has no evil spirits to send anyone! But since God's Spirit had departed, evil occupied that vacated seat in Saul. Darkness is simply the absence of light, and Saul's life was in darkness.

I have learned to stop rather than push beyond the Spirit in life and ministry. I've told pastors the same thing: the preaching and the meeting end when the anointing lifts. Start when the Spirit starts, and stop when the Spirit stops!

THE SPIRIT AND WISDOM

> *David was prospering* [or "acting wisely"[3]] *in all his ways for the Lord was with him.* (1 Samuel 18:14 NASB95)

The anointing on David to be king, prophet, and psalmist-priest included his having the spirit of wisdom. David would not have fulfilled any of those offices if he had been unwise in his daily affairs. The Spirit does not just endow us with power and might; He also endows us with wisdom. To walk fully in the anointing, we must walk in that wisdom.

3. NASB95, verse 14, footnote a.

2 SAMUEL

Adviser to the King

The ascension and reign of David are the focal point of the book of 2 Samuel.

David is considered Israel's greatest and most beloved king. Like all the other characters in the Bible, he wasn't a perfect man, but he did seek and experience the love and mercy of God. Continually seeking and experiencing God made David a man after God's own heart. (See, for example, Acts 13:22.) He nurtured his relationship with the Lord and cherished the anointing he had been given.

SAME SPIRIT, DIFFERENT MEN

In 1 and 2 Samuel, David's heart can be seen in stark contrast to Saul's heart.

Saul's anointing left him. But once David was anointed, *"from that day forward"* (1 Samuel 16:13, various translations), the anointing never departed.

Saul tried to kill David twenty-one times over the course of nine years and thought nothing of it. David begged God to retain the Spirit in his life after he committed adultery. (See Psalm 51:11.)

Saul sought out the witch of Endor (or En Dor) when he could not hear from God. (See 1 Samuel 28:3–20.)

After David's sin was exposed and his son died, David *"arose from the ground, washed, anointed himself, and changed his clothes; and he came into the house of the* LORD *and worshiped"* (2 Samuel 12:20 NASB95).

Both men had the same Spirit upon them. Both men had a kingly anointing.

Each of these men had moral and spiritual failures. Each responded to the Spirit differently.

The Holy Spirit and the accompanying anointing flow in our lives in the measure that we allow them to.

In 2 Samuel, the Spirit may be seen as David's Counselor, as David would often inquire of the Lord. The holiness of the Spirit may also be seen in Nathan's confrontation with David over his affair with Bathsheba and his arranged murder of her husband, Uriah.

We see the Holy Spirit operate through multifaceted manifestations centered on the anointing on King David.

SPEAKING BY THE SPIRIT

The last three chapters of 2 Samuel sum up David's life and reign.

In chapter 23, David reveals a key principle in his life: *"The Spirit of the* LORD *spoke by me, and His word was on my tongue"* (verse 2, various translations).

As a shepherd, a psalmist, and a king, David learned to yield his tongue to the Spirit so that the Spirit could speak through him. *The tongue was David's, but the words were God's.* This is a picture of how the Spirit inspires utterances on the earth. Utterances from God are always needed before manifestations of the Spirit occur. The psalm of David that is included in 2 Samuel 22:2–51 illustrates this.

I have found that we can "unhook" our tongue from our mind and "hook" it onto our spirit, where the Holy Spirit dwells. One means of doing this is to pray in tongues.

Our mind was made to study, inquire, and question. Our heart, our spirit, was made to believe. When we hook our tongue to our spirit, we allow the indwelling Holy Spirit to cause us to speak prophetically; this includes both foretelling and forth-telling. Foretelling is declaring the plans of God that are not yet manifest in the earthly realm. Forth-telling is supernatural insight and proclamation regarding the already revealed plans of God. We must learn to still ourselves, hear from the Spirit, and then speak forth what the Spirit says to us!

1 KINGS

Standard Against Wickedness

The historical books show that God is involved in the history of mankind. First Kings records the turbulence among God's people after the death of David. Sadly, internal and external pressures caused the kingdom to split in two. Despite the book's title, the main characters in this book are prophets such as Elijah and Elisha.

THE TANGIBLE PRESENCE

> *The priests could not stand to minister* [in the temple] *because of the cloud, for the glory of the* LORD *filled the house of the* LORD.
>
> (1 Kings 8:11 NASB95)

The Israelites had previously experienced God's presence in the tabernacle. (See Exodus 40:34.) The Spirit of God manifested in this way to signify His abode among the people. The people could worship at such a level because their worship came from their covenant relationship with God, established through Abraham and later Moses. It is the same for us today. By our covenant through Christ, we ourselves are now the Spirit's abode. When we take time to worship God and to honor His indwelling presence, we develop a sensitivity to that presence.

I've experienced a number of services where the worship was similar to that described in the above verse. Once, I led a youth service that lasted for five hours. The young people sat, knelt, or were prostrate in near absolute stillness and quiet. On another occasion, at a pastors' conference in Asia, the service went way past midnight, with the people in similar postures of worship and surrender. In both those occurrences, the worship team on the stage fell out under the power of God. I noted that each time we had the manifestation of a thick presence of God, it was usually after a series of meetings; it wasn't normally during the first meeting of the conference. People need time to adjust inwardly toward abandonment in worship. While there may have been some exhortation made at the beginning of the service for the people to worship, the presence became thick only when those leading the service led the people into engaging in deep worship together.

A high level of corporate reverence is needed to usher in that level of the presence of God. This is another reason why more than one meeting is usually needed to experience it. If you have people attending the service from different backgrounds and expectations, it takes a while for that synchronicity to happen.

At those meetings where there was a heightened corporate awareness of the Spirit's presence, many healings and deliverances took place without the laying on of hands or the calling out of words of knowledge. Once, a young man with scoliosis was healed, having his back straightened! The presence of God just seemed to roll into the building and engulf the people.

THE SPIRIT OF GOD, ELIJAH, AND ELISHA

Elijah and his protégé, Elisha, are a delight to study regarding the anointing! These men flowed easily with the Spirit of God. The manifestations they experienced are among the most spectacular in Scripture. Let's look at several of them.

TRANSLATIONS

> [Obadiah, the steward of King Ahab, said to Elijah,] *"It will come about when I leave you that the Spirit of the LORD will carry you where*

> *I do not know; so when I come and tell Ahab and he cannot find you, he will kill me, although I your servant have feared the LORD from my youth."* (1 Kings 18:12 NASB95)

Being caught up by the Spirit and being translated to another location is a phenomenon that is recorded at least twice more in Scripture. (See Ezekiel 37:1; Acts 8:39.) Since chronological time and space as we know them in the physical realm were created by God for us, translations occur when we are caught up physically in the Spirit and transported somewhere else.

FIRE

> [Elijah said,] *"Answer me, O LORD, answer me, that this people may know that You, O LORD, are God, and that You have turned their heart back again." Then the fire of the LORD fell and consumed the burnt offering and the wood and the stones and the dust, and licked up the water that was in the trench. When all the people saw it, they fell on their faces; and they said, "The LORD, He is God; the LORD, He is God."* (1 Kings 18:37–39 NASB95)

Elijah's victory on Mount Carmel resulted from an epic Spirit-led challenge to the prophets of Baal. His boldness to issue this challenge was the gift of faith in operation. Elijah expected God to accept his sacrifice with fire from heaven when he called on the Lord. He had such explosive faith that he drenched the offering and the firewood with four large pots of water—three times! (See verses 30–35.)

The result of the fire from heaven was not just the devastation of the prophets of Baal: the people *"fell on their faces"* and acknowledged the Lord.

The Spirit's purpose in demonstration is always twofold: first, so that the work and people of God will not be hindered; and, second, so that people will be free to know God's offer of redemption. We see both of these purposes in this occurrence of the gift of faith in Elijah.

RUNNING IN THE SPIRIT

> *Then the hand of the LORD was on Elijah, and he girded up his loins and outran Ahab to Jezreel.* (1 Kings 18:46 NASB95)

By a supernatural sign to Ahab, Elijah ran ahead of Ahab's carriage under the anointing of the Spirit. For Elijah to be able to physically do that demanded the power of God, which was again a sign to Ahab. This demonstration was the overflowing mercy of God to Ahab in case he had missed the previous demonstration of fire on Elijah's water-soaked offering!

When the supernatural power of God comes into contact with our physical being, we can be energized. Something has to happen when you come into contact with the supernatural. As we have seen, the Holy Spirit is a gentle Spirit. The Holy Spirit did not *make* Elijah run; instead, He *enabled* Elijah to run. Elijah had to yield to God in order to run, and then the Spirit enabled him. It is the same with any spiritual endowment. We have to want to yield to the anointing so that, when we do, the anointing can empower us with a heavenly endowment to do the natural supernaturally.

This is the case with speaking in tongues. *"And they were all filled with the Holy Spirit* [endowment] *and began to speak with other tongues* [yielding], *as the Spirit was giving them utterance* [empowerment]" (Acts 2:4 NASB95).

This concept is made even clearer in *The Amplified Bible*'s rendering of this verse: *"And they were all filled [that is, diffused throughout their being] with the Holy Spirit and began to speak in other tongues (different languages),* ***as the Spirit was giving them the ability to speak out*** *[clearly and appropriately]."*

The Holy Spirit didn't speak in tongues *for* them; He *empowered them* to speak in tongues as they yielded to Him.

The believers' tongues. The Holy Spirit's words.

Elijah's legs. The Holy Spirit's speed.

Our willing yieldedness. The Holy Spirit's manifestation.

RUNNING AWAY

> *And he was afraid* [because of Jezebel's threat to kill him] *and arose and ran for his life and came to Beersheba, which belongs to Judah, and left his servant there.* (1 Kings 19:3 NASB95)

Scripture records Elijah running again. But, this time, he was running not in the Spirit but in his flesh out of despair that led to depression. For all of his mighty encounters and experiences with the Spirit, Elijah stepped out from operating under the anointing and instead saw things according to his carnal mind. His carnal mind failed to remember all that God had done for and through him; sadly, it could see only in the desperate natural. Elijah saw Jezebel through his natural eyes instead of his spiritual eyes.

It's one thing to operate mightily under the anointing, but it's another thing to develop your spirit-man in your relationship with God.

Remember, the anointing *on* you and through you serves others. But your relationship with God sustains you in your personal life. You could say that one is a gift that is given, and the other is fruit that has to ripen. It is to our detriment to have one without the other.

> *Then he came there to a cave and lodged there; and behold, the word of the LORD came to him, and He said to him, "What are you doing here, Elijah?"*
> (verse 9 NASB95)

The faithfulness of God reached out to Elijah while he was having a one-man pity party in a cave. Similarly, we can expect the Holy Spirit to find and comfort us at our lowest point!

THE STILL, SMALL VOICE

> *Then He said, "Go out, and stand on the mountain before the LORD." And behold, the LORD passed by, and a great and strong wind tore into the mountains and broke the rocks in pieces before the LORD, but the LORD was not in the wind; and after the wind an earthquake, but the LORD was not in the earthquake; and after the earthquake a fire, but the LORD was not in the fire; and after the fire a still small voice.*
> (1 Kings 19:11–12 NKJV)

God wasn't found in the strong wind. God wasn't found in the earthquake. God wasn't found in the fire.

God was found in the still, small voice!

Some people have gotten so used to hearing about or experiencing the Spirit speak in a loud, booming voice that they forget that the Spirit also speaks in a still, small voice. This is especially so for us in the New Testament era because the Spirit now dwells inside us. The Spirit's still, small voice is the primary means by which we, as the church, are led. All other voices should only confirm what the still, small voice has already told us. As has often been said, don't miss the supernatural by looking for the spectacular!

SHEEP WITHOUT A SHEPHERD

Micaiah is another prophet whose ministry is recorded in 1 Kings. Not much is said about him, but what is said in chapter 22 reveals quite a lot about the spiritual realm.

Ahab, the wicked king of Israel—the northern kingdom—and Jehoshaphat, the righteous king of Judah—the southern kingdom—formed an uneasy military alliance. But before they marched their troops off to war, they called for prophets to see what additional direction they could receive.

Four hundred prophets from the northern kingdom were gathered, and they all chimed in unison, *"Go up, for the Lord will give it into the hand of the king"* (1 Kings 22:6 NASB95, ESV). Despite this word, Jehoshaphat was unsure, so he asked for another prophet to confirm it.

Ahab begrudgingly called for Micaiah, saying, *"But I hate him, because he does not prophesy good concerning me, but evil"* (verse 8 NASB95, NKJV).

At first, Micaiah mockingly mimicked the other prophets and proclaimed victory. (See verse 15.) Still, when pressed by Ahab, Micaiah delivered the true word: *"I saw all Israel scattered on the mountains, like sheep which have no shepherd. And the LORD said, 'These have no master. Let each of them return to his house in peace'"* (verse 17 NASB95).

Ahab misinterpreted this to mean he would not be successful in battle. However, a more likely interpretation is that Micaiah declared that Israel had no shepherd because Ahab was a false shepherd. Rather than let Micaiah's prophecy correct him, Ahab soon had Micaiah thrown in prison. (See verses 26–28.)

It takes the Spirit to prophesy accurately, and it also takes the Spirit to interpret prophecies accurately.

Regardless of the interpretation, it didn't bode well for Ahab.

MICAIAH'S VISION OF THE THRONE ROOM

> *Then Micaiah said, "Therefore hear the word of the LORD: I saw the LORD sitting on His throne, and all the host of heaven standing by, on His right hand and on His left. And the LORD said, 'Who will persuade Ahab to go up, that he may fall at Ramoth Gilead?' So one spoke in this manner, and another spoke in that manner. Then a spirit came forward and stood before the LORD, and said, 'I will persuade him.' The LORD said to him, 'In what way?' So he said, 'I will go out and be a lying spirit in the mouth of all his prophets.' And the LORD said, 'You shall persuade him, and also prevail. Go out and do so.' Therefore look! The LORD has put a lying spirit in the mouth of all these prophets of yours, and the LORD has declared disaster against you."*
>
> (1 Kings 22:19–23 NKJV)

This vision of a throne room provides us with a glimpse into the spirit realm during the time of the Old Testament.

Because Ahab had hardened his heart and set his will against God's will, lying spirits were allowed to influence him. Those lying spirits spoke through the four hundred false prophets and convinced Ahab to go into war and, ultimately, to his death. It is important to see that just as the Holy Spirit is the source of true prophecy, lying spirits are the source of deceiving prophecies.

Thus, as Elijah ran in the power of the Spirit, let us always obediently run in the path of God's commands. (See Psalm 119:32 NIV.)

2 KINGS

Giver of the Double Portion

The books of 1 and 2 Kings were originally one book that was a sequel to 1 and 2 Samuel. This book was divided by the translators of the Septuagint (the Old Testament in Greek, also known as LXX) into the two-book format we now have. Second Kings records the sad history of the divided kingdom.

A DOUBLE PORTION OF THE SPIRIT

The following is perhaps one of the most well-known portions of 2 Kings:

> *When they had crossed over, Elijah said to Elisha, "Ask what I shall do for you before I am taken from you." And Elisha said, "Please, let a double portion of your spirit be upon me." He said, "You have asked a hard thing. Nevertheless, if you see me when I am taken from you, it shall be so for you; but if not, it shall not be so."* (2 Kings 2:9–10 NASB95)

Elisha had followed after Elijah ever since Elisha's supernatural call in 1 Kings 19:19.

Even though there was a school of prophets nearby, Elijah had not been led to cast his mantle on any of those prophets but rather on a simple farmer's son who was plowing his fields. The Spirit has a way of choosing the seemingly unqualified. Later, Jesus would be seen doing the same in choosing His twelve disciples. Additionally, Paul wasn't one of those original disciples, yet the Spirit chose him to theologically frame the results of the new birth. Through such divine callings, the Holy Spirit rebukes, refreshes, and rejuvenates the ministry, thus keeping it on the cutting edge of what the Spirit is doing.

Elisha's response to Elijah's original invitation demonstrated a great readiness in him to obey the prophetic call. After bidding his parents farewell, Elisha threw a religious feast to signal his separation unto service for God. He was quick to heed the Lord's call. (See 1 Kings 19:19–21.)

When Elisha later asked, *"Please, let a double portion of your spirit be upon me,"* he was, in essence, asking for a double portion of the Holy Spirit that was upon Elijah. This means that *not only is the presence of the Spirit upon a person measurable, but it can also be increased.*

Elisha nurtured the call of God that was upon him through his faithful service in partnership with Elijah. The call on Elisha also caused him to be hungry enough to ask for a double portion. What are you hungry for? I have learned that I can be hungry only for things that exist. If they did not, I would not know to ask for them.

If you hunger for healing, it's only because healing is available.

If you hunger for abundance, it's only because abundance is available.

If you hunger for a more intimate walk with the Lord, it's only because a more intimate walk is available.

If you hunger for more of the Spirit, it's only because more of the Spirit is available!

I believe that the double-portion principle is for all of us.

Joshua conquered more land than Moses did.

Solomon built the temple that his father, David, had in his heart to build.

Jesus said that His disciples would do greater works than He did. (See John 14:12.)

> *He* [Elisha] *also took up the mantle of Elijah that fell from him and returned and stood by the bank of the Jordan. He took the mantle of Elijah that fell from him and struck the waters and said, "Where is the* Lord, *the God of Elijah?" And when he also had struck the waters, they were divided here and there; and Elisha crossed over. Now when the sons of the prophets who were at Jericho opposite him saw him, they said, "The spirit of Elijah rests on Elisha." And they came to meet him and bowed themselves to the ground before him.*
>
> (2 Kings 2:13–15 NASB95)

After Elisha picked up Elijah's mantle, or his outer garment, the Spirit demonstrated that He was now with Elisha by empowering him to repeat Elijah's last miracle.

The anointing we have upon us is one of transferability for generational continuity. The next generation is to double what the previous one accomplished for God.

The anointing oil described in Exodus 30:22–25 is a compound substance. It is composed of five specific ingredients, each adding to the other. If any ingredient were to be removed from the other ingredients (or were to stand alone), the anointing oil would be nonexistent or incomplete.

This is the principle of the double portion. Each individual anointing developed through a lifetime is supposed to add to the next wave of the anointing that follows.

The flip side of the flow of the double portion, or of any anointing, is that there must be qualified recipients. Receiving a double portion is not just the result of having had hands laid on you. *Double-portion impartations result from our serving and partaking in a Spirit-filled vision and anointing.*

HOW TO RECEIVE

> *Then he said, "Go, borrow vessels at large for yourself from all your neighbors, even* ***empty vessels****; do not get a few."... When the vessels were full, she said to her son, "Bring me another vessel." And he said to*

> *her, "**There is not one vessel more.**" And **the oil stopped.***
> (2 Kings 4:3, 6 NASB95)

A desperate widow sought Elisha out, asking for help because her sons were about to be enslaved due to the family debt. Her late husband, likely one of the sons of the prophets, was known to Elisha. What a sad picture of so many households today. Lack, in any area, is not God's plan for His people. It takes the anointing to destroy the yoke of lack! (See Isaiah 10:27.)

Elisha asked the widow what she had, and she replied that all she had was a jar of oil. (See verse 2.) This amount was insignificant compared to what was needed, but *God, in His faithfulness, always leaves something in your hand that can be multiplied*. We are *never* left with "nothing." There is always something we already have at hand that, if we allow the Spirit to lead, will bring multiplication to our lives.

Don't despise your "jar of oil"! In His mercy, God always gives seed to the sower.

Elisha asked the widow to borrow *"empty vessels"* because the Spirit can only fill what is empty. The widow started pouring oil with her insignificant jar, filling every empty vessel she had borrowed. The oil poured so freely that she could sell the surplus and redeem her debt, saving her sons. (See verses 5–7.) Self-righteousness, often cloaked as religion or an ideological "ism" of any kind, has a hard time receiving from the Spirit because it is so full of itself. May we be empty of ourselves so we can be full of Him.

The amount of oil the widow received was not determined by the Holy Spirit but by how many empty vessels she obeyed Elisha in acquiring. The oil stopped only when she could no longer provide an empty vessel for it to flow into. Assuming she would have been able to borrow ten times the number of vessels, her previously insignificant flask would have poured out that much more oil! There was no limit to the oil that could have been poured, but there was a limit to the receptacles. May we be enlarged so that we can have more oil poured into us!

AS MUCH AS YOU WILL ALLOW

> *He* [Elisha] *arose and went into the house, and he poured the oil on his* [Jehu's] *head and said to him, "Thus says the LORD, the God of*

> *Israel, 'I have anointed you king over the people of the* Lord, *even over Israel.'"*
> (2 Kings 9:6 NASB95)

> *The* Lord *said to Jehu, "Because you have done well in executing what is right in My eyes, and have done to the house of Ahab according to all that was in My heart, your sons of the fourth generation shall sit on the throne of Israel." But Jehu was not careful to walk in the law of the* Lord, *the God of Israel, with all his heart; he did not depart from the sins of Jeroboam, which he made Israel sin.*
> (2 Kings 10:30–31 NASB95)

After Solomon was anointed king, there is no record of the other kings having been anointed, officially or otherwise, except for King Jehu. King Jehu obliterated King Ahab's evil empire, Jezebel's network of prophets, and the temple of Baal. This was a major cleansing of evil in the land that could have happened only by the anointing's might to destroy the yoke. King Jehu "*destroyed every trace of Baal worship from Israel*" (2 Kings 10:28 NLT).

Yet, for all of his success, King Jehu compromised. His obedience was compartmentalized and incomplete. He wiped out the prophets of Baal, but he tolerated Jeroboam's golden calves. (See 2 Kings 10:29.) As with the widow's vessels, the anointing on Jehu to conquer stopped when he made no room for it.

The Holy Spirit will flow into any area of our lives that we allow; all we need to do is make room for Him!

To conclude this chapter, here is a list of the miracles of Elijah and his disciple, Elisha—who asked for and received a double portion of Elijah's anointing:

ELIJAH'S MIRACLES

1. Making the rain cease (1 Kings 17:1)
2. Multiplying a widow's food (1 Kings 17:13–16)
3. Restoring the widow's son to life (1 Kings 17:17–23)
4. Calling down fire on Mount Carmel (1 Kings 18:30–39)

5. Restoring rain to the land (1 Kings 18:41–45)
6. Calling down fire on soldiers (2 Kings 1:12)
7. Separating the waters of the Jordan (2 Kings 2:8)

ELISHA'S MIRACLES

1. Separating the waters of the Jordan (2 Kings 2:14)
2. Healing spring waters (2 Kings 2:19–22)
3. Cursing jeering young men (2 Kings 2:23–24)
4. Filling ditches with water and winning a battle (2 Kings 3)
5. Multiplying a widow's oil (2 Kings 4:1–7)
6. Prophesying a Shunammite woman's pregnancy (2 Kings 4:8–17)
7. Raising the Shunammite woman's dead son (2 Kings 4:18–37)
8. Rendering poison harmless (2 Kings 4:38–41)
9. Multiplying loaves to feed a hundred men (2 Kings 4:42–44)
10. Healing Naaman the leper; cursing Gehazi for greediness and dishonoring God (2 Kings 5:1–27)
11. Effecting the miracle of the floating ax-head (2 Kings 6:1–7)
12. Blinding and trapping the Aramean (Syrian) army (2 Kings 6:8–23)
13. Praying for his servant to see an angelic army (2 Kings 6:15–17)
14. Prophesying an abundance of food for besieged Samaria (2 Kings 6:24–7:20)

1 CHRONICLES

The One Who Calls

Just as there are four gospels that relate the story of Jesus Christ, there is more than one record of God's people in the Old Testament. Much of what is recorded in 1 and 2 Chronicles is similar to what is in 1 and 2 Kings, but the content is not identical. While 1 and 2 Kings cover both kingdoms, Israel and Judah, from a prophetic point of view, the books of 1 and 2 Chronicles, originally one book, focus on Judah from a priestly perspective.

"YOUR CALL CALLS OTHERS"

Once, the Spirit spoke to me and said, "Your call calls others. No one is called alone."

David found out this truth as well. Hiding from Saul in the town of Ziklag with a group of Saul's former troops, David was cautiously deciding his next move. He had the protection of skilled archers and could decide who had permission to have an audience with him. When some men from the tribes of Benjamin and Judah approached David, he went out to meet them.

> *David...said to them, "If you come peacefully to me to help me, my heart shall be united with you; but if to betray me to my adversaries, since there is no wrong in my hands, may the God of our fathers look on it and decide."* (1 Chronicles 12:17 NASB95)

David knew that he could get help from God to determine who was called to aid him in his divine destiny. As people of destiny, we must watch whom we allow into our inner circle. Those who have access to us can affect us. This does not mean we should isolate ourselves or be elitist; instead, we should be discerning and selective about those whom we permit to enter our circle of influence. *It is important for us to have people around us who can pour into and "pull" on the anointing in us in the right way.*

Too many believers have negligently allowed "anointing assassins" into their lives. Anointing assassins seek to shift you off God's path by overtly or covertly trying to divert you from God's plan. For every path, there is a plan.

Jesus encountered a covert anointing-assassin attitude when Peter "lovingly" rebuked Him for talking about His imminent death and resurrection. (See Mark 8:31–33.) Jesus also dealt with overt anointing assassins like the scores of Pharisees who openly questioned and plotted against Him.

Paul dealt with a covert anointing assassin when the girl possessed with the spirit of divination said all the right things and hoped to gain influence with the Macedonian advance team. (See Acts 16:16–18.) Paul also experienced Alexander the coppersmith overtly working against him. (See 2 Timothy 4:14–16.)

It has been said that when God wants to send blessings your way, He sends you people, and when the enemy wants to send problems your way, he sends you people. Obviously, that is not a biblical saying, but the principle is relevant: it matters whom you let into your life.

Again, just as David called on God to show him who should be allowed into his life, we should be diligent in guarding whom we let through the doors of our lives.

> *Then the Spirit came upon Amasai, who was the chief of the thirty, and he said, "We are yours, O David, and with you, O son of Jesse! Peace, peace to you, and peace to him who helps you; indeed, your God helps you!" Then David received them and made them captains of the band.* (1 Chronicles 12:18 NASB95)

Once more, there are no individual callings from the Spirit. An individual may receive a calling, but there are always others who are called to add to or to support that person's call in some way. No call stands alone without having secondary calls to others to undergird it.

Where would Paul's calling have brought him if Ananias had not also been called to lay hands on him, restore his sight, and gently introduce him to the rest of the body of Christ? (See Acts 9:10–19.) Later, Barnabas was called to open the door for Paul to be recognized by the other apostles. (See Acts 9:26–30.) Paul's call required these other callings—and additional ones—in order to reach fruition.

RECOGNIZING PEOPLE BY THE SPIRIT

Your calling is no different.

For every missionary called to the foreign field, partners are called to send them.

For every pastor called to minister in a church, members are called to be faithfully planted in that congregation.

For every traveling ministry, hearts and locations are called to receive from them.

For everyone called to start a business, others are called to help that business through their gifts, expertise, and investments.

Every call calls other callings. And when the other callings call, they'll call to you those of the same spirit!

We must return to recognizing people by the Spirit and not just by outward appearances.

I have spiritual elders in my life, people whom I consider spiritual fathers and mothers to me. They have helped to shape and protect me. Some have moved to heaven, while others are still here. I have noticed that, with each relationship that developed, it took my recognizing them for more than the anointed pulpit ministers that they were and are. I had to recognize that beyond blessing and teaching me with their public speaking, their ministry through books, and more, they had a supply that I was to tap into personally, at a deeper level. I did not initially set out to seek a personal relationship with them, but I did start financially partnering with them—because one's sowing must follow the direction of one's heart. I also made myself available to volunteer to serve in whatever way they needed. This positioned me to receive from them and to give to them; that is how covenant relationships are established!

2 CHRONICLES

The One Who Sustains

Second Chronicles tells us about King Solomon's reign, wealth, and wisdom. It also tells us about the twenty rulers of the southern kingdom of Judah, without giving too many insights into the northern kingdom of Israel.

Besides the accounts already covered in 1 and 2 Kings, there are three clear instances where the Holy Spirit speaks in this book: through Azariah (see 2 Chronicles 15:1–6), Jahaziel (see 2 Chronicles 20:14–17), and Zechariah (see 2 Chronicles 24:20). In all three accounts, God speaks a correcting word of encouragement, although that word was sadly not always received and heeded.

HEARING GOD'S PRECEPTS

> *Now the Spirit of God came on Azariah the son of Oded.*
>
> (2 Chronicles 15:1 NASB95, AMP)

The Spirit of God doesn't just show us the way; He can also show us what went wrong in our lives in the past so we can avoid repeating it.

King Asa had pleased the Lord by removing idol worship from Judah. This had brought the blessing of God on the land, and there had been peace. But, suddenly, an Ethiopian army arose threateningly. King Asa went to the Lord, and, in reply, the Spirit spoke through Azariah, *"For many days Israel was without the true God and without a teaching priest and without law"* (2 Chronicles 15:3 NASB95). This is how Asa responded:

> *Now when Asa heard these words and the prophecy which Azariah the son of Oded the prophet spoke, he took courage and removed the abominable idols from all the land of Judah and Benjamin and from the cities which he had captured in the hill country of Ephraim. He then restored the altar of the LORD which was in front of the porch of the LORD.* (2 Chronicles 15:8 NASB95)

There was idolatry in the land again because of the lack of a *"teaching priest."* Even though King Asa had decreed righteousness in the land, idolatry had secretly crept back in. As a result of having idols back in the land, the people were lawless—the king had ruled against idols. Where there is no *"teaching priest,"* the people are *"without law."* Faith for anything comes only by hearing (see Romans 10:17), but hearing implies that someone is speaking.

We need solid teaching in the body of Christ in order to be strong. It's good to want a worshipping priest, a prophesying priest, or a healing priest, but we also need a teaching priest! When people are without teaching, they are without God's laws, which leads to lawless living. The laws of God are simply His precepts that He put in His Word to enable us to live an overcoming life. These precepts must be taught so that they can be experienced.

King Asa's law to remove the idols wasn't enough to change the people's hearts; they needed teaching so that God's Word could enter their hearts and not just be a law enforced on them.

THE SUSTAINING SPIRIT

Peace was restored when King Asa heeded what the Spirit said through Azariah. Peace is not only what God wants to restore to us, but it is also the manner in which we are supposed to live as believers. I believe in restoration and revival for anything and everything, but consider this: something had to have been lost for it to be restored. Someone or something had to have fainted or passed out to be revived. This happened to King Asa's people; they had the victory, then lost it, and then had it restored.

God *sustains* all things, including our peace, *"by the word of His power"* (Hebrews 1:3 NASB95, NKJV). When we have His Word, not only can peace be restored to us, but it can also be sustained so we won't have to lose it again. The Word and the Spirit can set the altar of our heart on fire from heaven and keep the fire of God lit in us. No one needs to "burn out" if we keep oil in our lamp.

The battle is the Lord's, and He does not require us to be "sacrificed" for Him to be victorious! (See 2 Chronicles 20:14–17.)

EZRA

Restorer of God's Covenant People

The book of Ezra covers a span of some eighty years in the history of the Israelites. God was working during this time—a time in which a portion of the Jewish population was carried off in exile to Babylon, which was subsequently conquered by the Persians—to bring about restoration to His covenantal people. He did this by moving on the hearts of two Persian kings—Cyrus and, later, Artaxerxes—so that the temple in Jerusalem could be rebuilt, and His people could be reestablished in the land.

THE SPIRIT MOVES ON A KING

> *Now in the first year of Cyrus king of Persia, in order to fulfill the word of the* Lord *by the mouth of Jeremiah* [see Jeremiah 25:11], *the* Lord *stirred up the spirit of Cyrus king of Persia, so that he sent a proclamation throughout all his kingdom, and also put it in writing, saying: "Thus says Cyrus king of Persia, 'The* Lord*, the God of heaven, has given me all the kingdoms of the earth and He has appointed me to build Him a house in Jerusalem, which is in Judah. Whoever there is among you of all His people, may his God be with him! Let him go up*

> *to Jerusalem which is in Judah and rebuild the house of the* Lord, *the God of Israel; He is the God who is in Jerusalem. Every survivor, at whatever place he may live, let the men of that place support him with silver and gold, with goods and cattle, together with a freewill offering for the house of God which is in Jerusalem.'"* (Ezra 1:1–4 NASB95)

More than two hundred years earlier, the prophet Isaiah had also delivered a prophetic word of wisdom about this period in Israel's history—a word regarding a man named Cyrus. (See Isaiah 44:28; 45:1–4.) The Spirit who gave Isaiah that word was the same Spirit who moved upon King Cyrus. While we might consider two hundred years to be a long time to wait, we must remember that, in the spiritual realm, God sees everything from the perspective of an everlasting "now." God is not a Being with a lot of time. Rather, God is a Being outside of time because He is the One who created time. This declaration from the Spirit was given to and made by Isaiah so that the Spirit could move into the heart of King Cyrus.

The Holy Spirit fulfilled what He had said, and He will do the same for you! What the Spirit has promised you, He will be faithful to bring about. *The Spirit speaks so that the word might be fulfilled.*

The Spirit of God is not limited to moving upon the hearts of believers. Cyrus didn't worship the God of the Hebrews, but God stirred his heart, so Cyrus made a decree that favored them. God can give you favor even with people who don't know Him! We need to understand that the Spirit can still move on any secular politician or person of influence who might seemingly have no affiliation with the people of God, to work for their benefit. And if God can do that, He can also move upon those with whom you live and work!

I have seen this happen many times with my humanitarian outreaches in Southeast Asia. In some of the more hostile places I have gone to, permission to start a church must be obtained from the village headman. And, in those places, the village headman is usually also the Imam, or leader of the local Muslim mosque. There were even a few situations where we were required to gather fifty signatures of approval from the households surrounding the area where the church was to be built before we could receive approval. As daunting as that process sounds, my team and I have never failed to obtain the approval to build those churches. We had to believe in

God's favor and trust that the Spirit of God would stir the hearts of the local leaders.

> *Then the heads of fathers' households of Judah and Benjamin and the priests and the Levites arose, even everyone whose spirit God had stirred to go up and rebuild the house of the* Lord *which is in Jerusalem.* (Ezra 1:5 NASB95)

The Spirit moved on specific people to walk along the path that He had stirred King Cyrus to open up. Again, we see that *God is the Initiator and then the Enabler*!

The path that God has for you—that He has planned for you—He will also open up for you. If you sense a path calling out to you that doesn't yet seem open, hold on, because that means the Spirit is working on others to open that way for you.

King Cyrus and the people who responded to his decree obeyed the Spirit's call to rebuild the temple and establish God's people in the land. This is prophetically symbolic because it is the basis for all that God calls anyone to do.

Whatever you feel called to do, it will always be to build God's temple, which is you and the rest of the body of Christ, and to become established in the things of God.

Those who are called to win the unreached masses are, in a very real way, establishing the temple (body of Christ) by adding members to it. Those who are called to the marketplace do the same by working in the financial realm and channeling finances back to the temple. God gives callings and paths only to build the church—which the temple in Jerusalem symbolized—on the earth today!

THE IMPACT OF INTERCESSION

A few years after the rebuilding of the temple, Ezra, a priest and scribe, arrived in Jerusalem, and, to his utter dismay, he found that, despite the grace and mercy of God, the people had once again managed to fall into a sad spiritual state. Even some of the leaders were involved in rebellious behavior against God.

When Ezra saw this, his heart, already so hungry for the things of God, mirrored the Lord's heart by being *"crushed by their adulterous heart"* (Ezekiel 6:9 NKJV). (See Ezra 9:1–3.)

Ezra identified with and vocalized in prayer God's desires for His people. (See Ezra 9:6–15.) *This is the essence of intercession.* The Spirit birthed Ezra's intercession as He imparted the Father's heart to him.

> *Now while Ezra was praying and making confession, weeping and prostrating himself before the house of God, a very large assembly, men, women and children, gathered to him from Israel; for the people wept bitterly.*
> (Ezra 10:1 NASB95)

It was not just Ezra's distraught emotions that caused him to pray in that way. He was taking the place of the people before God, and the place of God before the people in showing them how much He wanted them for His own.

The Spirit births true intercession. That intercession reveals God's heart and draws us to call out in prayer for His heart to be fulfilled in the earthly realm.

We get God's heart by getting into God's presence.

We enter God's presence by allowing the Spirit to usher us into it.

Intercession is contagious. As Ezra prayed, others started gathering and crying out to God. The Spirit of intercession fell on them, and they began to weep as Ezra wept, resulting in national repentance. (See verses 2–5.) As always with this level of prayer, the result was that God answered, and the people turned back to the Lord. *Intercession, thoroughly "cooked," always gets results!*

NEHEMIAH

The Good Hand of the Good Lord

The book of Nehemiah is a sister book to Ezra. While the book of Ezra deals with the spiritual aspects of rebuilding the temple, Nehemiah—similar to the book of James in the New Testament—emphasizes that people's works should show their faith. The name *Nehemiah* means "Yahweh comforts" (*Strong's*, H5166), so we are immediately reminded of when Jesus, speaking of the Holy Spirit, promised us a *"Comforter."* (See John 14:26 KJV, AMPC.) True to his name, Nehemiah provided great comfort to the Israelites as they sought to fulfill the plan of God amid great opposition to rebuilding the walls of Jerusalem.

AN APOSTOLIC TYPE, AN APOSTOLIC SPIRIT

We can see that Nehemiah carried an apostolic call and anointing in a very real way. When he heard about the *"remnant there in the province who survived the captivity,"* that they were in *"great distress and reproach,"* and that *"the wall of Jerusalem* [was] *broken down and its gates* [had been] *burned with fire"* (Nehemiah 1:3 NASB95), he was moved by Spirit-birthed compassion. In response to the leading of the Spirit, he asked the king of Persia if he could return to rebuild the walls and was sent with that specific purpose. (See Nehemiah 2:5–6.) *Apostles are not just "sent ones"; they are always sent to a specific region or realm with a specific message for a specific purpose.*

Another apostolic aspect of Nehemiah was that he carried a building anointing. Apostles are foundation-laying builders and, in some cases, foundation re-layers and rebuilders.

Besides having a name meaning "Yahweh comforts," having an apostolic call is another area in which Nehemiah is an Old Testament type of the Holy Spirit. The Holy Spirit is an apostolic Spirit because He was specifically sent to earth and to the church for a specific purpose.

As believers today, not every one of us is an apostle, but we all have an apostolic Spirit in us!

THE GOOD HAND OF THE GOOD LORD

> *And I told them of the hand of my God which had been good upon me, and also of the king's words that he had spoken to me. So they said, "Let us rise up and build." Then they set their hands to this good work.*
>
> (Nehemiah 2:18 NKJV)

Throughout Scripture, the Holy Spirit is "the Hand of the Lord." Just as, in the natural, our hands are what we use to touch, lift, deliver, put on, or take off, the Hand of the Lord touches us, delivers God's "packages" to us, and places His anointing upon us. As with Nehemiah, today, the Hand of the Lord is still "good upon us." All that God delivers is good because God has no evil to deliver to anyone. He does not deliver darkness because, as we previously discussed, darkness is simply the absence of light. Evil is simply the absence of good, and good is God personified, so evil is the absence of God.

In the same way that the Hand of God was good to Nehemiah—and, through him, to the people—the people *"set their hands to this good work."* God has good *for* us so that good can come *from* us. (See Ephesians 2:10.) God has ordained good works for and from you!

THE LIGHT IN YOU LIGHTS YOU

The Holy Spirit in you energizes and lights up your spirit. One of the main benefits of having the Holy Spirit in us is that our spiritual senses are heightened. As our Guide, the Holy Spirit is always faithful to show us when there are plots against us. *Suspicion is not a gift of the Spirit, but the discerning of spirits is.* Being led by the Spirit through our spirit is a heritage of the children of God. God wills to *"deliver* [us] *from the **snare** of the fowler"* (Psalm 91:3, various translations). Where and when the enemy sets snares for us, the Holy Spirit is always faithful to alert us.

Three men—Sanballat, Tobiah, and Geshem—started whispering together against Nehemiah. They had unsuccessfully tried to frighten the people into stopping their work on the city walls. They had also tried to get the Persian king to stop supporting the project. But they did not understand what Nehemiah understood about this mission. When the Hand of God—His Spirit—is on a matter, He clothes it with favor. These men were soon to find out that with divine favor comes divine protection!

They tried to get Nehemiah to meet with them a few times, but Nehemiah stayed focused on the work God had entrusted to him and refused to be drawn in. (See Nehemiah 6:1–9.) That is wisdom. Don't be pulled downward into conversations, debates, and negotiations with those who have decided to set themselves against the call of God on your life.

Next, Shemaiah, who was *"a secret informer,"* offered to meet Nehemiah in the *"house of God,"* pretending to want to counsel and protect him. (See verse 10 NKJV.) But Nehemiah immediately rejected this offer because, since he was a layman, and not a priest of the tribe of Levi, it would have been unlawful for him to enter the temple in that way.[4] Nehemiah was protected by his obedience to the written Word of God! He did not need to pray and ask God if he should meet Shemaiah. He knew Shemaiah was not sent from God because Shemaiah was trying to get him to disobey God's already established Word. God's Word and God's will are one because God is not the author of confusion, and He never contradicts Himself. The Word and the Spirit always agree.

There is protection available to us when we obey God's Word.

As Nehemiah obeyed the Word of God, he *"perceived that surely God had not sent him* [Shemaiah], *but he uttered his prophecy against me because Tobiah and Sanballat had hired him"* (Nehemiah 6:12 NASB95).

4. Charles F. Pfeiffer and Everett F. Harrison, eds., *The Wycliffe Bible Commentary* (Chicago: Moody Press, 1981), 440.

Evidently, Tobiah and Sanballat, their threats having failed, had employed and assembled false prophets to spook Nehemiah into stopping the work on the walls. Nehemiah had prepared his heart to hear from God by obeying God's Word. Too many times, believers ask for a supernatural leading from God while choosing to ignore the written leadings of God. The first thing the Spirit will lead you to do is to obey God's Word!

INSTRUCTIONS AND ADMONITIONS FROM THE GOOD SPIRIT

> *You gave Your* ***good*** *Spirit to* ***instruct*** *them, Your manna You did not withhold from their mouth, and You gave them water for their thirst.*
> (Nehemiah 9:20 NASB95)

> *In your love, you were patient with them for many years. You sent your Spirit, who* ***warned*** *them through the prophets. But still they wouldn't listen! So once again you allowed the peoples of the land to conquer them.*
> (Nehemiah 9:30 NLT)

I love how clearly Nehemiah identified that the Spirit is not just *"good"* but also instructs and warns us. Since the Spirit is good, it stands to reason that His instructions and warnings are also from a place of good. The Spirit instructs us in the way of good for our good, and He warns us so that we can stay on the path of goodness.

Things change when we see God as good: we suddenly realize that, since there is nothing He does that is not good, we can trust Him regardless of His instructions and warnings. *Disobedience is always and only the result of not trusting that God's ways are best.* Knowing that God is good is a prerequisite for even wanting to hear any of His instructions and warnings.

The Spirit instructs in two primary ways: through *illumination*—that is, expanding a thought or idea; and by *revelation*—that is, uncovering something not previously seen. With illumination and revelation, we can make a course correction in life. In Nehemiah 9, the instructions of God are likened to manna and water. Manna feeds and fills. Water refreshes.

Too many times, people have misunderstood the warnings of God as negative messages of doom and gloom, and therefore have stayed away from them.

There was a time when I stayed away from ministering about the warnings and judgments of God. It wasn't that I didn't believe in the warnings of Scripture or that I thought everything would always be sunshine and roses; I just wasn't always sure that people needed me to remind them about these warnings. Then, one day, the Spirit arrested me about it and showed me that every message I ministered about the goodness of God was for the purpose of offering people an alternative to the evil of the enemy. When God issued a warning, it was simply to let people know about this alternative so that they can choose life!

ESTHER

The One Who Crowns Us with Favor

The book of Esther predates the previous books of Ezra and Nehemiah. Esther's marriage to the king of Persia would later lead to the rebuilding of Jerusalem during Ezra and Nehemiah's time. The events in this book are commemorated during the annual Jewish Feast of Purim, which is observed by Jews to this day.

The name *Esther* means "star" or "concealed, something hidden," so it should come as no surprise that the book of Esther does not directly mention the name of God, worship, or prophetic predictions of the Messiah. However, as we have seen, in keeping with His character, the Holy Spirit moves as powerfully in the background as He does in the open.

Whenever I think of the book of Esther, I consider how obedience to the promptings of the Holy Spirit is vital to accomplishing the plan of God. None of the godly people in the book of Esther had spectacular supernatural encounters. There were no burning bushes, pillars of fire and cloud, supernatural dreams, or angelic visitations. Yet a supernatural result was spectacularly accomplished—the saving of an entire race of people as they sought to obey the quiet leading of God.

In searching for the Holy Spirit in the book of Esther, we are specifically looking to see how the omniscient, all-knowing Holy Spirit has His hand on individuals' lives and prompted them toward doing His will. This is not to say that the characters in the book of Esther were puppets that merely acted out the will of God, but rather that the Holy Spirit moved on them and offered them an opportunity to yield to Him.

THE HOLY SPIRIT MAKES ROOM FOR US

The book of Esther reads like a movie script.

King Ahasuerus (*Xerxes* in Greek; this was not his name but a title like Pharaoh or Caesar) threw a lavish banquet and asked for Queen Vashti to make an appearance so that he could parade her beauty. Men and women did not dine together in Persia outside the privacy of domestic life. But Queen Vashti spurned the king. With his pride bruised and his anger mounting, King Ahasuerus listened to the other nobles and hastily made an example of the queen, stripping her of her royal position.

The king then searched the land for a new queen from candidates handpicked and sent to him.

Esther, the orphaned cousin of Mordecai, a Jew from the tribe of Benjamin, was brought to the palace by the king's officials to be one of the candidates.

Since the Holy Spirit, as God, is all-knowing, He knows the past, the present, and the future; His provision for our future begins in the choices He offers us today.

Pharaoh's daughter didn't know that the baby she saved—Moses—would one day be used by God to deliver a nation. (See Exodus 2:1–10.)

Jesse didn't know that sending David on a routine lunch delivery to his brothers would propel his youngest son toward becoming king of Israel. (See 1 Samuel 17:17–54.)

The Persian king Ahasuerus didn't realize the impact that his decision to find a new wife would later have on the destiny of Esther and all the Jews living in his land.

Moses, David, and Esther all had the call of God on their lives. Even before there was any proof of the greatness that God had called them to,

God used the actions of others to propel and position them so that when occasion and calling met, He would have His representatives in place.

If Pharaoh's daughter, Jesse, or Ahasuerus had chosen not to participate in the Spirit's prompting in those moments, the Spirit would have raised up someone else to do so because God doesn't allow the disobedience of others to alter the course of the obedient.

The Holy Spirit prompts us today because He knows what is needed tomorrow.

Our obedience to God's promptings of today becomes the manifestations that we need tomorrow.

THE HOLY SPIRIT GIVES US FAVOR

> *Now the young lady* [Esther] *pleased him* [Hegai, the king's chamberlain assigned to look after the candidates for queen] *and found favor with him. So he quickly provided her with her cosmetics and food, gave her seven choice maids from the king's palace and transferred her and her maids to the best place in the harem.* (Esther 2:9 NASB95)

Favor paves the way for the fulfillment of the call! Favor is the result of our having the Holy Spirit in our life. Once you are born again, the best gift given to you is the Holy Spirit because, as God, the Holy Spirit personifies all the attributes and abilities of God. Since the Holy Spirit lives in you, all of God and His abilities are now available in and through you! That is the favor of God. This doesn't mean we won't ever have any challenges but that the Spirit of favor and might will cause us to overcome those challenges. We see this reality in abundance in Esther's life.

Wisdom and favor go together. Both are the result of the Spirit's presence. The Holy Spirit is the Spirit of wisdom. (See, for example, Isaiah 11:2; Ephesians 1:17.) Esther's favor caused her to receive seven times more! (See Esther 2:9.) We see that not only did Esther trust the favor of God on her life, but also that she was wise in her dealings with Hegai. You can imagine that in a palace full of women who were all vying to be queen, the demands and pressures on Hegai must have been great. Esther made no demands but rather trusted Hegai to do his job and prepare her as he saw fit. (See Esther 2:15.) The level of trust that Esther walked in allowed the favor of

God to flow unhindered and gain her favor with Hegai. This spirit of favor on Esther shortly caused Ahasuerus to *"set the royal crown upon her head and* [make] *her queen instead of Vashti"* (Esther 2:17, various translations).

God's favor places a crown on your head!

Because *"Jesus grew in wisdom and in stature and in favor with God and all the people"* (Luke 2:52 NLT), we can, too!

HE WILL REMIND THEM OF YOU

I am convinced that the Holy Spirit not only reminds us of what Jesus has said (see John 14:26), but He also reminds others about us when we have been forgotten. This is another aspect of the Spirit of favor because favor will ensure that we are not deprived by the disregard of others.

Mordecai had uncovered a plot to assassinate the king. (See Esther 2:21–23.) He had informed Esther, who, in turn, had told the king. After the would-be assassins were apprehended, Mordecai's role in protecting the king had been overlooked, and he had not been rewarded for it; however, the incident had been recorded in the royal records.

> *During that night the king could not sleep so he gave an order to bring the book of records, the chronicles, and they were read before the king. It was found written what Mordecai had reported concerning Bigthana and Teresh, two of the king's eunuchs who were doorkeepers, that they had sought to lay hands on King Ahasuerus. The king said, "What honor or dignity has been bestowed on Mordecai for this?" Then the king's servants who attended him said, "Nothing has been done for him."* (Esther 6:1–3 NASB95)

God has set in operation the laws of seedtime and harvest. (See, for example, Genesis 8:22.) The apostle Paul said it in this way: *"Do not be deceived: God is not mocked, for whatever one sows, that will he also reap"* (Galatians 6:7 ESV). A divine spiritual rhythm runs across our lives. God will not allow seed, once planted, to fail to reach the harvest stage.

Once, after I had taught in a service along these lines, a man came up to me looking worried. He told me that before he was born again, he had done much harm to others and was worried that he had a bad "harvest" coming his way. I had him read 2 Corinthians 5:21 (NKJV): *"For He made*

Him who knew no sin to be sin for us, that we might become the righteousness of God in Him." Then I asked the man, "Do you know what that means?" He said he didn't, so I explained that Jesus became our "bad"—our sin—so that we could become His "good"—His righteousness. Contrary to what some ideologies teach, we are not trapped in a hopeless, merciless cycle of "karma," where everything we do comes back on us. We have the blood of Christ and the mercy of God to intervene on our behalf. Jesus took our sin harvest and left us with His righteousness harvest!

The Spirit of God kept King Ahasuerus awake because Mordecai had a harvest due him. There are people whom God will keep awake so that a harvest of favor and promotion can come on you.

> *So the king said, "Who is in the court?" Now Haman had just entered the outer court of the king's palace in order to speak to the king about hanging Mordecai on the gallows which he had prepared for him.*
> (Esther 6:4 NASB95)

The king asked Haman, without telling him whom he meant, how the king should honor a man with whom he was pleased. By this time, Haman had already devised a plan to eradicate all the Jews. (See Esther 3:5–15.) Ever prideful, Haman assumed the king meant to honor him, so he made some lavish suggestions, only to have the king tell him to oversee having those honors bestowed on Mordecai! (See Esther 6:6–11.)

I believe that God orchestrated this circumstance for two reasons: first, to honor and promote Mordecai; second, out of mercy, as a sign to Haman that His favor was on Mordecai and to allow him to reconsider his plans.

The Spirit of God is the Hand of the Lord that turns the heart of a king *"wherever He wishes"* (Proverbs 21:1 NASB95, NKJV). Never be intimidated when people plot against you. Not only is your life in the hands of God, but the hearts of those who oppose you are also in His hands. *God can use the mouths and the hands of those who oppose you to promote and honor you!*

WHY GOD WANTED ESTHER TO BE CROWNED

> [Mordecai said to Esther,] *"For if you remain completely silent at this time, relief and deliverance will arise for the Jews from another place,*

but you and your father's house will perish. Yet who knows whether you have come to the kingdom for such a time as this?" (Esther 4:14 NKJV)

Haman had been promoted above all the other nobles and officials of the king. He demanded and received their subservience—all except for Mordecai's. Some theologians think Haman was an Amalekite, and that would have added to Mordecai's suspicions of him. Of course, the Spirit of God was on Mordecai, so I expect that Mordecai had both a spiritual and a natural sense that Haman would be trouble. Not used to being ignored, an enraged Haman devised an unholy plan to wipe out the Jewish race because of his anger against Mordecai. (See Esther 3:1–6.)

Ignorantly, the king gave Haman his signet ring, symbolizing his authority, to sanction the plan to exterminate the Jews. When Mordecai found out about Haman's plot, he responded with loud mourning and sackcloth. He was so deeply distressed that Esther heard about it within the palace walls. Inconsolable, Mordecai reminded Queen Esther that if she remained passive, she and her family would ultimately be outed as Jews and face the same fate as the rest of her people. Mordecai was certain that even if Esther refused to intervene, God would save the Jews by raising up someone else. (See Esther 4:1–14.) This speaks of Mordecai's deep faith and relationship with God. I wrote this earlier in this chapter, but it is worth repeating: God doesn't allow the disobedience of others to alter the course of the obedient!

Mordecai ended his admonition with what is likely the most well-known verse from the book of Esther: *"Yet who knows whether you have come to the kingdom for such a time as this?"*

Every call, every anointing, has the element of timing attached to it. The Holy Spirit is a Master Planner. Nothing from or about the Spirit is without specificity. *There is a specific time and location for the delivery of the anointing that is deposited on you.*

Of course, as we know, Esther yielded to the Spirit's guidance, and, through shrewd wisdom and favor, she saved the Jews; in addition, the king used the gallows that Haman had designed for Mordecai to execute Haman himself. (See Esther 4:15–5:8; 7–9.)

The all-knowing Spirit of God made provision for the Jews before Haman had time to hatch his plot to destroy them. The provision required the obedience of Mordecai and Esther, and when they yielded, the Spirit positioned them so that when the need arose, God's supply was already available. No need, challenge, or lack comes your way without the Spirit's having first made a supply for your provision. The Holy Spirit is a Spirit of provision!

PART THREE

THE HOLY SPIRIT IN THE WISDOM BOOKS

JOB

The Faithful and Sure Counselor

Job was a wealthy gentile, and he knew God in a way consistent with the revelation, or the lack thereof, that was available to him at the time. Since the life of Job is considered among the earliest records in the Bible, it is important to remember that Job lived during pre-covenant times. This means he had no Spirit-breathed Scriptures or Spirit-structured ordinances to reveal God and His ways to him.

Over thirty references in Job use the term *El Shaddai*, the Almighty, for God. God refers to Job as "My servant." (See, for example, Job 1:8.) Job was a real person who had real challenges and discovered a real God. Both Ezekiel (see Ezekiel 14:13–20) and James (see James 5:11) make mention of Job.

HOW TO READ THE BOOK OF JOB

I think the book of Job is among the most misinterpreted, or at least the most misquoted, of all the Scriptures.

It is vital in reading the book of Job—or any portion of Scripture—to remember that *everything in the Bible is truly stated, but not everything included is a statement of truth.*

Imagine you were present at a board meeting for a corporation or a church. At this meeting, the chairman of the board suddenly gets up and declares, "All elephants flap their ears to fly, are fuchsia pink, and have lime-green tails!" The appointed secretary of the meeting faithfully and studiously types all that is said so that the board will have a record of the minutes to refer to in future meetings. The meeting closes, and everyone is dismissed. The following month, at the next gathering of the board, the chairman calls the meeting to order, and, before the board members start discussing the business at hand, he asks the secretary to read the minutes from the previous meeting. She stands up and, as she reports the minutes, reads, "All elephants flap their ears to fly, are fuchsia pink, and have lime green tails!"

What the secretary read *had been* truly stated by the chairman, but it was not a statement of truth!

The Bible is 100 percent God-breathed as far as what God intended to be recorded for us, and it "*is profitable for doctrine, for reproof, for correction, for instruction in righteousness*" (2 Timothy 3:16 NKJV). But it is important to remember that the biblical record includes statements from people who didn't know God, who were perhaps new and immature in their walk with God, or were just operating in open rebellion toward Him.

Did you know that this statement is recorded in the Psalms: "*There is no God*" (Psalm 14:1, various translations)? When we look at this verse carefully, we see that it was the fool who said that. *It was truly stated by the fool, but it was not a statement of truth.*

Why was it recorded about Stephen, the deacon, that he spoke "*blasphemous words against Moses and against God*" (Acts 6:11 NIV, NASB95)? Because those words were *recorded truly* in Acts as having been spoken about Stephen by false witnesses who were stirring up trouble—and a mob—against him. *It was true that the false witnesses stated it, but it was not a statement of truth.*

Will Lucifer really do the following? "*I will ascend to the heavens; I will raise my throne above the stars of God; I will sit enthroned on the mount of assembly, on the utmost heights of Mount Zaphon. I will ascend above the tops of the clouds; I will make myself like the Most High*" (Isaiah 14:13–14 NIV). No! *This was truly stated by Satan from his rebellious heart, but it was not a statement of truth.*

Therefore, knowing the context, including who was speaking and to whom they were speaking, is important in reading and understanding the Bible.

What makes a statement true? A statement is true when it squares with the whole character of God, which can be seen only through the whole counsel of God's Word. In other words, *the best way to interpret a verse is with and alongside other verses.* The Bible is its own best commentary.

WE'VE ALL HEARD THIS

We've all likely heard this verse from Job read by someone at a funeral, perhaps in a dramatically somber voice:

> *Naked I came from my mother's womb, and naked I will depart. The LORD gave and the LORD has taken away; may the name of the LORD be praised.* (Job 1:21 NIV)

This is just one of many quotes from Job; Job truly stated it, and this has left many people scratching their heads.

When you read through the dialogue between Job's three friends in chapters 3–26 and the accusatory counsel they gave Job, you find that they all had a very cursory understanding of the personhood of God. Not only did they falsely blame Job for harboring some secret sin, but they also made accusations against God Himself.

God kept quiet throughout the "counsel" given by the three friends. In chapter 38, God finally spoke through the whirlwind of the Spirit, and, by the time He got through speaking, Job confessed, "*I put my hand over my mouth*" (Job 40:4 NIV), and "*Surely I spoke of things I did not understand, things too wonderful for me to know*" (Job 42:3 NIV).

In other words, Job took back what he had said in the earlier portions of the book. Yet people still preach and quote those portions as truth without realizing that Job himself repented of these statements!

As for Eliphaz, Bildad, and Zophar, Job's three counselors, we read this: *"After the Lord had said these things to Job, he said to Eliphaz the Temanite, '**I am angry with you and your two friends, because you have not spoken the truth about me**'"* (Job 42:7 NIV). Their advice to Job was so far off that God was angry with them and instructed them to offer sacrifices and to have Job make intercession for them! (See verse 8.)

JOB'S FOURTH COUNSELOR

Elihu was the fourth and last of Job's visitors to speak. He remained silent while the others spoke, probably because he was the youngest, yet he seemed to have the deepest revelation of God. In fact, in the first five verses of chapter 32, it says no fewer than four times that the advice that had been previously offered to Job angered Elihu!

Elihu's name means "My God is He," and he seemed to represent God the best. Unlike the other three visitors, Elihu wasn't rebuked by God and wasn't required to offer a sacrifice and have Job intercede for him.

> *But there is a spirit in man, and the **breath** of the Almighty gives him understanding.* (Job 32:8 NKJV)

The Hebrew word translated *"breath"* (*nshamah, Strong's*, 5397) here could be rendered as either "spirit" or "breath." In the context of this verse, we could say that it is "the Spirit of the Almighty" who gives man's spirit understanding.

Elihu knew, undoubtedly by inspiration of the Spirit, that it was the Holy Spirit alone who could bring inspiration and understanding to man. The counsel from the previous three visitors was all humanistic and soulish and came from their limited knowledge and religious biases. That is why they didn't help Job and needed to repent.

We have access to two realms of knowledge. One realm is accessed by our soul. Our soul gets information through study, observation, inquiry, and processing. Soul knowledge is not always bad but is always limited to the natural. The other realm from which we can obtain knowledge is accessed through our spirit. Since God is Spirit and lives in our spirit, our spirit is where the Holy Spirit speaks and teaches us. The knowledge we can obtain through our spirit is unlimited. Not because we know everything but because the Holy Spirit in our spirit knows all things; when and if necessary, the Holy Spirit can give us a portion of His wisdom and knowledge. This is also how the gifts of the Spirit operate.[5]

As believers, we need to return to operating and ministering from the higher realm of Spirit-based revelation. We should have the same attitude of looking to the Spirit when we seek help from experts and professionals in any field, whether legal, financial, medical, business, or otherwise. That doesn't mean we disregard any help available in the natural, but it does mean that, as believers, we see the Spirit as our ultimate Source of help and life.

Elihu said to Job, *"The Spirit of God has made me; the* ***breath*** *of the Almighty gives me life"* (Job 33:4 NIV). Elihu's understanding of the breath of God expanded as he continued talking to Job. He came to see that the Spirit had made him, and the breath—the Spirit—of God had given him life.

The Holy Spirit is a life-giving Spirit. This quality was in direct contrast to all that was happening to Job.

The thief came to steal, kill, and destroy. But the Spirit of Christ came that we might have life, and have it more abundantly! (See John 10:10.) The Spirit who brings life does not also bring death and destruction. We have a life-giving Spirit in, on, and around us!

The life that the Holy Spirit is and gives extends even to those who don't yet know Jesus personally. He extends life to them out of His mercy and kindness but also to sustain them so they can yet have opportunities to hear about and receive the fullness of life: Jesus!

THE SPIRIT MEDIATES FOR US

> [Job said to Bildad,] *"Nor is there any mediator between us, who may lay his hand on us both."* (Job 9:33 NKJV)

5. For more information on how the gifts of the Spirit operate, see my book *Releasing the Miraculous* (Shippensburg, PA: Harrison House Publishers, 2020).

Job didn't know that a Mediator was coming, but he knew that he needed one. One main role of a mediator is intercession. To intercede is to plead a case on behalf of someone else. The mediator has one hand on the one for whom they are interceding, and the other on the one to whom they are interceding. Jesus is our Intercessor today. (See Hebrews 7:25.) But whereas Job had no mediator interceding on his behalf, we have two! The Holy Spirit is our other Intercessor. (See Romans 8:26–27.)

This is why believers today need not think of themselves as Job Jr.!

Part of the reason why Job went through his trials was that he had no shield around him. But we have the shield of intercession around us by virtue of our Intercessors.

When we pray in tongues, we both activate and participate in the intercessory ministry of the Holy Spirit. The divine Helper assists us in and through intercession. The Holy Spirit enables and offers the utterances, and we allow and receive that help by vocalizing those utterances.

I don't believe the enemy would have been able to bridge the hedge around Job (see Job 1:10) if intercession had been made for him.

Pray in the Holy Spirit, in tongues, anytime you feel prompted by the Spirit because that's when the all-knowing Intercessor knows you need intercession and intercedes *for* you *through* you!

PSALMS

Inspirer of Spiritual Stanzas of Instruction and Worship

The Psalms are the Spirit-inspired songbook of Israel. We can identify with the various psalmists through their highs and lows as they prophetically inspire edification, exhortation, and comfort. (See 1 Corinthians 14:3.)

Nearly half of all Old Testament references to Jesus mentioned by the New Testament writers come from the Psalms.

Jesus Himself relied on the Psalms. He and His disciples would have recited Psalms 113–118, the Hallel (Hebrew for "Praise"), at the Last Supper. (See Matthew 26:20.) After the resurrection, Jesus told His disciples that what had been written about Him in the Psalms had to be fulfilled. (See Luke 24:44.)

There are five divisions to Psalms; interestingly, each corresponds to a book in the Pentateuch:

1. Psalms 1–41 (Genesis) deal with God's sovereignty and mankind.
2. Psalms 42–72 (Exodus) speak of deliverance and redemption.
3. Psalms 73–89 (Leviticus) instruct us on how to approach God in the sanctuary.

4. Psalms 90–106 (Numbers) give the history of God's people as they wandered in unrest in the wilderness.
5. Psalms 107–150 (Deuteronomy) emphasize the Word of God.

David was a major contributor to the book of Psalms. Seventy-three of the Psalms are credited to him. We know that David was anointed by the Spirit both as a king (see 1 Samuel 16:13) and as a prophet (see Acts 2:30). The lyrics of David's songs were anointed by the inspiration of the Spirit. (See 2 Samuel 23:1–2.) There was an anointing on David as he composed and sang. Even the plans David had when he appointed the chief musicians, choir, and musicians had an anointing. (See 1 Chronicles 28:12–13.) So, the book of Psalms is a collection of anointed songs.

The Holy Spirit is all over these songs!

THE HOLY SPIRIT ANOINTS OUR HEAD

The anointing can be said to be both the ability of the Holy Spirit and the dwelling of the Spirit.

In the Psalms, there are many references where the psalmist acknowledged the anointing of God, such as Psalm 23:5 (NIV):

> *You prepare a table before me in the presence of my enemies. You anoint my head with oil; my cup overflows.*

The Holy Spirit can "anoint your head" so that you have inspired ideas and wisdom. *An anointed head leads to a cup that overflows.* God can give you witty ideas and inventions that can bring you prosperity! The anointing of your head speaks of at least three things: first, the giving of direction so you know what next step to take and where to go; second, the giving of wisdom—the ability to see things the way they really are; and, third, the granting of access to knowledge or the ability to know things. The way to receive a cup that overflows in any area of life is to let the Holy Spirit anoint your head for direction, wisdom, and knowledge!

The psalmist outlines a spiritual blueprint for us: the Holy Spirit anoints our heads when we come to the table He prepares, but the table the Lord prepares is in the presence of our enemies.

When we have enemies lined up in battle against us, we must come running to the table of the Lord. The table of the Lord is where a feast of the Word and the Spirit is laid out for us. As we partake of the spiritual feast God spreads for us, the Holy Spirit anoints us to seal all that we eat at the table. Don't stay away from God when you see enemies on the horizon! Run to His table: the Lord always lays out a spread of everything you need to be nourished and victorious.

I enjoy a good meal, and people know me to be a foodie. So, I love it when the Lord uses food analogies with me. Once, when I was in prayer, I saw a table laden with every possible food imaginable. It was as if each platter of food was piled high on top of another. It was a heavily laden table! As I sat at this table, servers came out and scooped sizable food portions onto my plate. I was aware of a hustling and bustling around me as people fixed and served the meal. And the Lord said to me, "Those are apostles, prophets, evangelists, pastors, and teachers. They are the ones whom I use to prepare, cook, and serve My meals!"

Make sure you surround yourself with seasoned and mature people with ministry gifts (see Ephesians 4:11–12) who can serve you a good meal from God's table. Attending church, reading biblically based books, traveling to conferences, and listening to messages are simple ways in which we allow those with ministry gifts to serve us at the Lord's table. Personally developing a life filled with the Word, prayer, and worship is a way in which we eat of God's feast!

ANOINTED WITH GLADNESS

> *You love righteousness and hate wickedness; therefore God, your God, has set you above your companions by anointing you with the oil of joy.* (Psalm 45:7 NIV)

Psalm 45 is a messianic psalm, prophetically speaking of Christ the King and His bride, the church. This psalm is quoted in Hebrews 1:8–9 to establish the deity of Jesus and His superiority over angels. Being anointed with the oil of joy is not just for Jesus but for the whole body of Christ.

I love how this psalm describes the Messiah as hating wickedness—and *doesn't* say that He hates wicked people. This old saying is true: "God hates the sin but loves the sinner." God is not an angry old man in heaven, and we ought not to be angry, grumpy believers here on earth. If all that believers do is "hate on" and get upset over the wickedness or the wrongs of the world as they see these things occur around them, they will turn bitter and angry and not be of much good to those whom they are trying to reach for Christ—or even to themselves. We must allow the Spirit to anoint us with the oil of gladness to balance our experience of seeing the wrongs, injustices, and wickedness in the world. However, it is not just the wickedness that we generally see around us that can affect us. The wickedness and wrongs committed directly against us can also cause us to become bitter if we don't allow the oil of gladness to anoint and heal us.

There is a stream of strength that enables us to live and overcome adversity that comes only from the joy of the Lord. (See Nehemiah 8:10.)

I've seen young people who engaged in self-harm, such as cutting themselves, walk into a service, have the presence of the Spirit come upon them, end up on the floor laughing under the power of the Spirit, and then get up, having been set free, just from having the joy of the Lord hit them! The Holy Spirit still has the oil of gladness available today for anyone who wants it.

I was once asked if I would minister to a woman who used to attend my revival services but had moved away quite a few years earlier. She had not connected to a local church in the area where she moved and wasn't in touch with any believers. She had become a shut-in and had not been out of the house for over two years because she was suffering from severe depression and a myriad of phobias. This woman was under psychiatric care. Now, let me say that I am not against anyone getting any kind of medical advice or care. But, as believers, we need to recognize God as the Source of healing and life and let Him have the final word.

When I visited this woman, she came out of her room after much coaxing from her relatives who had asked me to see her. She looked down at the floor and wouldn't make eye contact with me. I greeted her and read Acts 10:38 to her, reminding her that Jesus was able and willing to go about doing good and healing all who were oppressed by the devil. I laid my hands on her, bound and broke the power of darkness over her, and then started to worship God in tongues. The others who were with me joined in the worship, and, in about ten minutes, the woman lifted her head a little, and tears began to stream down her cheeks.

I encouraged her to join us, and she hesitantly did. Her countenance changed as she worshiped for a little while longer, and she started worshiping more joyfully. I sensed the oil of gladness flowing in the room, so I told her to yield to it. She began to laugh a little. The rest of the team sensed that flow of the Spirit, so they also yielded to it. Soon we were all laughing under the anointing! When that anointing lifted, and as we were all leaving, I encouraged the woman to get back into the Word, to fellowship with a local church, and to yield to that anointing every time she sensed it. About a year later, she attended one of my meetings and told me that after I visited her, she would yield to that flow of joy anytime she sensed it, and now she was free from depression and phobias. The oil of gladness destroys the yoke of the enemy!

THE FAVOR OF THE ANOINTED

> *O God, behold our shield, and look upon the face of Your anointed.*
> (Psalm 84:9 NKJV)

This is one of the psalms written by the sons of Korah. Their father had been judged by God because he led a rebellion against Moses (see Numbers 16:1–35); yet, by God's grace and mercy (see Numbers 26:9–11), his sons came to God, served in the Lord's tabernacle and temple, and had eleven of their psalms recorded in the book of Psalms for us to read. Reading any psalm by the sons of Korah always reminds me that our family's past need not be repeated by us today. Negative family cycles can be broken!

The anointing is the favor of God, and God looks in the direction of the face of the anointed.

The anointing that God has placed on you causes His favor to be upon you in multiple areas of your life.

DAVID TREASURED THE HOLY SPIRIT

Psalm 51 shows David in sorrowful repentance after he was confronted by Nathan the prophet because of his affair with Bathsheba. David's response to Nathan's visit was one of brokenness. He was contrite.

> *Do not cast me away from Your presence, and do not take Your Holy Spirit from me. Restore to me the joy of Your salvation, and uphold me by Your generous Spirit.* (Psalm 51:11–12 NKJV)

When I was a young believer attending a local charismatic church, one of the songs we used to sing regularly included the line "take not thy Holy Spirit from me." I remember always thinking afterward that I had better live right, or else the Holy Spirit might be taken away from me, and I would be "God-less." I also heard some sermons about this. It always made me see the Holy Spirit as a little flighty and touchy.

The truth is, as I have mentioned in our studies of some of the other biblical books, in the Old Testament, the Holy Spirit didn't reside in anyone. He merely rested on people; even then, it was mainly the prophet, king, or priest who qualified for this. Before Jesus's sacrifice on Calvary, God's covenant people tried to keep the law but were not saved in the New Testament sense because the law did not give them a new nature through the new birth. (See John 3:3.) So, the Holy Spirit would rest upon certain people to anoint them for a task, but He would not reside within them. In that regard, *"Do not take Your Holy Spirit from me"* was an Old Testament prayer because losing the presence of God's Spirit was a possibility.

If we study this psalm, we see that David was making this statement from a place of sincere contrition and not actual fear of losing the Holy Spirit. In the following sentence, he says, *"Uphold me by Your* ***generous*** *Spirit."* How could David say that God's Spirit was generous if He was afraid that the Spirit would be taken from him?

Immediately after Nathan delivered the word of the Lord to David, *"David said to Nathan, 'I have sinned against the LORD.' Nathan replied,* ***'The LORD has taken away your sin. You are not going to die'"*** (2 Samuel 12:13 NIV).

Sadly, there were consequences to David's actions, including the death of his newborn son, but the generous Holy Spirit spared David's life.

Immediately after David's son died, *"David got up from the ground. After he had washed, put on lotions and changed his clothes, he went into the house of the LORD and worshiped. Then he went to his own house, and at his request they served him food, and he ate"* (2 Samuel 12:20 NIV). How could David have had the strength to get up, get dressed, go to the house of the Lord, and worship if the Spirit had been taken from him? We don't see David pausing before he worshiped to see if God would accept his worship. He knew that the generosity of God would accept his sincere worship.

Nathan's prophecy and judgment did not include any word that the Holy Spirit would be taken from David.

If the Holy Spirit was generous to people under the old covenant, how much more is He generous to us, as God's sons and daughters, under the new covenant?

Jesus said about the Holy Spirit, *"And I will ask the Father, and he will give you another advocate to help you and **be with you forever**"* (John 14:16 NIV). Other translations say, *"...that He may **remain with you forever**"* (AMPC) and *"...who will **never leave you**"* (NLT).

Now that Jesus has ascended to heaven, the Holy Spirit represents Jesus in and through us. If the Holy Spirit were ever to leave us, we would be orphans in a real sense because we would be without our heavenly Father, whom we access through the Spirit; that is why Jesus promised, *"I will **not leave** you as orphans"* (John 14:18, various translations).

The Holy Spirit is the One who draws people to Jesus, and the Holy Spirit is the strength that walks them back to Jesus when they stray. How could we ever return to Jesus if the Holy Spirit were to leave us whenever we sinned? That is why the Holy Spirit within us doesn't leave us!

People can be dull to the Spirit's presence in their lives, numbed to it because they are not being intentional about remaining aware of His presence, but that doesn't mean He isn't there. It just means they are distracted and therefore unmindful that He is with them. But we can treasure the Holy Spirit, as David did, and be intentional about acknowledging His presence in and with us.

HE'S NOT TOUCHY...BUT SENSITIVITY IS REQUIRED

I've led many services where the Spirit would move, and there would be demonstrations of people spontaneously laughing, dancing, running, and travailing with groanings in intercession. I've led services where people were caught up in trances, lost in the Spirit. In one of these services, a pastor's wife went into a trance and stood in one spot, unmoving, with her hands uplifted, for over ninety minutes. At another time, there was a service where a spontaneous forty-five-minute offering broke forth as people came forward to bring offerings to the altar.

The Holy Spirit is not touchy or overly sensitive, but we need to be sensitive to Him when He is moving so that we can flow with Him.

The key to sensitivity to the Holy Spirit—both individual and corporate—is reverence.

We need to learn how to respond when the Holy Spirit is moving in a corporate setting.

There is a time to sing. There is a time to be still.

There is a time to clap. There is a time to lift our hands. There is a time to dance. There is a time to lie prostrate.

In services where I've ministered, there have been times when the tangible presence of God rolled into the room, and I sensed a spirit of prophecy coming on me. Some people in the congregation would sense it, as well, but they wouldn't know how to respond, so a few of them would start clapping loudly, and it would distract others from the presence, and the presence would lift. This grieves the Spirit.

I have seen the same thing happen in prayer lines where people have come to have hands laid on them for various needs. Going down the lines, I'll often have a word for the people. But, sometimes, when I get to them and lay hands on them, they'll become so excited that they start speaking very loudly in tongues; I can hardly even hear myself talk, much less give them the prophecy I sensed rising up. I've had that anointing lift off me, and the prophecy for them with it.

Such clapping or speaking in tongues couldn't have been in the Spirit because why would God interrupt Himself? If God is trying to do or say something, but no one can hear it or partake of it, then we're all wasting our time gathering together!

There have been other times when I've had the anointing come on me to minister prophetically, but then people would come in late to the service or some people would get up and start moving around. That lack of reverence grieved the Spirit, and He left, meaning that the tangible anointing left. The Holy Spirit Himself didn't leave. But the anointing, to the point of manifestation, left.

Reverence is the key.

THE EVER-PRESENT PRESENCE

> *Where can I go from Your Spirit? Or where can I flee from Your presence? If I ascend into heaven, You are there; if I make my bed in hell, behold, You are there. If I take the wings of the morning, and dwell in the uttermost parts of the sea, even there Your hand shall lead me, and Your right hand shall hold me.* (Psalm 139:7–10 NKJV)

The Holy Spirit is omnipresent. This psalm of David clearly shows that David understood he could go nowhere to escape the Spirit's presence.

The Holy Spirit is not with us because we are good. He is with us because *He* is good. The Holy Spirit is not faithful because we are faithful. He is faithful because *He* is faithful.

"*If I make my bed in hell....*" People sometimes think God won't help them out of situations that are of their own making. If God left us every time we made a mistake, He would have left us all long ago! David said, "*If I make my bed in hell*"—not "If someone else makes their bed in hell," not "If I fell into hell," and not "If I was pushed into hell"! No doubt, David was talking from experience that God's presence would be with him and available to him even when he knowingly or unknowingly made a mistake.

That demonstrated faith in the goodness and mercy of God.

Why can you always expect the help and the Hand of God? Because the Holy Spirit is with you all the time.

LED IN THE LAND

> *Teach me to do Your will, for You are my God; Your Spirit is good. Lead me in the land of uprightness.* (Psalm 143:10 NKJV)

As we saw in our discussion of Psalm 51, the Holy Spirit doesn't just lead people *to* God; the Holy Spirit also leads people *back to* God.

Psalm 143 is the last of the penitential psalms. Historically, the penitential psalms (the others in this category are Psalms 6, 32, 38, 51, 102, and 130) were written to express a heart turned or returned to God.

We can go to God and ask, "*Teach me to do Your will*" because He is "***my** God.*" Where do we get this confidence that He is "my God"? By His good Spirit leading us to *"the land of uprightness."* Once, when I read this verse, the Lord ministered to my spirit, saying, "My good Spirit leads you *up, to the land of what is right."*

Often, people think of "uprightness" as just righteous living. While it most certainly involves that, uprightness in God's eyes also involves living in the land where we have all that Jesus bought for us on the cross—which was what God intended for mankind all along before we lost it through disobedience to Him in the garden of Eden. Jesus became our sin so that we could become His righteousness. (See 2 Corinthians 5:21.) For the children of God, uprightness means having *"every good and perfect gift"* (James 1:17 NIV) that comes down from Him. These good and perfect gifts are the privileges of His children.

God has salvation for our spirit, soundness for our soul, and wholeness for our body. In His eyes, it is not upright for His children to be robbed of their heavenly privileges!

Because He is good, the Holy Spirit leads us to the land of God's uprightness, which is His best for us. If we allow Him to, the Holy Spirit will lead us to complete salvation—uprightness for our spirit, soul, and body.

PSALMS TODAY

> *Singing psalms and hymns and spiritual songs among yourselves, and making music to the Lord in your hearts.* (Ephesians 5:19 NLT)

Psalms are not just poetic prose, but, like the rest of Scripture, they are a direct result of *"holy men of God* [speaking] *as they were moved by the Holy Spirit"* (2 Peter 1:21 NKJV). The same Spirit who moved on the *"holy men of God"* now lives inside us!

Even though they are like spiritual poems, psalms don't always have to rhyme. And, as we see in the book of Psalms, the psalmists benefit from, and are often encouraged in their private times with God by, the psalms that come forth. Psalms stir us and remind us that God is on our side.

Hymns are praise and worship songs that are directly sung to God. With hymns, the emphasis is not on a catchy beat or melody but lyrics about the majesty and goodness of God. Hymns still our souls and open our spirits.

Paul encourages us to speak in psalms, hymns, and *spiritual songs*. This would mean that not all the songs we sing in church and in other meetings are spiritual; otherwise, why would Paul have had to specify *"spiritual songs"*? The songs we sing as believers should not just be songs to motivate and encourage us or even songs about how great and good God is; we need to sing worshipful songs that minister directly to the Lord.

When we minister to Him, He speaks! (See, for example, Acts 13:2.)

The songs we sing can set the atmosphere for the Spirit to speak. We need to have Spirit-welcoming, Jesus-honoring, God-uplifting songs. Spiritual songs are songs that invite the Spirit's presence into our midst as we sing forth revelation from God.

> *Let the message of Christ dwell among you richly as you teach and admonish one another with all wisdom through psalms, hymns, and songs from the Spirit, singing to God with gratitude in your hearts.*
> (Colossians 3:16 NIV)

In Ephesians, Paul tells us to speak to one another, making melody in our hearts; and, in Colossians, he tells us that we are to teach and admonish one another. Psalms, hymns, and spiritual songs are not just to entertain us or fill up time in a church service before the minister comes to preach. Psalms, hymns, and spiritual songs come from the inspiration of the Holy Spirit and are part of our spiritual makeup and function to build us up individually and corporately. Psalms, hymns, and spiritual songs are the *"worship…in spirit and truth"* that Jesus said the Father is looking for. (See John 4:23, various translations.) Because they come by the unction of the Holy Spirit as we yield to Him, this level of worship is from the same stream of the Spirit from which prophecy flows; prophecy is simply an utterance inspired by the Holy Spirit that edifies, exhorts, and comforts. (See 1 Corinthians 14:3.)

> *Do not get drunk on wine, which leads to debauchery. Instead, be filled with the Spirit.* (Ephesians 5:18 NIV)

In the original Greek, the word translated as *"be filled"* is in the continuous present tense, giving the verse the meaning, "Be continually filled with the fullness of the Holy Spirit." The phrase could then also be translated as "Be being filled...." Being filled with the Spirit is not just a onetime occurrence but an ongoing filling as we grow through life. This is part of the Spirit's ministry of never leaving us and of empowering us.

There is a "filling cycle" that we can get into: psalms, hymns, and spiritual songs come to and through us as we continue to "be being filled," but psalms, hymns, and spiritual songs also are what fill us.

I have noticed that a flow of prophetic utterance, in any form, comes the most quickly when I allow the Holy Spirit to help me by my praying and speaking in tongues. I learned that, as I spoke in tongues, if I was watchful, words or phrases in English (my only known tongue) would come up—and that, if I spoke out those words and phrases, and then went back to praying in tongues, more words and phrases in English would come. While most of these words were interpretations of the tongues I was speaking, rather than psalms, hymns, or spiritual songs, it was the beginning of my learning how to flow with the Spirit in yielding to have utterances. As time went on and as I grew in my relationship with the Spirit, learning to sense His presence, there would be many times when I would sense Spirit-inspired prose come up.

Praying and speaking in tongues will simultaneously fill us and overflow from us. Keep yourself filled, and all kinds of inspired utterances will overflow from you!

I appreciate good music, but I am not musically gifted in the natural. I don't play any instruments or sing with a microphone in front of me. But that has not stopped me from accessing the prophetic flow of psalms, hymns, and spiritual songs, which can be spoken just as easily as they can be sung. After all, most times, we don't sing the Psalms—we just read or speak them.

If we take time to consciously yield to the Spirit as we speak in tongues, there will come a flow of inspired utterances, psalms, hymns, and spiritual songs from us!

PROVERBS

Dispenser of Divine Wisdom

The book of Proverbs is unique because it is a collection of divine wisdom mainly penned by Solomon with contributions from two other named authors, Agur and King Lemuel.

One meaning of the Hebrew word for "proverb" is "like."[6] Its root word means "to rule," or "to have dominion,"[7] so these proverbs refer to a standard or a rule of God.

"TO KNOW WISDOM AND INSTRUCTION"

Solomon received God's wisdom because he specifically asked for it above wealth or a long life. (See 2 Chronicles 1:6–12.) Thus, the wisdom that Solomon records here is from God Himself.

Solomon's objective in scribing these proverbs is summed up in this way: "*To know wisdom and instruction, to discern the sayings of understanding, to receive instruction in wise behavior, righteousness, justice and equity....*

6. Strong's Lexicon, "4912. mashal," Bible Hub, https://biblehub.com/hebrew/4912.htm.
7. Strong's Lexicon, "4910. mashal," Bible Hub, https://biblehub.com/hebrew/4910.htm.

The fear of the Lord *is the beginning of knowledge; fools despise wisdom and instruction*" (Proverbs 1:2–3, 7 NASB95).

Wisdom is the recurring theme of this book. So we see that knowing wisdom and receiving the instruction of wisdom lead to and constitute the fear of the Lord. Knowledge is the acquisition of facts and truths. Wisdom is the correct and beneficial application of those facts and truths.

Wisdom is such a focus in this book that it is personified as a woman. (See, for example, Proverbs 1:20.) This tells us that divine wisdom is not just about spiritual matters in heaven but also has tangibility in the physical realm. Additionally, the term "*my son*" is used almost thirty times, which, again, highlights the idea that this book is personal and is meant to be the kind of practical advice someone would receive from a father or mother.

Wisdom, for which the Hebrew word is *chokmah* (*Strong's*, H2451), occurs forty-five times in Proverbs and is described as eternal (see Proverbs 8:22–26), present at creation (see verses 27–29), and the delight of God (see verses 30–31). It's very clear that the wisdom recorded in these proverbs is not of any earthly, human origin but of divine origin.

The divine wisdom in Proverbs is carried over into the New Testament and is quoted several times in the Epistles.

Of course (perhaps unbeknownst to Solomon), when he asked for wisdom, what he received was the "*Spirit of wisdom*" (Isaiah 11:2, various translations), which is the Holy Spirit Himself! So, although we see no direct mention of the Holy Spirit in this book, throughout it, we do see one of the Holy Spirit's main manifestations.

Joshua received the Spirit of wisdom when Moses laid hands on him. (See Deuteronomy 34:9.)

As Jesus began His ministry, He declared that He had this same Spirit on Him. (See Luke 4:18.) Paul later prayed that we, the church, would also receive the "*Spirit of wisdom*" (Ephesians 1:17 NIV, ESV).

THE HOLY SPIRIT IS WISDOM

Understanding that the Holy Spirit shows up in the book of Proverbs as divine Wisdom helped me to reread Proverbs in a different light.

> *Wisdom is the principal thing; therefore get wisdom. And in all your getting, get understanding.... My son, give attention to my words; incline your ear to my sayings. Do not let them depart from your eyes; keep them in the midst of your heart; for they are life to those who find them, and health to all their flesh. Keep your heart with all diligence, for out of it spring the issues of life.* (Proverbs 4:7, 20–23 NKJV)

How a person responds to wisdom dictates the quality of their life. As believers, we could say that how we respond to the Spirit of wisdom, the Holy Spirit, is what determines the success we have. The wisdom of God answers everything that life can throw our way. The Holy Spirit can bring you in and out of anything!

The only way we can "*give attention*" to Wisdom's words is to incline our ears. The Hebrew word translated as "incline," *natah* (*Strong's*, H5186), means "to bend" or "to bow." In order to bend or bow, a person needs to lower themselves. This speaks of humility. We need to bow to God's Word to really hear it. The proud see no need for God or His wisdom. But if we bow to His words, both what is recorded in Scripture and what is spoken by inspired utterance, we will find life.

If we allow God's wisdom in our hearts, life and health will be ours!

Wisdom in our hearts is more valuable than knowledge in our heads. I often organize humanitarian outreaches in third-world nations, and we legally need a local doctor on site, even though the team I bring includes doctors. Once, we drove to a nearby hospital to pick up the local doctor we had hired to be a part of our outreach that day. When we arrived, we noticed a group of perhaps a dozen or so medical personnel, all dressed in scrubs and doctor's lab coats, standing in circle outside the hospital, chatting and happily puffing on cigarettes, evidently having a "smoke break" underneath a huge sign that said, "Stop Smoking—Lung Cancer Kills"! Besides the irony of their standing under that sign after having been medically trained, they must have known what those local, unfiltered cigarettes could do to a person. Still, they lacked the wisdom to apply that knowledge.

Wisdom tells us to be diligent to keep God's wisdom in our heart because from out of our heart—our spirit—flow the issues of life. The *New International Version* renders Proverbs 4:23 as, "*Above all else, guard your heart, for everything you do flows from it.*" "*Everything*" must include our health, finances, relationships, emotions, and all else that life includes.

So, we could say it in this way: If we bow to the words from the Spirit of wisdom, keep those words in our heart, and guard our spirit with all diligence, then health and all other issues that pertain to life will spring forth for us. If we hide the seed of God's wisdom in our hearts, we will harvest God's wisdom in our lives!

ECCLESIASTES

Revealer of Eternity

The book's title, "Ecclesiastes," comes from a Greek word that implies someone who calls or gathers an assembly. So, it makes sense that the author identifies himself in Ecclesiastes 1:1 by the Hebrew word *qoheleth*, rendered in many translations as *"Preacher."*

The book of Ecclesiastes features Solomon as the preacher reflecting on his season of disobedience to God. (See 1 Kings 11.) Looking back at that season, Solomon realizes that life's only meaning and value come from wisdom in obedience to God and in relationship with Him. Unlike his other book, Proverbs, this is not a collection of precepts but a cumulative message that looks beyond the frailty of this physical life. Solomon finally wisely asserts that, to make sense of this life, a grasp of eternity is required.

Since Solomon is looking back to a time when his relationship with God was estranged, he makes no reference to Jehovah God; rather, he uses the word *Elohim*. In using *Elohim*, Solomon refers to God less personally than usual, which is symptomatic of how people who don't know God think of Him. However, *Elohim* also references the Trinity of the Father, Son, and Holy Spirit.

The references to "spirit" in this book are not necessarily to the Holy Spirit but rather to the life force that animates living beings. (See Ecclesiastes 3:18–21.) Yet, throughout Ecclesiastes, Solomon acknowledges that he received wisdom from God.

THE SPIRIT GIVES WISDOM AND KNOWLEDGE

> *For to a person who is good in His sight He has given wisdom and knowledge and joy, while to the sinner He has given the task of gathering and collecting so that he may give to one who is good in God's sight.* (Ecclesiastes 2:26 NASB95)

Solomon recognizes that the gifts of God—wisdom and knowledge—are given to those who are "*good in His sight.*" You might think, "Well, who is good enough?" The church, the redeemed ones, are! We are "*good in His sight*" because we are the righteousness of God in Christ. (See 2 Corinthians 5:21.) We are the recipients of the good and perfect gifts from the Father. (See James 1:17.)

Here is the alternative to receiving the wisdom and knowledge that God gives: those who don't know God gather and collect in their own strength only so that God will give the effort of that toil to those who know Him! We saw an example of that type of transfer when the children of Israel left Egypt with gold and other goods of the Egyptians. (See Exodus 12:35–36.)

Solomon may have had this in mind when he wrote in Proverbs 13:22 (NIV) that "*a sinner's wealth is stored up for the righteous.*" The wisdom of God enables us to plunder the toil of the enemy, Satan. The enemy's plan is to divert the material resources of the earth away from the people of God and into the hands of the ungodly. Wisdom makes a path so that the resources that God intends for His plans and people are redeemed and released to them.

> *I tried cheering myself with wine, and embracing folly—my mind still guiding me with wisdom. I wanted to see what was good for people to do under the heavens during the few days of their lives.... I became greater by far than anyone in Jerusalem before me.* ***In all this my wisdom stayed with me.*** (Ecclesiastes 2:3, 9 NIV)

Solomon had some very dark days when he walked away from the Lord. During those days, the wisdom he had received from God was not removed from him or absent. Solomon was simply choosing not to yield to God's wisdom. It is a sobering truth that *"God's gifts and his call are irrevocable"* (Romans 11:29 NIV). This means that God doesn't change His mind concerning the gifts He bestows on us. It speaks to His unchanging faithfulness. *God is available and faithful even when we are not.* It also means that, once given, all of God's power and resources are available to us, but, as happened with Solomon, we can choose to mute them by our attitudes, decisions, and actions.

If we ever stray from God's best, all we need to do is simply go back to where we last were and pick up whatever we have let go of. We will find that God has not removed anything from us. We'll be able to paraphrase what Solomon said: "In all this mess that I created, my wisdom, the gifts that God gave me, stayed with me!"

ETERNITY IN US, AND US IN ETERNITY

> *He has made everything beautiful in its time. He also has planted eternity in men's hearts and minds [a divinely implanted sense of a purpose working through the ages which nothing under the sun but God alone can satisfy], yet so that men cannot find out what God has done from the beginning to the end.* (Ecclesiastes 3:11 AMPC)

Blaise Pascal, the seventeenth-century French Catholic mathematician, said,

> What else does this craving, and this helplessness, proclaim but that there was once in man a true happiness, of which all that now remains is the empty print and trace? This he tries in vain to fill with everything around him, seeking in things that are not there the help he cannot find in those that are, though none can help, since this infinite abyss can be filled only with an infinite and immutable object; in other words by God himself.[8]

8. Blaise Pascal, *Pensées* (New York, Penguin Books, 1995), 45.

Man was created with an innate need for eternity, a life beyond this temporal biological existence. All cultures, far and wide, have an ideological thread that seeks to connect them to eternity. This need, this awareness, was put in mankind by God Himself.

The Holy Spirit's role on earth is to bring people to Jesus, who is the Way, the Truth, and the Life, without whom no one can go to the Father. (See John 14:6.) The Spirit's method is to equip and empower believers so that they can be witnesses to this truth.

There is a primary call on all believers to be witnesses. The Holy Spirit was specifically sent so that we *"will receive power when the Holy Spirit come on* [us]; *and* [we] *will be* [Jesus's] *witnesses in Jerusalem, and in all Judea and Samaria, and to the ends of the earth"* (Acts 1:8 NIV). I love talking and ministering about the Holy Spirit and the anointing. However, it's vital to remember that the Holy Spirit was not *just* sent to be our Guide and Comforter; a major aspect of the Holy Spirit's ministry is to equip us to be witnesses of Jesus.

Mankind's need for what is eternal can be satisfactorily met only by an encounter with the Holy Spirit revealing Jesus!

DIVINE WISDOM FOR SPIRITUAL MANIFESTATIONS

> *For a dream comes through much activity, and a fool's voice is known by his many words.* (Ecclesiastes 5:3 NKJV)

Just as the apostle Paul would later do in 1 Corinthians, Solomon cautions against an overemphasis on spiritual manifestations. While it is scriptural that the Holy Spirit has spoken and still does speak through dreams and other manifestations (see Joel 2:28–32; Acts 2:17–21), Solomon reminds us that not every dream is the voice of God or even has a spiritual origin. He wisely points out that dreams can have natural causes, like an overactive mind.

If we are not careful, it's easy to forget that what are sometimes perceived as spiritual manifestations can come from one of three sources: God, the enemy, or man himself. It takes the wisdom of God to determine which it is.

I have known people who claimed to have dreams almost nightly that they thought had some significance. Dream interpretation guidelines are similar to those of basic prophetic protocol:

- Does the dream agree with Scripture?
- What is the fruit of the dream?
- Does it offer redemption, or does it condemn?
- Does it inspire faith or fear?
- Are the goodness and greatness of Jesus presented?
- Is it all doom and gloom—stealing, killing, and destroying—or does it lead to life, and life abundantly?
- Does it lead to a deeper relationship with God through the Word and the Spirit?
- Does the dream produce liberty or bondage?
- Does it loose the dreamer to receive more of God?
- Does the dreamer become "dream dependent," replacing the usual leading of the Spirit—by the Word and the inward witness—with dreams?

It takes the wisdom of God to govern the proper administration of spiritual manifestations. Human wisdom will either reason away the need for any spiritual manifestations or take all manifestations, fleshly or demonic, as coming from God without any exercise of discernment. It's prideful to think that human reasoning alone can decipher manifestations of the Spirit. Both the Word and the Spirit are required to grasp what God is doing and saying. *The Spirit illuminates what the Word says, and the Word solidifies what the Spirit does.*

SONG OF SOLOMON

Sealer in the Love of God

On the surface, Song of Solomon seems to be a poetic telling of the passionate love between the Shulamite woman and King Solomon. But, deeper than that, it portrays covenantal love, the basis for God's relationship with mankind: Christ's love for the church.

The Holy Spirit is the One who pours out the Father's love into our hearts. (See Romans 5:5.) The Holy Spirit is the One who bonds us with love to the Father. The way this book is written—through song and rich symbolism—is characteristic of how the Holy Spirit speaks.

The Holy Spirit, the breath of God (see, for example, Psalm 104:29–30) that brought the clay body of Adam to life (see Genesis 2:7), may be seen in this poetic song as the "breaking" (various translations) or the "breathing" (ESV) of the day in Song of Solomon 2:17 and 4:6, as the wind blowing on the Shulamite's garden in 4:16, and as a fragrance in 7:8.

THE GENTLE WOOING OF THE SPIRIT

Arise, come, my darling; my beautiful one, come with me.

(Song of Songs 2:13 NIV)

The Holy Spirit is pictured as gently and lovingly drawing the unsaved to salvation as tenderly as Solomon and his beloved whisper sweet nothings to each other. Not only is the Holy Spirit gentle with those He is wooing to salvation, but He is also as gentle as a dove with us who are in the church. Even when manifesting as fire to the one hundred and twenty disciples on the day of Pentecost (possibly the Holy Spirit's most intense symbolic manifestation), the Holy Spirit "***settled** on each of them*" (Acts 2:3 NLT). Other translations use the wording "***rested** on each one of them*" (NASB95) and "***came to rest** on each of them*" (Acts 2:3 NIV).

The Holy Spirit is gentle because gentleness is an aspect of love, and God is love!

However, we should not mistake gentleness for weakness. *The Holy Spirit is so strong that He can afford to be gentle!*

I have witnessed the forceful gentleness of the Holy Spirit many times, and I have noticed it in this way: the Holy Spirit is gentle with people but forceful in enforcing the kingdom rule in their lives. I think that some of the clearest examples I have seen of this in ministry have been when people were delivered from demonic oppression.

I remember one woman who had been a nominal church member, and whose family had brought her to one of my meetings seeking help. She had been alone one afternoon, shopping in an area of the town that was popular with tourists, and she had just walked by a row of fortune tellers with booths selling charms and idols when she suddenly passed out. When she came around and was brought home, she started occasionally speaking in a different voice, would react violently whenever anyone in her home put on praise and worship music, and refused to have anyone pray for her. This had gone on for a few months before they brought her to the meeting. In the service, after the ministry of the Word, as we transitioned to the ministry part, her family helped her go up to the prayer line. As I made my way to her, I sensed a gentle wave of the Holy Spirit flowing her way. I stretched my hands toward her, and she fell gently under the power of the Spirit. She peacefully lay there for a while as I went down the line ministering to others. When I was about five or six people down the line from her, I sensed a stronger, more forceful wave of the Spirit as I ministered to those people, and I felt nudged by the Spirit to turn back toward her. When I did, I said firmly, "Now, in Jesus's name, leave and don't come back!" She started screaming and writhing around as if she were in great pain. I sensed another wave of the anointing as I said, "Out! Now! In Jesus's name!" She let out another loud cry and then went still. She woke up about thirty minutes afterward and has been free ever since! The anointing was gentle with her but forceful with what held her bound because the Holy Spirit is gently forceful.

THE WELL OF THE SPIRIT

> *You are a fountain [springing up] in a garden, a well of living waters, and flowing streams from Lebanon.* (Song of Songs 4:15 AMPC)

Since the children of Israel and the people Jesus ministered to were primarily living in desert regions, they understood the necessity of access to water. Water did not simply refresh them but was essential for life itself. It's no wonder, then, that both water and wells are used throughout Scripture to symbolize eternal life and the Holy Spirit. (See, for example, John 4:10; 7:37–38.)

The Holy Spirit seeks to communicate with us in language we can relate to. That is one of the reasons there are so many translations of the Bible. Language evolves, and since God is eager to speak to people, He allows for updates of the language—but not of the message or the intent—that will be relevant to the hearer. I have always been grateful for this truth as I have traveled and studied the world's religions. God does not restrict His communications with us in arcane and ancient speech. He seeks communication with us in wording that we can comprehend. The God of Abraham, Isaac, and Jacob wants to communicate with us, and the Holy Spirit is a master Communicator!

"A well of living waters." It was primarily through wells that those desert communities obtained their water. Water washed, refreshed, and sustained life. What an accurate picture of what the Holy Spirit does for us!

"Flowing streams" speaks of water that is living, not stagnant or dead. We must choose to flow with the river of the Spirit, moving in the Spirit's manifestations, if we want to be streams of living water!

SEALED AND LOVED

> *Place me like a seal over your heart, like a seal on your arm; for love is as strong as death, its jealousy unyielding as the grave. It burns like blazing fire, like a mighty flame. Many waters cannot quench love; rivers cannot sweep it away. If one were to give all the wealth of one's house for love, it would be utterly scorned.*
>
> (Song of Songs 8:6–7 NIV)

We are sealed in our salvation by the Spirit. (See, for example, Ephesians 1:13.) The gifts of the Spirit (see 1 Corinthians 12:8–10) empower us to demonstrate the life of Jesus, and the fruit of the Spirit (see Galatians 5:22–23) allow us to live the life of Jesus.

The Holy Spirit's love for us is like a mighty flame—like the flames that rested on the one hundred and twenty disciples on the day of Pentecost. The love of the Holy Spirit outlasts death and burns bright!

PART FOUR

THE HOLY SPIRIT IN THE MAJOR PROPHETS

ISAIAH

Purification and Outpouring

Isaiah is the first of the books of the Bible that are commonly termed the "Major Prophets." Although they are classified as such, the major prophets were not superior to the minor prophets in terms of their walk with God or the weight of their prophetic utterances. Rather, they were simply more prominent in their social/political involvement, and thus their recorded writings were longer. All the major and minor prophets are woven into the larger tapestry of God's plan. They, like us, contribute to what *"every joint supplies"* (Ephesians 4:16, various translations). Regardless of how others may classify us in life—whether as major or minor players in society—we can rest assured that if we will let the Holy Spirit move in our lives and order our steps, we too will have our part in God's plan for our generation.

The name *Isaiah* means "Yahweh is salvation." Isaiah prophesied when the kingdoms of Judah and Israel faced a crucial time in their history. Both kingdoms had prosperity and power but had fallen into moral and spiritual decline. Isaiah preached a no-nonsense message. In this book, he used almost all the Hebrew words available for "sin." But as strongly as he preached judgment, he also passionately offered hope for redemption and restoration to God's people.

ISAIAH SAW JESUS!

Isaiah has been called an evangelistic and messianic prophet because of his message of salvation and his prophecies, which stretch into the millennial reign of Christ. (See Isaiah 65:17–25.) Here are other prophecies about Jesus in the book of Isaiah:

- Isaiah 9:1–7 prophesies about the coming King.
- Isaiah 7:14 prophesies about the birth of Jesus.
- Isaiah 40:3–5 prophesies about the forerunner ministry of John the Baptist.
- Isaiah 42:1–4 prophesies about Christ the Servant.
- Isaiah 42:1; 49:6 prophesy about Christ's ministry to the gentiles.
- Isaiah 52:13–53:12 prophesies about Jesus's suffering and death.
- Isaiah 6:9–12 prophesies about Israel's rejection of Jesus.

In true prophetic fashion, Isaiah decried the openly sinful lifestyle of Israel and Judah, rebuked them for their hypocritical observance of Jewish orthodoxy, warned them of the consequences, and also pointed to the coming Christ. With all of the solemn pronouncements against sin and immorality, the Holy Spirit, through Isaiah, inserted seventeen chapters containing prophetic references to Jesus, including chapter 53, which details the Old Testament's single most detailed prophecy of the Messiah's work of atonement. How like the Holy Spirit to magnify Jesus in the midst of sin and darkness! This is still the standard today for all prophetic manifestations; *the Spirit never arrests our wrongdoings without also pointing us to God's way of atonement.*

Prophecies become "heart-less" when Jesus is left out of them because Jesus is the heart of everything the Spirit has to say!

Through Isaiah, the Spirit also described many attributes of the Messiah. To list some of these instances, Jesus is spoken of, in various Bible translations, as *"Immanuel"* (Isaiah 7:14; 8:8), *"Wonderful Counselor"* (Isaiah 9:6), *"Mighty God"* (Isaiah 9:6), *"Everlasting Father"* (Isaiah 9:6), *"Prince of Peace"* (Isaiah 9:6), *"Redeemer"* (Isaiah 59:20), and "Anointed One" (see Isaiah 61:1).

No wonder the Spirit revealed all this about Jesus through Isaiah, whose name means "Yahweh is salvation" or "the salvation of Jehovah." Salvation is a recurring theme of this book, so giving a clear picture of Jesus is necessary. In describing Jesus, the Holy Spirit was describing the One through whom salvation would come!

THE SPIRIT OF JUDGMENT AND FIRE

> *The Lord will wash away the filth of the women of Zion; he will cleanse the bloodstains from Jerusalem by a spirit of judgment and a spirit of fire.* (Isaiah 4:4 NIV)

Isaiah uses the Hebrew word *ruwach* (*Strong's*, H7307) over fifty times in his writings, including in the above verse. This word can be translated as "wind," "breath," "mind," or "spirit." A dozen or so of these instances refer directly to the Holy Spirit.

Here, it is used as a double reference to the Holy Spirit. God's *"spirit of judgment"* is more than mere doom, gloom, and destruction. When the fire of God consumed Elijah's offering on Mt. Carmel (see 1 Kings 18:38), it was a *judgment that the offering was accepted*. God's fire doesn't just destroy or purify; it can also be a sign that the offering is accepted!

God is *"a consuming fire"* (Hebrews 12:29) and *"a refiner's fire"* (Malachi 3:2). So the Holy Spirit consumes and refines us in heavenly flames.

John the Baptist prophesied that the Messiah would baptize *"with the Holy Spirit and fire"* (Matthew 3:11; Luke 3:16). That is precisely what happened on the day of Pentecost. The disciples, in the upper room, were an altar offering that God found acceptable because of the finished work of Jesus.

THE EFFECTS OF THE SPIRIT

> *The Spirit of the LORD shall rest upon Him, the Spirit of wisdom and understanding, the Spirit of counsel and might, the Spirit of knowledge and of the fear of the LORD.* (Isaiah 11:2 NKJV)

The Messiah is the central figure of chapters 7 through 12 of Isaiah. The above verse is not necessarily about the Spirit Himself but about the effects of the Spirit on and in manifestation.

Many Spirit-filled believers rightly associate the Spirit with demonstrative power manifestations, such as healings and deliverances. However, they forget that the Spirit also manifests as wisdom (skill and insight), understanding (discernment), counsel (advice), might (strength), knowledge (inner knowing, learning, and information), and the fear (reverence) of the Lord.

The flow of the Holy Spirit's ministry to believers causes us to be able to have both a stable inner life and the outward demonstrative ministry of Jesus.

When I was a new believer, I was led to ask God for wisdom daily. I did not have a Bible-based background at home when I was growing up, and I was not surrounded by many godly influences. I didn't even know you could ask for God's wisdom until, once, when I was praying through tongues and interpretation, I started crying out for the wisdom of God. Afterward, I discovered in James 1:5 that believers were offered God's wisdom if they would ask for it. I have seen God do many miracles in my life, services, and other ministry, but what has privately kept me going was not just the power demonstrations of the Spirit but the inner workings of the Spirit in my personal life.

I have seen that the churches and ministers that have asked me to be a voice in their lives benefit more from the wisdom of God flowing through me than from the miraculous signs and wonders in my ministry.

Job's fourth friend, Elihu; Joshua; and Joseph all received the Spirit's wisdom. There aren't any records of outwardly miraculous signs and wonders in Joseph's life, but the wisdom of God promoted him in Pharaoh's court and positioned him to save both his brothers and the nation of Egypt. (See Genesis 41.)

Don't limit the Holy Spirit in your life to just miracles. Allow Him to lead you to live in all the blessings of God!

THE FUTURE OUTPOURING UPON ISRAEL

> *Until the Spirit is poured upon us from on high, and the wilderness becomes a fruitful field, and the fruitful field is counted as a forest.*
>
> (Isaiah 32:15 NKJV)

This promise for Israel will be fulfilled in the millennial reign of Christ.

God's love for Israel, codified by His many promises to them—despite the fact of their repeated repudiation of Him—should be a constant reminder for us that God's faithfulness is independent of our faithfulness or lack thereof. Remember, God is not just good when we are good. He is good even when we are not good!

JESUS THE SERVANT

> *Behold! My* **Servant** *whom I uphold, My Elect One in whom My soul delights! I have put My Spirit upon Him; He will bring forth justice to the Gentiles. He will not cry out, nor raise His voice, nor cause His voice to be heard in the street. A bruised reed He will not break, and smoking flax He will not quench; He will bring forth justice for truth. He will not fail nor be discouraged, till He has established justice in the earth; and the coastlands shall wait for His law.* (Isaiah 42:1–4 NKJV)

In coming to earth, Jesus chose subservience to the Father. *Ebed* (*Strong's*, H5650), the Hebrew word used for "*Servant*" in the above passage, means "bondservant" but could also mean, in a unique sense, people like prophets or Levites.

In His role, Jesus is the Servant in whom God delights; He embodies all that God called Israel to be. So, Jesus is the fulfillment of the law. (See Matthew 5:17.)

In the Old Testament, God had servants but no sons. It took a Son to be the ideal Servant and fulfill all that God required under the law for servants.

In the New Testament, God has sons who minister as servants. Jesus was the Seed (see Genesis 3:15); His seed was one of sonship. He was the firstborn (see, for example, Colossians 1:18), and from the seed of Jesus, the Son, came a harvest of sons! *The Son-Seed did not produce a harvest of servants: we are a son-harvest from a Son-Seed!*

A SERVANT SPIRIT

Isaiah records a series of passages collectively known as "Servant Songs." (See Isaiah 42:1–9; 52:4–9; 52:12–13; 61:1–3.) These passages prophetically portray and point to Jesus as a Spirit-endowed Servant.

So, not only did the Spirit speak into the millennial reign of Christ, but He also revealed an unexpected aspect of the Messiah's ministry. The Messiah would appear as a suffering Servant who had the ability to heal, set free, and bring light and justice to the nations. (See Isaiah 42:1–9.)

This was something that most of the people of Jesus's day were not expecting. They were eagerly looking for the Messiah to come as the King and to conquer all their natural enemies, not to have the Messiah come as the Servant who would serve and suffer at the hands of those He came to save. They were looking for the Messiah to bring external change, but the Messiah's first priority was internal change. The work of the Spirit in and through the Messiah was to offer man "root" change before "fruit" change. Religion works on the outside to try to change, or at least mask, the inside of man. But the work of the Spirit is to change the inside of man and thus affect the outside. *The way of the Spirit is always "root before fruit."*

AN ANOINTING TO SERVE

> *Behold! My Servant whom I uphold.... I have put My Spirit upon Him.... He will not cry out, nor raise His voice, nor cause His voice to be heard in the street.* (Isaiah 42:1–2 NKJV)

The world seeks to lead, but we see in the Spirit's empowerment of Jesus that He *first* anoints and empowers to serve. Jesus came first as a sacrificial Servant; later, He will return as a conquering King. *Serving paves the way to leading.*

We should remember the serving aspect of Jesus's ministry when considering His quotation of Isaiah at the beginning of His ministry, with the announcement that *"the Spirit of the LORD is upon Me..."* (Luke 4:18 NKJV; see also Isaiah 61:1). Although this verse is usually seen as Jesus announcing His Spirit-empowered ability to heal, set captives free, and preach, the original context of the Spirit's empowerment of Jesus was that of serving! Jesus did serve by demonstrations of power, but He also served by demonstrations of love and compassion. Actually, Jesus's motivation to move in power was the love of God. When we discuss having the Spirit empower us to do Jesus's *"greater works"* (John 14:12, various translations), we should include a greater capacity to love, walk in humility, have compassion, and serve. *The Spirit empowered all the works of Jesus!*

"YOUR SONS AND YOUR DAUGHTERS..."

> *For I will pour water on him who is thirsty, and floods on the dry ground; I will pour My Spirit on your descendants, and My blessing on your offspring.* (Isaiah 44:3 NKJV)

I ministered for many years without any thought about writing books. Occasionally, people would suggest the idea to me, but I always put it off. I felt like I didn't have anything "new" to say that hadn't already been said better by other, more experienced ministers. I am not saying that this attitude was right, but it was the way I felt. One day, I had a visitation from the Lord, and one of the things He said to me was, "Revelation only lives one generation! Every generation must have a fresh voice!"

This did not mean that every new generation does away with what the previous generation received from the Spirit. Nor did it mean that each generation had to receive some new revelation that was unheard of in previous generations. It simply meant we should not live on the previous generation's manna. We have to receive for ourselves truths that the earlier generations received and then stand on those generations' shoulders, as it were, to go higher!

To receive "new" revelation means to receive what is new to us because we either had not previously known about it, or it had been formerly known but forgotten. It should not be totally unique in that no previous generation had ever heard of it. "*There is nothing new under the sun*" (Ecclesiastes 1:9, various translations), and I always tell the pastors to whom I minister that if a "truth" is completely unique in that it has never been heard of before in church history, then it is too new, and they should run from it! God, in His faithfulness, will never let the truth be snuffed out completely from the earth. It may be marginalized, hidden, or lost, but if you look at history, even through the dark ages, there was always a remnant that walked in a level of truth regarding salvation and the Holy Spirit. Every generation needs men and women who will hear God for themselves and proclaim what the Word and the Spirit are saying to their generation.

Of course, the moves of the Spirit effected through God's "generals" in previous generations should continue to inspire and disciple us by means of those generals' printed and recorded messages, the example of their lives, and their testimonies. Still, every generation needs to raise up generals.

> *And it shall come to pass in the last days, says God, that I will pour out of My Spirit on all flesh; your sons and your daughters shall prophesy....*
> (Acts 2:17 NKJV)

Since God is the God of generations—past, present, and future—introducing the work and the ways of the Holy Spirit to the next generation is the most significant inheritance that we can leave them. And being introduced to those works and ways ourselves is the most important inheritance we can receive from previous generations.

DIVINE SPECIFICITY...YOUR DESCENDANTS' DESCENDANTS

> *For I will pour water on him who is thirsty, and floods on the dry ground; I will pour My Spirit on your descendants, and My blessing on your offspring.*
> (Isaiah 44:3 NKJV)

In the book of Isaiah, there are at least fifteen places where the Holy Spirit is directly mentioned, and there are multiple indirect references to the Spirit's influence.

The Holy Spirit was active in creation (see Isaiah 40:12–13; 48:16) and in God's workings to protect and preserve Israel (see Isaiah 59:19, 21). One of the most far-reaching aspects of the Spirit's ministry in Isaiah was to reveal how the Spirit would anoint the soon-coming Messiah to rule as King on David's throne in His millennial reign. (See Isaiah 11:1–12.) The Spirit was speaking into the Messiah's ministry *at the second coming before the first coming!*

In speaking prophetically into the distant millennial age, the Holy Spirit again showed Himself to be fully in control and to have plans for the generations to come.

It is *always* the will of the Spirit to fill a generation so full that there will be an overflow for the next generation. I often ponder this thought: God intends not just to fill me but to *overfill* me so I can spill over on others. This overflow is part of God's plan as *"my cup runneth over"* (Psalm 23:5 KJV).

I am a first-generation believer—the first in my immediate family to be born again and Spirit filled. The gravity of that fact has never left me. I have the privilege of being a vessel from which the Spirit will pour forth to the next generation. And this is true for all of us!

Many times, while I am preaching, teaching, or ministering in the Spirit, I become keenly aware of a shift in the flow of the Spirit, and I tangibly sense, almost like a coat that is thrown on me, anointings that were on elder ministers whom God had used to pour into my life and spiritual development, either by their teaching ministry or by my personal association with them. When that happens, it is as if an additional charge of the anointing is added to me. This is part of the overflow of the Spirit available to all of us. In addition to the anointing that God has deposited in us, we can have access to the anointings on others whom God places in our lives. As I have mentored and discipled others, I have heard similar testimonies from people who have sensed the grace on my life come on them.

In a very real way, all of us are now, generations later, to various degrees, partakers of the anointings of Paul, Peter, and the rest of the early church, by their writings and by the Spirit who was upon them.

Understanding this, we should all develop an expectation that what God has done for and in us will overflow into the next generation!

THE SPIRIT AND THE WORD

> *"As for Me," says the* Lord, *"this is My covenant with them: My Spirit who is upon you, and My words which I have put in your mouth, shall not depart from your mouth, nor from the mouth of your descendants, nor from the mouth of your descendants' descendants," says the* Lord, *"from this time and forevermore."* (Isaiah 59:21 NKJV)

The first thing that happens when the Spirit comes upon someone is that His words are *"put in* [their] *mouth."*

This does not just happen when we search out a passage of Scripture to stand on and confess over our lives. It is right and proper to confess God's Word in that way; the speaking and the hearing of the Word cause faith to come. (See Romans 10:8–10, 17.) Confessing what God says allows us to possess what God promises. Confessing the Word of God is part of the process of renewing our minds with the Word.

But when the Spirit comes upon you and puts a word in your mouth, that is not a faith *confession* of the Word but an authoritative *declaration* of a word from God (whether it comes from Scripture or by direct revelation).

When Jesus commanded, *"Peace"* to the storm (see Mark 4:39), that was not a Word confession that Jesus was standing on in faith, awaiting its manifestation; it was an authoritative declaration of the Spirit through the lips of Jesus!

In confessing the Word, we assimilate the Word into our heart.

In declaring the Word (or a Spirit-inspired word), we release the Word/word from our heart.

In a broader sense, a declaration by the Spirit is when God gives revelation to someone that shapes a generation. When Martin Luther declared that *"the just shall live by faith"* (Romans 1:17 NKJV, KJV), it shook the religious and social world. It opened a door in the Spirit that many people are still walking through today. This is how *"the worlds were framed by the word of God"* (Hebrews 11:3 NKJV, KJV).

What a promise for the generations to come that the age-defining, prophetic declaration that the Spirit releases *"shall not depart…from the mouth of your descendants, nor from the mouth of your descendants' descendants."* God intends that the revelatory declarations given in our age remain to define, shape, and establish our descendants.

THE SPIRIT ON JESUS

> *The Spirit of the Lord GOD is upon Me, because the LORD has anointed Me to preach good tidings to the poor; He has sent Me to heal the brokenhearted, to proclaim liberty to the captives, and the opening of the prison to those who are bound; to proclaim the acceptable year of the LORD, and the day of vengeance of our God; to comfort all who mourn.*
> (Isaiah 61:1–2 NKJV)

This prophecy in Isaiah was fulfilled in Jesus and, again, was declared at the launch of His ministry. Luke 4:18–19 tells us that Jesus ended the quote with *"to proclaim the acceptable year of the LORD,"* choosing not to mention *"the day of vengeance."* Jesus was not here to proclaim vengeance but acceptance to all! (See John 3:17.)

Even in Isaiah's original text, it was an *"acceptable* ***year,****"* but only a *"****day*** *of vengeance."* That is God's love, grace, and mercy in action!

JEREMIAH

The Compassionate Weeping of Heaven

For anyone sensing a call to a prophetic office, studying the work of the Spirit throughout the life and ministry of Jeremiah will bear much fruit because it showcases the life and function of a prophet. Jeremiah was a young man with a weighty call on his life: God tasked him to speak forth warnings and judgments against Judah and Jerusalem. A depth of compassion balanced the severity of these heavenly pronouncements through Jeremiah, reflecting God's heart.

PROPHETIC LIVES AND ACTIONS

Jeremiah didn't just deliver prophetic messages verbally—the Spirit also directed him to act them out. He didn't marry or have children in order to symbolize that there essentially wouldn't be a next generation, except among the remnant that would be exiled, because the pending judgment would sweep away most of that generation. (See Jeremiah 16.) Why would the Holy Spirit inspire such an unusual instruction to Jeremiah? Because just as we see parents of newborn babies making gurgling, cooing sounds to them that have no meaning—other than to communicate with their infants—the

Holy Spirit seeks to communicate with us through speech and symbols by every means available. That is the mercy and grace of God in action.

Similar to Jeremiah, I believe there is a company of young prophetic voices that have arisen and are still emerging that will not just deliver messages from heaven but will also demonstrate by their prophetic lives and actions what God wants to be known.

I see them being raised from deathbeds of sickness and sin so others can see that God has power over death and destruction.

I see them being delivered from the clutches of the darkness of addiction and confusion as a sign of the deliverance through Christ that is available to mankind.

I see them being promoted in the "courts of Pharaoh," having governmental authority so that the Spirit's light and voice can influence a nation.

I see them being given voices of favor, influence, and authority so that the goodness and life of God can be proclaimed through every form of media.

I see a prophetic Jeremiah company arising that calls mankind back to God!

Today, many people refer to Jeremiah as "the weeping prophet" because he was not just consumed by a message of judgment and repentance but was also engulfed by the compassion of God. In the church, it seems as if, with every generation, there arises a host of prophetic voices that are eagerly poised to declare a message of doom and gloom against the sins of society and the lukewarmness of God's people. No doubt, some of these prophets are called by God, their messages being warranted and even necessary; but to declare judgment without encasing it in the heart of the Father's love and compassion is always a mark of an immature believer. From the Father's love, warnings and judgments flow—not to bring about damnation but to redeem and separate people from the coming destruction. Jeremiah went so far as to pray for his people even when the Lord told him not to! (See Jeremiah 7:16; 11:14; 14:11.)

SHAPING THE UNSHAPED

> *Then the word of the Lord came to me, saying: "Before I formed you in the womb I knew you; before you were born I sanctified you; I ordained*

> *you a prophet to the nations." Then said I: "Ah, Lord GOD! Behold, I cannot speak, for I am a youth."* (Jeremiah 1:4–6 NKJV)

I am well convinced from the Word that God had plans for us before we ever arrived in this world and celebrated our first birthday, and He intends for us to have an impact well after we cease having birthdays. His plans for us began long before we appeared on the physical earth and extend until after we will depart from it. God intends for us to leave a legacy of lasting fruit on the earth when we leave it.

The call and plans God had for us before we were born are part of the mysteries that we pray out when we speak in tongues. (See 1 Corinthians 14:2.) Since it is the Spirit who calls us from before our birth, it is only the Spirit who knows all that is planned for us. It's a mystery to us, but, by the enabling of the Spirit, we can pray out these mysteries in the Spirit.

The mysteries of God are kept for us, not from us!

Just as, in Genesis, the Holy Spirit hovered over the formless earth, He hovers over any part of our life and calling that is still formless, waiting for the command of "Light, be!" so that He can manifest the Word and will of God in us. There are still parts of our life, steps to take, and places to go that God has ordained for us that are not fully formed "in the womb."

The Spirit knows people, things, and situations that are not yet formed or visible to the natural eye, and He makes plans for these unseen aspects, calling them, just like He did Jeremiah, into the will of God. You can trust the unseen parts of your life to Him. The all-knowing Spirit of God has ordained and called into being the unformed aspects of your life that you do not yet see, to be a "prophet," a testimony to the nations!

THE FIRE OF LONGEVITY

> *Therefore thus says the LORD God of hosts: "Because you speak this word, behold,* ***I will make My words in your mouth fire, and this people wood, and it shall devour them.****"* (Jeremiah 5:14 NKJV)

The fire of the Holy Spirit burns through everyone who is called to preach and proclaim His Word. There is an aspect of Spirit-led teaching and preaching that will not just inspire and instruct us but will also douse us in the fire of the Spirit! This speaks of the Word and the Spirit consuming us wholly. Even Balaam's donkey (see Numbers 22:28) and Peter's rooster (see, for example, Mark 14:30, 66–72) could bring forth a Spirit-inspired utterance, but to be consumed by the fire of the Spirit speaks of a lifestyle and longevity in following the Lord. It is not those who start a race but those who finish it who win a prize.

> *Then I said, "I will not make mention of Him, nor speak anymore in His name." But* ***His word was in my heart like a burning fire shut up in my bones****; I was weary of holding it back, and I could not.*
> (Jeremiah 20:9 NKJV)

Later, when Jeremiah felt like quitting, God's *"word,"* like a burning fire, sustained him. You need both the Word and the Spirit to finish the race set before you. The Lord once showed me a candle and said, "You need both the wick and the wax for that candle to produce light. The wick draws from the wax [oil] to have something to burn, and the wax flows through the wick to burn!"

Longevity in the things of God requires a balance of having the wick of the Word and the wax of the Spirit burning in unison in our life.

The Word was in Jeremiah's heart, and the fire was deep in his innermost being—*"shut up in my bones"*—so his encounter with the Word and the Spirit was not just on the surface; there was a depth in his relationship to them.

The Jeremiah company goes deep in its walk with God.

THE HOLY SPIRIT WRITES DEEPLY

> *But this is the covenant that I will make with the house of Israel after those days, says the Lord: I will put My law in their minds, and write it on their hearts; and I will be their God, and they shall be My people.* (Jeremiah 31:33 NKJV)

The Spirit seeded God's Word in the depth of Jeremiah's heart, and it developed into a deep walk with God. The Holy Spirit speaks and plants deeply in us as we learn to yield to Him. This is what the Pharisees and religious leaders of Jesus's day failed to understand. If the law of God remained in the intellectual realm alone, it would be a burden that leads to death; but if the Spirit were allowed to move the Word of God into the hearts of man, it would be a wellspring of life. What a tragedy that those religious leaders committed their lives to proclaim and preserve God's Word, yet their hardened hearts failed to recognize the One whom the Scriptures wrote about when He stood in their midst!

The Word renews our minds, but only if we first approach it with our hearts.

THE INTERCESSORY GRIEF OF THE SPIRIT

Jeremiah's weeping was more than just human sympathy; it demonstrated prophetic identification with those who were estranged from God. (See Jeremiah 9:1, 18; 31:15.) Jeremiah wept because he sensed God's grief over the state and plight of the people. Jesus also wept—over the death of Lazarus (see John 11:35) and over the hard-heartedness of the people (see Luke 19:41). There are places in the Spirit that we enter into through prayer and intercession where we get a sense of the God's heart and perspective. Weeping while in intercession and travail is often an expression of that.

When we think about the disobedience and hard-heartedness of those in Jeremiah's day and in Jesus's time, let us remember this: we are told not to grieve the Holy Spirit. (See Ephesians 4:30.) If we choose our strength and ability over His, even in a noble pursuit like pleasing Him, we grieve Him because whenever we try to exclude the Spirit's strength and ability, we set ourselves up for certain shortfalls and failure. This is the essence of all man-made religion: attempting to reach and placate God through man's strength and with man's own prescribed method. Such ideologies, even those within the church, are *always* about seeking to earn favor and standing with God through works instead of resting on Calvary's finished work and receiving God's grace and mercy. Man's attempt to reach God outside of receiving His love and mercy is what grieves the Spirit because it is the ultimate rejection of God.

Jeremiah grieved as God grieves, and for the only reason for which He grieves: when His goodness is rejected. God does not grieve out of self-pity because His goodness has been spurned but rather out of love because those who reject His goodness must live by their own means and efforts without Him, which always leads to destruction.

Such identification with the Spirit as Jeremiah had is a high form of intercession. When we are in this position of identification, the Spirit can move through us, making intercession *"with groanings which cannot be uttered"* (Romans 8:26 NKJV).

Not all intercessors are prophets, but all prophets are intercessors. Being grieved by what grieves the heart of God is what separates the mature prophets from the immature prophets.

LAMENTATIONS

The Lament and Love of God

Jeremiah is traditionally recognized as the author of Lamentations. Second Chronicles 35:25 records Jeremiah composing laments.

Five laments or poems are recorded in Lamentations. Although there are other laments in Scripture, this book is a collection of the longest of them.

Lamentations looks at concepts of suffering. There is not a more sorrowful book in the Bible.

This book also speaks to us about the depths of God's grieving-but-compassionate heart. Our moving to that level of God's compassion requires us to have a heart like Jeremiah's. After the destruction of Jerusalem, Jeremiah did not gloat or rejoice that the prophecies he had delivered about it were fulfilled; rather, he wept bitterly.

> *My eyes fail with tears, my heart is troubled; my bile is poured on the ground because of the destruction of the daughter of my people, because the children and the infants faint in the streets of the city.... Their heart cried out to the Lord, "O wall of the daughter of Zion, let tears run*

> *down like a river day and night; give yourself no relief; give your eyes no rest."* (Lamentations 2:11, 18 NKJV)

> *My eyes overflow with rivers of water for the destruction of the daughter of my people. My eyes flow and do not cease, without interruption.* (Lamentations 3:48–49 NKJV)

Not only do we see Jeremiah reflecting God's heart, but we also see his maturity in both his walk with God and his advancement in the prophetic office. *The true test of the prophetic office is not just in the accuracy of the words delivered but in the accurate presentation of the Father's heart.* The Holy Spirit doesn't just give us prophetic utterances; He seeks to express all of God's attributes and qualities through us!

AN ANGRY GOD...A SPIRIT OF COMPASSION

Those who are tasked with delivering prophetic utterances must take time to be absorbed into the Father's presence so that they reflect the whole of His personality. Redemption is at the heart of God. This can be easily seen when Adam and Eve fell in Eden, and God immediately provided them with tunics of skin to cover their nakedness. (See Genesis 3:21.) Redemption is always post-judgment. In fact, without the possibility of judgment, redemption would be unnecessary.

Judgment is the fruit of the integrity of God. Redemption is the fruit of the compassion of God. The Holy Spirit is both the Spirit of truth and the Spirit by which we call out, *"Abba, Father!"* (Galatians 4:6 NKJV).

For God, the warning of judgment and the offer of redemption always go hand in hand. Judgment and redemption are two sides of the same coin. To present one without the other would be to misrepresent God.

> *He has cut off in fierce anger every horn of Israel; He has drawn back His right hand from before the enemy. He has blazed against Jacob like a flaming fire devouring all around.* (Lamentations 2:3 NKJV)

Throughout the second chapter of Lamentations, verses like this portray an angry God. God's anger is principled and coupled with grief. It is principled because His anger is based on mankind's stubborn departure from His ways despite His many warnings and offers of redemption. Yet, because God is, in essence, love, He is grieved when mankind makes choices that invariably lead to death and destruction. God's parental compassion is expressed through His sending prophets to warn the people. And, of course, it is through the Holy Spirit that prophets are called and inspired with messages of hope from heaven!

THE LOVE OF GOD

> [The Lord said,] "*Yet you have forsaken Me and served other gods. Therefore* ***I will deliver you no more....*** *" And the children of Israel said to the* LORD*, "We have sinned! Do to us whatever seems best to You; only deliver us this day, we pray." So they put away the foreign gods from among them and served the* LORD*. And* ***His soul could no longer endure the misery of Israel.***" (Judges 10:13–16 NKJV)

I've spent many moments pondering these verses from Judges, nourishing my soul. Once again, the children of Israel had gotten into apostasy and fallen away from God and into the hands of the Philistines. They had done so, again, despite God's many warnings and wooings. This so angered God that He declared there would be no deliverance for them; but the nature of God, which is love, overcame the anger of God! God was moved by love and compassion toward them. *The impetus of our deliverance, by the power of the Holy Spirit, is the love of God.*

Once, the Spirit said to me, "'*For God so loved the world that He gave His only begotten Son*' [John 3:16 NKJV].... For the Son so loved the church that He sent the Holy Spirit [see John 15:26]!"

Similar to what we see in the book of Jeremiah, in the above passage from Judges, the Holy Spirit is shown to experience and express grief over the people's departure from the ways of God. But the Holy Spirit is also seen working redemption for and through the people.

NEW EVERY MORNING

In Lamentations, amid the people's sin, suffering, and loss, the solution is revealed in the heart of God.

> *Through the* Lord*'s mercies we are not consumed, because His compassions fail not. They are new every morning; great is Your faithfulness. "The* Lord *is my portion," says my soul, "therefore I hope in Him!"* (Lamentations 3:22–24 NKJV)

God is a God of mercy, love, and faithfulness even when we fall on hard times due to our straying from Him.

God is not good only when we are good. God is good even when we are not good.

As believers, vessels of the Holy Spirit, we have access to the grief and anger of God, but we must never forget to allow the love of God to be our determining factor!

EZEKIEL

A Foretaste of the River

Ezekiel, whose name means "God strengthens," was a prophet who was given to many mystical experiences. Whereas Jeremiah ministered about the Father's heart, and Isaiah had a revelation of the Son, Ezekiel records rich experiences with the Spirit. Ezekiel seemed to have had easy access to and been in contact with the Spirit realm through visions and prophecies.

The prophet Ezekiel is an Old Testament type of the New Testament Spirit-filled believer. Prophetic revelation and demonstration are abundant throughout the book of Ezekiel. There are so many spectacular demonstrations of the Holy Spirit that this book has sometimes been called "the book of Acts of the Old Testament." The prophet experiences spiritual manifestations of signs, visions, prophetic acts, and verbal utterances.

The Holy Spirit inspired Ezekiel to perform seemingly unusual prophetic acts, such as lying on his right and left sides for a total of four hundred and thirty days (see Ezekiel 4:4–8), shaving himself bald (see Ezekiel 5:1–4), and even enacting being a refugee of war (see Ezekiel 12:1–16). The Spirit didn't just speak through Ezekiel verbally, but He also demonstratively dramatized and enacted through the prophet some of what He was saying. Again, prophetic acts are within the sphere of God's methods of communication with man.

This was perhaps not as dramatic as Ezekiel's many experiences, but, once, when I was in private prayer for a series of upcoming meetings with a group of more conservative, traditional ministers, I breathed out and exhaled loudly, almost as if I were blowing onto kindling to start a fire. At the same time, I began to fan my arms about in a bladelike fashion. When I came out of this deep place of prayer, I thought back on that occurrence, and my natural mind was tempted to think how foolish that action must have looked. A few weeks later, when the series of meetings came around, rather unexpectedly, during one of the evening services, it seemed as if a sudden whooshing sound came into the room. Some of the ministers in attendance were knocked off their seats, and others in the room were filled with the Spirit without anyone laying hands on them or any altar calls being made for them to respond to, and they spontaneously started speaking in tongues! I did not immediately connect the earlier prayer episode with what happened in the meeting until the Holy Spirit prompted my remembrance and told me that I had prophetically acted out in prayer what the Holy Spirit wanted to accomplish in that meeting. Prophetic acts are often a form of intercession for and declaration of things to come.

Ezekiel saw deeply enough into the Spirit realm that he even saw heavenly creatures: the four-winged cherubim. (See, for example, Ezekiel 1:5.) The Spirit of God is the One from whom *all* life originates and is sustained. It's easy to forget that it is not just life in our physical realm that comes from the Spirit but life in all realms. I was once asked if I believe in aliens from other planets, and I replied, tongue in cheek, "I am not sure, but if they do exist, they'll need a Savior, and His name is Jesus!"

In Ezekiel's experiences in the Spirit, he caught prophetic glimpses that pointed him to the coming Messiah. Additionally, the messianic title "*son of man*" is used about ninety times throughout this book. Although it does so in reference to the prophet, Jesus would later give Himself this title. (See, for example, Matthew 12:8.) So we can see that, prophetically, Ezekiel was an Old Testament type of Christ.

By the Holy Spirit's inspiration, Ezekiel even spoke about the divine Shepherd. (See Ezekiel 34; 37:24–25.) This prophetic picture speaks powerfully of Jesus the Good Shepherd. (See John 10:1–30.)

The Holy Spirit always points us to Christ and can show us things to come.

Again, the Holy Spirit and the Word of God operate in divine unison. *The Spirit demonstrates the details of the Word, and the Word details the Spirit.* So, it's not a surprise that the phrase *"the word of the LORD came"* is used about fifty times in the book of Ezekiel.

HE SETS YOU ON YOUR FEET

> *And He said to me, "Son of man, stand on your feet, and I will speak to you." Then the Spirit entered me when He spoke to me, and set me on my feet; and I heard Him who spoke to me. And He said to me: "Son of man, I am sending you...."* (Ezekiel 2:1–3 NKJV)

We know from the final verse of the previous chapter, Ezekiel 1:28, that Ezekiel was on his face, overcome by all that the Spirit had shown him. In that position, Ezekiel could still hear when the Holy Spirit spoke, but the Spirit wanted Ezekiel upright before He continued talking to him. Ezekiel said that when the Holy Spirit spoke to him, *"He...set me on my feet"*! Hearing the word of the Lord will first cause you to fall on your face, but then it will set you on your feet. His words will lift you up so that you will be upright. It was when Ezekiel was in this position of standing upright that the Holy Spirit said to him, *"I am sending you."*

I have witnessed that those who have longevity in spiritual fruitfulness, those who are supernaturally sent out in power by the Spirit, are ones who were first overwhelmed by the Spirit's person and presence in their private life. They then dwelt and fed on what He had said to them until it strengthened them to stand before they were divinely sent. We must get back to waiting on the Word and the timing of the Spirit before we "go." I am convinced that too many people have rushed ahead to what might otherwise have been the will of God for them without first waiting to hear clear instructions or waiting for the seasons of the Spirit. The same Spirit who calls us also intends to instruct us and send us in the appropriate window of time; we need to stay in His presence long enough to hear all that He has to say.

Some are called, some are sent, and others just bought a loudspeaker and went!

This is not proper grammar, but it is only the "sending" that gives the "wenting"—the divine stamp of the Spirit's presence.

THE SPIRIT GIVES US A NEW SPIRIT

> *Then I will sprinkle clean water on you, and you shall be clean; I will cleanse you from all your filthiness and from all your idols. I will give you a new heart and put a new spirit within you; I will take the heart of stone out of your flesh and give you a heart of flesh. I will put My Spirit within you and cause you to walk in My statutes, and you will keep My judgments and do them.* (Ezekiel 36:25–27 NKJV)

Ezekiel prophetically saw into the new covenant and our new birth (see John 3:1–8) and said that we will be given a "*new spirit*" and "*a heart of flesh,*" and that God "*will put* [His] *Spirit within*" us. The primary work of the Spirit is internal before it is external.

Once more, all religious ideology is man's attempt to regulate and fix the outside of people, hoping to get to the inside. But the work of the Spirit is to change people from the inside out. Religion tries to fix man's roots by getting him to change his fruit, but by giving us a new heart and a new spirit, God provides us with a new root that will produce new fruit. One is the effort of man; the other is the work of God. A can of peaches doesn't change into a can of creamed corn just because someone puts a different label on it! The work of God, through the Spirit in us, is the beginning of all the godly fruit that we will bear in life.

THE RIVER OF THE SPIRIT

> *And when the man went out to the east with the line in his hand, he measured one thousand cubits, and he brought me through the waters; the water came up to my ankles. Again he measured one thousand and brought me through the waters; the water came up to my knees. Again*

> *he measured one thousand and brought me through; the water came up to my waist. Again he measured one thousand, and it was a river that I could not cross; for the water was too deep, water in which one must swim, a river that could not be crossed.* (Ezekiel 47:3–5 NKJV)

The Spirit brought Ezekiel from the outer courts to the inner vestibule of the temple to show him streams of water gushing forth at various depths. Using this imagery, the Spirit showed Ezekiel that there are depths to our progression in spiritual things that we can swim into. The river of the Spirit is ever-flowing and inviting us toward total submergence. Not only is this part of the living waters that Jesus prophesied would flow from believers (see John 7:38), but it tells us that ongoing growth in the experiential spiritual realm is possible.

Some people stop at the waters of being baptized in the Spirit with the evidence of speaking in tongues and the manifestations of the Spirit in operation.

Some go still deeper and stop at the river of the Spirit to partake of healing, deliverance, and provision.

Even hungrier ones wade more deeply into Spirit-led meetings where the Spirit overcomes them in waves of holy joy, dancing, visions, trances, and Spirit-birthed intercession.

But the hungriest of us all swim into the channel, the deepest part of the river, so that, beyond physical manifestations and reactions alone, we are fully submerged in the water of the Spirit, where all those manifestations are regular occurrences. More important, in this realm, we experience a oneness with God Himself!

As I travel the world and spend time with believers from various streams, I sense an increased hunger for the reality of the Holy Spirit. May we all sense the stirring of the waters and jump into the river of the Spirit!

DANIEL

Excellence in all Things

Daniel, whose name means "God is my Judge," was a teenager, likely from an upper-class family in Jerusalem, when he and thousands of others were deported to Babylon in the exile. The book of Daniel has great apocalyptic depth. While many Old Testament passages speak about the Messiah's first coming, Daniel saw into the second coming and reign of the Messiah. Jesus referred to Daniel as a prophet and quoted him three times in the book of Matthew (see Matthew 24:15, 30; 26:64), as well as in other gospels. Many New Testament end-time writings, like Jesus's Olivet Discourse (see Matthew 24–25) and Paul's revelations (see Romans 16:25; 1 Corinthians 15:51), require an understanding of Daniel's writings for them to come into focus. Daniel's visions of the end times are paralleled by the revelation the apostle John received, which is recorded in the book of Revelation. Daniel is one of only two biblical characters (the other is Joseph) of whom no wrongdoing is spoken.

There is such rich Spirit activity in this book! From the prophetically far-reaching implications of Nebuchadnezzar's dream (see Daniel 2) to the well-known "fourth Man" account of Shadrach, Meshach, and Abed-Nego in the fiery furnace (see Daniel 3:8–25) to Daniel in the lions' den (see Daniel 6:1–23) to the pivotal "seventy-week" prophecy (see Daniel 9:20–27), the Holy Spirit ministered in some very dramatic but typically hidden ways.

Daniel does not explicitly mention the Holy Spirit, but who can deny that the dreams and their interpretations, the visions, and the predictive prophecies in their contemporary and future contexts were all supernatural revelations given to Daniel by the power of the Holy Spirit Himself? I always walk away from reading Daniel remembering that there is an experiential, demonstrative side to the Holy Spirit that goes beyond merely knowing about Him to seeing Him at work!

THE BABYLONIANS SAW "AN EXCELLENT SPIRIT"

> *There is a man in your kingdom in whom is the Spirit of the Holy God. And in the days of your father, light and understanding and wisdom, like the wisdom of the gods, were found in him; and King Nebuchadnezzar your father—your father the king—made him chief of the magicians, astrologers, Chaldeans, and soothsayers. Inasmuch as an excellent spirit, knowledge, understanding, interpreting dreams, solving riddles, and explaining enigmas were found in this Daniel, whom the king named Belteshazzar, now let Daniel be called, and he will give the interpretation.* (Daniel 5:11–12 NKJV)

Even though Daniel himself is not recorded as having talked about the Holy Spirit, the Babylonians noticed something spiritually different about him and identified it as the Spirit of God. The manifestations of the Spirit on Daniel that they identified are perhaps not ones most people would normally mention because we don't have any record of the Spirit of God healing anyone or doing any sea-parting miracles through him.

The initial things the Babylonians listed about Daniel were not dramatic power manifestations of the Spirit but rather manifestations of mature internal qualities and gifts: *"an excellent spirit, knowledge, understanding...."*

Daniel's promotion and longevity in serving the secular heathen kings resulted from the favor of God, but that favor initially manifested as excellence, knowledge, and understanding. Many believers want a spiritually supernatural life but are not as concerned with living a natural life supernaturally. They want power demonstrations but don't understand that the Holy Spirit wants to empower us to live a balanced life, where our spirit, soul, and body are endued with, and are demonstrations of, divine power. Excellence is attractive!

We believers make it hard for our witness to be accepted when we are sloppy at work and in life. For example:

- Someone is late for work every day but wants to tell everybody that Jesus is coming soon.
- An individual is so disorganized that they can't find anything, but they want to tell people how the Holy Spirit can be their guide.
- A person with dangerously unhealthy eating habits seeks to talk to others about a healing Jesus.
- Someone repeatedly gets into debt because they can't control their credit-card spending, but then they try to tell their family members about how God provides.

I am not saying that Jesus won't return to earth if a person is late all the time, that the Holy Spirit isn't a guide if someone keeps losing things, that Jesus doesn't heal if an individual has unhealthy eating habits, or that God doesn't provide when people get into debt by overspending. The very nature of God's goodness is that He helps us even when we don't deserve it! But why limit the Holy Spirit to being only the cleanup crew in our lives? Why not allow the Holy Spirit to help us shape up so we won't need as much cleanup? I am thankful that the mercy and grace of God are always available any time I mess up, but as soon as God saves me from any destruction, my next prayer after thanking Him is to ask for wisdom so that I won't fall into that pit again. And if I do fall again (and again!), His grace and mercy meet me and get me up and out so that I can ask for more wisdom, so that I can become better and wiser for the next time an occasion to fall comes my way. Having an excellent spirit is as much a demonstration of the Holy Spirit as any other miracle we can think of; and maybe if we thought about it more, we'd ask for and allow the Spirit to manifest in that way in our lives.

Daniel could also interpret dreams through the power and inspiration of the Holy Spirit. I've been asked what I think of people taking courses or reading materials that would enable them to be interpreters of dreams. You get better at anything that you give your attention to, but dream interpretation is not something that we see any biblical characters study to do. You can better interpret dreams by getting to know the Word of God more completely so you'll understand and recognize biblical symbols and languages, and then by training yourself to be sensitive to the Holy Spirit while you are awake. Dreams are just one of the ways in which the Spirit can speak; we should seek to be able to interpret all the ways the Spirit communicates with us, even when we are asleep. There are prophetic dreams that are symbolic and have interpretations, but we should also remember that just as not everything negative that we experience is a demonic attack, not every dream is significant, either. We are three-part beings—spirit, soul, and body. While we are fundamentally spiritual beings, we are also composed of soul and body, and each of those parts can speak to us.

THE FINGERS OF GOD

> *In the same hour the fingers of a man's hand appeared and wrote opposite the lampstand on the plaster of the wall of the king's palace; and the king saw the part of the hand that wrote....* [Daniel said to the king,] *"Then the fingers of the hand were sent from Him, and this writing was written."*
> (Daniel 5:5, 24 NKJV)

God holds our lives in His hands. He desires to direct and guide us. The Holy Spirit is the Hand of God that seeks to point us in the way we should go. King Belshazzar had a firsthand encounter with the Hand of God! During a lavish party for his nobles, the king called for the goblets that Nebuchadnezzar had taken from the temple in Jerusalem so that he and his guests could use them and toast in celebration of the Babylonian gods. (See verses 1–4.) The Hand of God was swift to respond in judgment to this.

The Holy Spirit delivers the judgments of God!

The Holy Spirit still points us, blood-bought believers, to judgment—the complete, finished judgment of the cross. When we fail in any area, the Holy Spirit, the Hand of God, seeks to guide us back to our redemption and the finished work of Calvary to restore us.

PART FIVE

THE HOLY SPIRIT IN THE MINOR PROPHETS

HOSEA

The Restorative Rain

Hosea means "salvation." This prophet had the distinct privilege of being chosen by God to prophetically dramatize His pain over and patience toward Israel's unfaithfulness. God led Hosea to marry Gomer, a woman who was a *"wife of harlotry"* (Hosea 1:2, various translations). They had children together, but she was repeatedly unfaithful to Hosea. Each time, he went after her and took her back. This symbolized how God repeatedly went after Israel and received her back from the mess she had gotten herself into.

Hosea ministered during a time of seemingly outward peace and prosperity for Israel, but chaos was brooding internally, leading to Israel's political collapse a few years later. Socially, corruption, immorality, and idolatry were rampant and accepted.

The book of Hosea shows us the outrageous love of God for a people who repeatedly turned their back on Him. The people had developed a warped sense of love. They thought that love was self-gratification (see Hosea 2:5) and could be bought (see Hosea 8:9), and that showering their love on material things could satisfy them (see Hosea 9:10). In contrast, God tirelessly sought out Israel to let them know that He had loved the people unconditionally ever since they were *"a child"* (Hosea 11:1, various translations) and that His heart toward them was never changing (see Hosea 11:8).

Moved by love for a people who would not hear Him, God decided to illustrate His love by having Hosea prophetically live out this message with Gomer, his ever-unfaithful wife. Hosea's being able to do this was clearly supernatural, beyond any man's ordinary love and tolerance for a wandering wife. The anointing of the Spirit can even extend to our emotions if we let it!

God led Hosea to marry a harlot, love her, start a family with her (see Hosea 1:3, 6, 8), and repeatedly go after her when she strayed (see Hosea 3:1–2). This was and is the kind of love God has for people. His love is unrelenting!

PATIENT, GENTLE, TENDER

> *But then I will win her back once again. I will lead her into the desert and speak tenderly to her there.* (Hosea 2:14 NLT)

God's approach to the backslidden people of Israel, as it is with all people, was to go to them tenderly and patiently. God intends to *"win* [us] *back* ***once again,***" meaning that He is patient even after someone strays repeatedly. Then God tries to *"lead* [us] *into the desert."* This implies that He guides us gently, without force or coercion. Once God has us where He can talk to us alone, without distraction, He speaks to us *"tenderly."*

Patiently, gently, and tenderly—this is how God approaches us.

AN UNHOLY SPIRIT OF HARLOTRY

The absence of the Holy Spirit in someone's life, resulting from a rejection of the Spirit, leaves a void that will soon be occupied by unholy spirits. Likewise, when believers do not honor and make room for the Holy Spirit, it is the beginning of all kinds of weakness among them. The presence of God in our midst, in and through the person of the Holy Spirit, is our safe hiding place. It is where we are under the shadow of the Almighty. (See Psalm 91:1.)

Hosea twice identifies *"the spirit of harlotry"* (Hosea 4:12; 5:4 NKJV, AMPC) that caused the people to stray and to not know God. Just as the Holy Spirit leads us to a close relationship with God, unholy spirits, attitudes, and ideologies lead us away from God. This is not to say that those who are insensitive or resistant to the Holy Spirit are possessed by evil spirits. The term *possessed* has unfortunately been inaccurately used, and this has popularized the idea that believers can be thoroughly the property of demons. It is misleading because "possessed" implies the concept of ownership. Seldom are people *fully* possessed by demons, and this is especially *never* so if they are believers. However, if believers don't know their authority or exercise it, they can be harassed, oppressed, and influenced by demons—but not possessed by them. The Holy Spirit lives inside believers; how could a demon occupy the same space as the Holy Spirit? We'll receive more light on demons and deliverance when we study some of the New Testament books.

Even though *"the spirit of harlotry"* shadowed the people, this did not stop God from pursuing them and offering them redemption!

THE RAIN OF THE SPIRIT

> *Let us know, let us pursue the knowledge of the LORD. His going forth is established as the morning; He will come to us like the rain, like the latter and former rain to the earth.* (Hosea 6:3 NKJV)

Using the symbols of seasons and rain, the Holy Spirit, through Hosea, prophesied the great outpouring that would take place on Pentecost.

In desertlike, arid Israel, the rains in winter and, especially, in spring that soaked the ground and ushered in a season of new life in nature were much anticipated.

The tremendous outpouring on the day of Pentecost that led to an immediate harvest of three thousand people (see Acts 2:41) continues today worldwide. The Spirit's overflow upon the one hundred twenty initial disciples in the upper room still impacts millions. But a greater harvest is still coming when the *"latter and former rain"* will meet on the earth. God has ordained us to be alive during this season, in which the precious fruit of the earth is being harvested and is still to be harvested.

THE SPIRIT OFFERS RESTORATION

> *O Israel, return to the LORD your God, for you have stumbled because of your iniquity; take words with you, and return to the LORD. Say to*

> *Him, "Take away all iniquity; receive us graciously, for we will offer the sacrifices of our lips. Assyria shall not save us, we will not ride on horses, nor will we say anymore to the work of our hands, 'You are our gods.' For in You the fatherless finds mercy." "I will heal their backsliding, I will love them freely, for My anger has turned away from him. I will be like the dew to Israel; he shall grow like the lily, and lengthen his roots like Lebanon. His branches shall spread; his beauty shall be like an olive tree, and his fragrance like Lebanon."* (Hosea 14:1–6 NKJV)

The book of Hosea ends with God's call for the people to return to Him. That message comes through Hosea, but he is inspired and empowered to give it by the Holy Spirit.

It has been wrongly said that the "God of the Old Testament" was all about judgment and punishment, in contrast to the "God of the New Testament," who was all about mercy and love. But the God of the Old Testament is the same Being as the God of the New Testament—and He is about love, mercy, and forgiveness!

The Father, the Son, and the Holy Spirit share the same heart to bring people everywhere to a place of restoration in their relationship with the Lord.

In Hosea 14, God again graciously asked that the people return to Him, promising that the fatherless would find mercy, that He would heal their backsliding and would love them freely, and that His anger would be turned. These are not the words of an angry God but a God of love who wanted good for His people.

> *O Israel, return to the LORD your God.... Say to Him, "Take away all iniquity; receive us graciously, for we will offer the sacrifices of our lips."*

God made it easy for the Israelites to accept His invitation of restoration. All they needed to do was return to Him and ask Him to *"take away all iniquity."* They didn't have to take away their own iniquity; they couldn't—but they could return to Him and ask Him to do it for them! This pattern of going to God still holds true today. We don't need to clean up our lives before we go to Him. We go to Him as we are, and He cleans up our lives! If we could clean up ourselves without Him, then the sacrifice of Jesus would have been unnecessary. What grace and mercy He affords us!

JOEL

A Preview of the Upper Room

Most theologians agree that Amos and Isaiah borrowed from some of the writings of Joel. That would make this book one of the earliest of the minor prophets.

Joel, which means "Yahweh is God," is a short, three-chapter book that significantly impacts us New Testament believers. Most of us are familiar with the quotation from Joel's prophecy that Peter declared on the day of Pentecost. (See Joel 2:28–29; Acts 2:16–18.) Today, we are still experiencing the fulfillment of Joel's prophecy. This is the impact that a "small" prophetic word can have—it can transcend time and generations! Joel prophesied the beginning of the church age.

In Joel's day, an unusually large and destructive swarm of locusts descended on the entire land of Judah. The locusts stripped the land of all vegetation, right down to the bark of the fig trees. This, in turn, affected the pastures of the sheep and cattle. The locust infestation devastated the land. Famine and drought followed throughout Judah. The death and destruction of man and animals were commonplace. (See Joel 1.)

Joel was raised up to sound the alarm that such a plague of locusts was a judgment from God and was a direct fulfillment of Moses's proclamation that locusts would come if Israel strayed into disobedience. (See Deuteronomy 28:38–46.) So, the prophetic utterance that Joel delivered was based, at least in part, on a previous verbal and then written prophecy given through Moses.

Peter would repeat the same prophetic protocol on the day of Pentecost, quoting Joel to provide scriptural justification for the outpouring of the Spirit.

This is the divine blueprint for prophetic utterances and spiritual manifestations. As with Joel, when prophetic utterances are delivered, those utterances should be based on previously recorded utterances. In other words, all prophetic utterances should be based not just on "thus saith the Lord" but also on the previously expressed will of God, which for us today means the written Word of God.

After declaring, by the Spirit, the reason for the plague of locusts, Joel saw into the future when *"the sun shall be turned into darkness, and the moon into blood, before the coming of the great and awesome day of the LORD"* (Joel 2:31 NKJV). So the Spirit showed Joel not only the beginning of the church age but also the end of the age!

WHAT WAS SPOKEN BY JOEL

But this is what was spoken by the prophet Joel.... (Acts 2:16 NKJV)

Again, when a demonstration of the Spirit occurred on the day of Pentecost, rather than leaning on the demonstration itself as proof of God's approval, Peter, led by the Holy Spirit, immediately referred to Joel's written prophecy to confirm and validate the spiritual manifestation. So, the Spirit of God confirmed His actions on Pentecost by what the Word had recorded in the book of Joel. As has been emphasized previously, the Word and the Spirit always agree. The Word will confirm what the Spirit does, and the Spirit will demonstrate what the Word says.

If we see manifestations that the Word does not support, how will we know what manner of spirit is behind it? Amos 3:7 says that God does nothing without first revealing it to the prophets. If it wasn't first revealed to the prophets and recorded for us, then we must question its origin.

Once, when I taught this principle, a pastor afterward asked me about the occurrence when Jesus made clay of His spittle and healed the blind man. (See John 9:1–7.) I answered that while that method wasn't previously specified in Scripture, the principle of "*I am the Lord that healeth thee*" (Exodus 15:26 KJV) applies.

God has tied Himself to this standard: "*By the mouth of two or three witnesses every word shall be established*" (2 Corinthians 13:1 NKJV).

It would be against the character of God to have one standard for us and demonstrate another for Himself!

WHAT WAS SPOKEN BY MOSES

> *And it shall come to pass afterward that I will pour out My Spirit on all flesh; your sons and your daughters shall prophesy, your old men shall dream dreams, your young men shall see visions.*
>
> (Joel 2:28 NKJV)

This passage from Joel, which Peter quoted on the day of Pentecost, was itself a reaffirmation by the Spirit of what Moses had once declared: "*Then Moses said to him, '...Oh, that all the Lord's people were prophets and that the Lord would put His Spirit upon them!'*" (Numbers 11:29 NKJV).

So, by the mouths of three witnesses—Peter quoting Joel, who reaffirmed Moses—the outpouring of the Spirit was confirmed. This is the biblical pattern that God has established.

The Spirit will confirm the Word, and the Word will confirm the Spirit!

THE PLACE OF PROPHECY

Let us look at this passage once more:

> *And it shall come to pass afterward that I will pour out My Spirit on all flesh; your sons and your daughters shall prophesy, your old men*

shall dream dreams, your young men shall see visions.

(Joel 2:28 NKJV)

The context of the second chapter of Joel is that the outpouring of the Spirit would happen after the people had repented and turned back to God. The immediate result of the outpouring of the Spirit would be that "sons and daughters shall prophesy."

So, prophecy was a sign that the Spirit had been poured out, and the Spirit being poured out was a sign that the people had returned to God.

Prophesying is the right of those who have returned to God. Prophesying is not just predicting the future; at its most basic function, prophesying is saying what God says about something. This is what Peter was doing in quoting Joel, and what Joel was doing in referencing what Moses had said. We can take God's Word, put it in our heart, and then declare it from our mouth and be a channel for prophecy to flow. We are a prophesying generation!

The Holy Spirit, the omnipresent One, is poured out on all flesh, anywhere and everywhere that hearts are turned to God. The outpouring of the Spirit crosses denominational, gender, ethnic, and economic borders.

Joel's original prophecy was delivered during a time of famine and severe lack due to the locust infestation. But the fulfillment of that prophecy was at a time of abundance, during the agricultural grain harvest of Pentecost.

Prophecy can come at the lowest points in our lives and usher us to the highest peaks. That is the power of a prophetic utterance!

AMOS

Agreement with God's Will and Word

Amos means "burden bearer." This prophet was a shepherd (see Amos 1:1) and cultivated sycamore fig trees (see Amos 7:14). Amos was not part of the recognized schools of the prophets. He was also not part of a priestly or noble lineage. He was the only prophet who stated his secular occupation before declaring his divine commission. He did not try to hide his background. Yet God magnified Amos's voice so that he delivered the word of the Lord throughout the northern kingdom of Israel.

The call of God is not reserved for a "spiritually elite" class. Our background and current social and economic standing don't determine how much of a voice for God we can be on the earth. It is our heart for God that tunes our ears to hear Him.

While the people of Amos's day interpreted the prosperity they were experiencing as a sign of the approval of God, the prophet declared that idolatry, immorality, oppression of the poor, and a corrupt judicial system were moving the nation toward destruction and judgment. Amos was a messenger of impending judgment in a time of seeming peace and prosperity.

"THUS SAYS THE LORD"

Like many of the experiences and writings of most of the prophets, with Amos, there is no clear distinction of whether it was the Lord God or His Spirit who was specifically speaking. This book has no direct references to the Holy Spirit, but who else could have called Amos to the prophet's office and empowered him in it? As we have seen throughout the Old Testament, and as we will see even into the New Testament, many times, the Holy Spirit operates incognito. The person and presence of the Holy Spirit are like the wind: not recognizable by sight but by the effect. (See John 3:8.)

Throughout Amos's writings, you see the phrases *"thus says the LORD"* and *"says the LORD"* (various translations). Both communicating the voice of God and giving people the ability to hear that voice are functions of the Holy Spirit. Our delivering to others what God has said requires an unction from the Spirit. How else could a vessel of clay receive, contain, and be a dispenser of a divine message? That takes the power of God the Holy Spirit!

PROPHETS AGREE WITH GOD

> *Can two walk together, unless they are agreed?* (Amos 3:3 NKJV)

> *Surely the Lord GOD does nothing, unless He reveals His secret to His servants the prophets.* (Amos 3:7 NKJV)

Agreement with God is the basis for walking with Him. Whenever we agree with Him, we are in unity and alignment with Him. Whatever we agree with Him about becomes true for us.

When we agree with Him that He, the Son, is our Savior, He is!

When we agree with Him that He is our Healer, He is!

When we agree with Him that He is our Deliverer, He is!

When we agree with Him that He is our Provider, He is!

When we agree with Him that He is our Protector, He is!

God was all those things before we agreed with Him about them, but *until we agreed, He wasn't those things to us.*

Agreement is the place of unity and power.

There is the understanding here that we, the lower, agree with Him, the Higher, and not the other way around. When we agree with Him, it means that we agree with His already-spoken Word, the Bible; but it also means that we agree with what the Holy Spirit says. The Spirit's word can come in two forms besides what He has previously said to others as recorded in the Word. First, the Spirit speaks to us personally and directly, often inwardly. Second, the Spirit speaks to us externally through others' preaching, teaching, or prophecy. Regardless of how we hear Him speaking, what He intends to do for us always occurs *after* He speaks. The word "*surely*" in Amos 3:7 means that God's speaking indicates His intention. I have found that I never need to ask Him to speak, but I have often asked Him to help me hear.

For God to reveal His secrets to the prophets and for them to declare His secrets to His intended audience would mean that God and the prophets are in agreement. Hopefully, those who hear the prophets will also be in agreement. That is the purpose of prophecy: in order that faith for what God intends can come by hearing (see Romans 10:17) so that the people can agree with God.

Since God cannot contradict Himself, any message His true prophets deliver will always agree with His Word. This is primarily how the prophecy's accuracy and the prophet's maturity are judged. Does the prophecy agree with God's already-spoken and written Word, and does it agree with the spirit in which the Word was written?

The company of prophets that King Jehoshaphat and King Ahab consulted prophesied contrary to God's will, inspired by a lying spirit. (See 1 Kings 22:1–38.)

The Pharisees in Jesus's day agreed with what was written in the Word, but not with the spirit in which it was written. (See, for example, Luke 11:42.)

True and mature prophets who speak on God's behalf will always agree with God!

OBADIAH

Always a Word of Comfort

Obadiah is the shortest book in the Old Testament. The prophet Obadiah was a messenger of comfort from God the Father to a people who were mourning over the deaths of loved ones, friends, and neighbors and the destruction of Jerusalem. Humiliatingly, they were now confined to a small portion of a rubbish heap in what had once been their own city.

In comforting them, the Comforter, through Obadiah, assured the people that God had neither forgotten nor forsaken them.

The Holy Spirit *always* speaks comfort....even when we are on a rubbish heap!

The book of Obadiah speaks to an agelong rivalry of brother against brother. Conflict originating from the twins Esau and Jacob had now resulted in their descendants' living in different, competing regions. (See, for example, Numbers 20:14–21.) When the Babylonians invaded the southern kingdom of Judah, where Jacob's descendants had settled, Esau's descendants, the Edomites, took advantage of this by aligning with the Babylonians.

The Spirit moved upon Obadiah to comfort and assure the people of Judah that God had not forsaken them and to warn Edom of judgment.

I love the fact that, amid an invasion, the Spirit of God took time to deal with the issue of brotherly conflict, pride, and resentment. This tells us how much God values relationships.

> *As you have done, it shall be done to you; your reprisal shall return upon your own head.* (Obadiah 1:15 NKJV)

God is just and honors His covenants. Those qualities—*not* harshness and hate—are the basis for divine judgment. God had promised to bless those who bless His people and curse those who curse them. (See Genesis 12:3.) Out of blind jealousy, the Edomites chose to stand against Judah. Through Obadiah, God warned them of impending judgment.

FIRE ON YOUR HOUSE

> *"The house of Jacob shall be a fire, and the house of Joseph a flame; but the house of Esau shall be stubble; they shall kindle them and devour them, and no survivor shall remain of the house of Esau," for the* LORD *has spoken.* (Obadiah 1:18 NKJV)

In response to the devastation of betrayal and invasion, God declared that a holy fire would consume the house of Jacob. Fire from heaven on your *whole house* is *still* God's answer to devastation and invasion! We see a picture of this on the day of Pentecost when the sound of a mighty rushing wind filled the upper room, and there appeared tongues of fire on each of the one hundred and twenty disciples. The Holy Spirit met them personally and intimately as they gathered in faithful obedience, seeking direction as to what was to follow after the ascension of Jesus.

JONAH

Unrelentingly Merciful

Many of us remember the story of Jonah from Sunday school. This is a unique book among the Minor Prophets because it doesn't contain prophecies with a message; rather, the narrative itself is the message.

The prophet Jonah, whose name means "dove," was sent as a messenger of God's love and mercy to the undeserving and otherwise lost Assyrians. Similarly, the Holy Spirit is sent to lost humanity so that people can find salvation in the redemption that God offers through His Son.

GOD IS LOVING AND COMPASSIONATE

Whenever I meet people who believe that, in the Old Testament, God is an angry, vengeful God, I am reminded of the book of Jonah. God sent Jonah on an eight-hundred-mile journey through land and sea to bring a message of love and forgiveness to the hated and hateful Assyrians. Even with Jonah's detour through Tarshish and the deep sea, God's love and compassion confronted and confounded Jonah, who did everything he could to avert the mission God wanted him to fulfill.

By reaching out to the Assyrians, God proved that He could not be confined by geography or nationality. His mercy knows no boundaries!

Again, there was never an "angry God of the Old Testament," but there is a just, holy God…and there were plenty of rebellious people, set in their ways, who *did not have a mediator.*

Jonah's nationalistic hesitancy to bring God's message to the Assyrians was not just because he hated the Assyrians due to what they had done to the Israelites so far, but also for practical reasons: he was concerned that if the Assyrians responded to this message and were spared by God, they would soon return to their old ways and turn around to harm Israel again. (See Jonah 4:2.) God must surely have thought of this, but it wasn't enough to stop Him from offering redemption to the Assyrians. His offer of love and redemption comes *without* an insistence on our future sinlessness. In other words, not sinning again in the future isn't a prerequisite for our receiving the grace and mercy of God today. Yet when someone truly receives God's forgiveness, grace, and mercy, it will humble them and cause them to look at their past sins with disdain. God's offer of forgiveness and mercy is truly a free gift!

THE WIND OF THE SPIRIT

> *But the Lord sent out a great wind on the sea, and there was a mighty tempest on the sea, so that the ship was about to be broken up.*
>
> (Jonah 1:4 NKJV)

The wind of the Spirit is sent to keep us in the way that God has ordained for us. It can blow us into the callings of God, but it can also blow us out of the entrapments of the enemy.

It comforts me greatly to know that, even in the midst of a storm caused by our disobedience, the Holy Spirit can send a gust of wind to propel us in the right direction. The wind of the Spirit fans the flame of our calling, envelops us in His will, and transports us to our place of ministry.

GOD'S GREAT CARE FOR HUMANITY

In this book, not only do we see the Spirit speaking to and empowering Jonah for the Assyrians' sake, but we also see the Spirit's tenderness in God's dealings with Jonah's resistance to his calling.

The great fish that swallowed Jonah was not divine judgment sent to devour the unwilling prophet; it was a means of preserving him and transporting him to where he could continue his mission (see Jonah 2), perhaps depositing him right on the shores of Nineveh, to which God had called him. God has a way of preserving us and escorting us to the places He has ordained for us to be.

Jonah's heart was unmoved after the Ninevites responded with repentance to the message he delivered. Despite their fasting, sackcloth, and ashes, in which even their animals were made to partake (see Jonah 3:5–10), Jonah still failed to see their sincerity. Reacting angrily, he pouted under the sun on a hill overlooking the city. God caused a plant to grow overnight, providing the sulking prophet with shade. God then caused a worm to gnaw through the stem of the plant, killing it. Next, God sent a hot east wind to intensify the heat, scorching Jonah further.

With Jonah mourning the loss of shade, God used all these things to illustratively show the prophet how much He cares for humanity. (See Jonah 4:5–11.)

In all this, God demonstrated His encompassing love for both those who know Him and those who do not.

WORKER OF GODLY SORROW

> *But let man and beast be covered with sackcloth, and cry mightily to God; yes, let every one turn from his evil way and from the violence that is in his hands. Who can tell if God will turn and relent, and turn away from His fierce anger, so that we may not perish?*
>
> (Jonah 3:8–9 NKJV)

The Holy Spirit is the One who convicts us of our need for God. (See John 16:8.) Nineveh's mass repentance was a mass move of the Spirit in convicting the people of their need for the mercy offered by God. Not only did the Holy Spirit inspire Jonah's message, but He also opened the hearts of the Ninevites to receive that message. *The Holy Spirit is the Giver of the seed and the Reaper of the harvest.*

JONAHS TODAY

The Spirit who sought out the Ninevites is the same Spirit who is seeking out those today who seem to be the furthest from Him. I believe *God is raising up unlikely Jonahs to go into unlikely Ninevehs.*

There is an awakening "Jonah generation" whom God is calling because, in His mercy, He desires to reach out to a lost Nineveh generation. The Jonahs whom God is calling may be hesitant to go to the adversarial-looking Ninevites, but God's offer of redemption must be heard!

MICAH

Faithful to Forgive

Picking up in our review of the Minor Prophets from Jonah's encounter with the relentless mercy and redemption God offers, Micah receives visions and prophecies about the Lord, who is without rival in compassion and in forgiving sins. God continues to display to Abraham's descendants this faithfulness to compassion. From the very start of this book, He is shown to come down from heaven to be among the people. This sets the tone for God coming to our level, not demanding that we rise to His.

A younger contemporary of Isaiah, who ministered to those in the upper echelons of society, Micah spoke the common man's language. They both presented the same message but to different crowds.

Like Isaiah, Micah received messianic prophecies. When the town of Bethlehem was virtually unknown, the Holy Spirit revealed with specificity that the Messiah would be born there. (See Micah 5:2.) In Micah 5:4, the Holy Spirit revealed that the Messiah would be the divinely anointed Shepherd. It is appropriate that with such a revelation of mercy and compassion, Micah also received personal details about the Messiah—who was the personification of mercy and compassion!

GOD'S WORDS DO GOOD TO THOSE WHO LIVE BY THEM

> *You who are named the house of Jacob: "Is the Spirit of the LORD restricted? Are these His doings? Do not My words do good to him who walks uprightly?"* (Micah 2:7 NKJV)

Many times, not only will prophets prophesy liberating truth to the people of God, but they will also often speak out, under the anointing, against lying prophets. When Micah did this, the false prophets commanded him to stop. Micah's pure messages from God showed up their soulish, watered-down, compromised messages. Micah responded to the false prophets, reminding them that when they challenged him, they were rebuking the Spirit of God, who had given him the words to say. (See Micah 2:6–11.)

Utterances from the soul always cater to emotions and never to the spirit of man. Soulish "prophecies" seek to soothe man without bringing the order and correction of God.

At best, soulish prophecies come from a place of spiritual immaturity. At worst, they come from a place of willful deceit. Either way, soulish prophecies do not lead anyone to God-ordained paths.

Generally, I have noticed that immature believers usually give soulish prophecies because they are so eager to start moving in the things of the Spirit that they do so *without* the leading of the Spirit. This is generally because their zeal far outweighs their spiritual development. How much better and safer it would be if younger believers would seek to be discipled in the movement of the Spirit. Of course, this would also mean that we need the more mature believers to have a heart big enough to disciple them. Without discipleship in the movement of the Spirit, believers will be like role-playing children who merely pretend to be astronauts or firemen.

Sadly, there are also those who make it their profession to bring forth soulish prophecies for the purpose of control, manipulation, and personal gain. These hard-hearted ones need to be disciplined, not just discipled!

Micah also reminds the people that rather than complain against what God has said, they should realize that God's words will "*do good*" to those who seek to live by them. Many times, what people have erroneously called the judgment of God was simply the result of individuals' willful wrong living. The prophecies didn't cause the judgment. They merely warned of what was coming due to the people's choices. The judgment of God does not always come in the form of His doing something against someone. Sometimes it comes in the form of God simply doing nothing when someone's actions lead to self-inflicted calamity. We can, however, be assured that God's Word and His Spirit always seek to warn us and guide us toward paths that lead to life.

FULL OF POWER BY THE SPIRIT

> *Thus says the LORD concerning the prophets who make my people stray; who chant "Peace" while they chew with their teeth, but who prepare war against him who puts nothing into their mouths.... But truly* ***I am full of power by the Spirit of the LORD****, and of justice and might, to declare to Jacob his transgression and to Israel his sin.*
>
> (Micah 3:5, 8 NKJV)

Micah boldly declares a significant difference between the false prophets and himself. The false prophets *"chant 'Peace,'"* meaning they typically say that everything is all right, regardless of the state of people's walk with God. They also set themselves to war against God, who *"puts nothing into their mouths"* (since none of their utterances comes from Him), by their spreading of falsehood. In contrast, Micah is *"full of power by the Spirit of the LORD."* This is a bold declaration by Micah, since most Old Testament prophets would declare only an association with the Holy Spirit. You could not be filled with the Holy Spirit and not be filled with power.

One aspect of the power of the Holy Spirit upon Micah was that the prophet could distinguish truth from error amid a confused society. How we need that power today! Seeing truth from error, the Holy Spirit kept Micah on the path of rightness and holiness. The Holy Spirit *only* leads us to holy things and places...He couldn't be the *Holy* Spirit otherwise. So, holiness is not a product of our doing or not doing something; holiness is a result of our yielding to the empowerment of the Holy Spirit.

Thus, holiness is not the result of our human effort. Holiness is the result of our giving in to divine empowerment!

NAHUM

Prolonged Mercy Delays Judgment

About a hundred years after Jonah prophesied and saw Nineveh repent, God raised up Nahum, who began prophesying the city's destruction because the Assyrians had gone back to their evil ways. Sadly, Nineveh was finally destroyed around a hundred years after that. So, it was two hundred years from the time of Jonah before the Assyrian capital of Nineveh was finally annihilated. What a demonstration of God's long-suffering and mercy!

Although Nahum's theme was about the severity of sin and the coming destruction of Assyria, he also offered a lot of comfort to the people of Judah. As long as the Assyrians oppressed them, they cried out to God for deliverance and vindication. Nineveh's fall could not have come soon enough for them. Yet, for the Assyrians, it came too soon. I have often pondered this regarding the judgment of God: what the oppressed would like to see sooner, the oppressor would like to see delayed...and God has to weigh between judgment and mercy in His dealings with mankind.

Under the inspiration of the Holy Spirit, Nahum said it in this way: "*The* L*ORD* *is slow to anger and great in power, and will not at all acquit the wicked*" (Nahum 1:3 NKJV).

As painfully horrific as a crime or injustice may be, what holds back *immediate* divine judgment is that God offers the oppressor an opportunity to repent.

He could not be a merciful God otherwise.

However, as with the Assyrians, there is a finality to what God will allow before judgment follows.

He would not be a just God otherwise.

As believers, we must understand that God is both merciful and just. I have found that understanding this truth affects the way in which I pray. It tempers my need to see the justice of God on the earth with the understanding that God, in His justice, has also ordained mercy. There are seasons when it may seem that His mercy overshadows justice, but just as surely as God has set seasons in place (see Genesis 8:22), judgment will follow unless His mercy and redemption are accepted.

THE VISION OF THE SPIRIT

> *The burden against Nineveh. The book of* ***the vision of Nahum*** *the Elkoshite.* (Nahum 1:1 NKJV)

The work of the Holy Spirit, manifested as Nahum's vision, may be seen from the very start of the book. One aspect of heavenly visions is that God allows us to see what He sees, and the way in which He sees it.

The Spirit allowed Nahum to have God's view of sin and rebellion. No one can stand in the way of God's righteous judgment once it is unleashed. When judgment comes, no one who is judged will be able to say that God is unjust because they will know they had ample opportunity and time to turn from their ways back to God.

The fact that God is merciful does not take away from the truth that He is also holy and does not tolerate sin in His presence. Sin is severe in the sight of God. Sin is so severe that it cost God His Son!

There was a season in my life when I traveled quite a lot in an Asian country that was known for child trafficking. As I ministered there, working with the churches, I was aware of the situation. I always felt sadness and sympathy whenever I thought of the children. Sometimes I would pray about it and would even be moved to tears. But even as I did dutifully pray about the situation, my heart never seemed to connect with what I was praying about. When praying, I would rattle off the few facts I knew from my mind.

One day, while I was getting ready to return to those churches, the Spirit said to me, "Sympathy is from your soul. Compassion is from Me!" I suddenly saw that while I had sympathy and felt bad about the situation with the children, I had kept it to the arena of my soul and not allowed God to move me to the realm of the Spirit to see what He felt about it. That's why I could not pray about it beyond my head knowledge. My spirit was not connected. I pondered that word, and, the next time I prayed, I said to the Lord, "Father, help me see this situation the way You see it. Not my eyes, but Your eyes!" I waited in stillness before the Lord for a while. Then I started to tear up a little and suddenly found myself saying, "Divine intervention! Father! Interventions from heaven!" I repeated this for approximately fifteen minutes, and then there was a shift in the flow of prayer. It moved from asking God to commanding the enemy. I started saying forcefully, "Stop! Stop in your maneuvers! I speak confusion to your plans!" After about fifteen to twenty minutes, I felt as if a weight had been lifted off me. I closed out the prayer time just praising and thanking God.

A few weeks later, I received a call from one of the pastors in that country who told me that one of the prominent leaders involved in the trafficking syndicate had been accidentally killed by one of his own henchmen in a smuggling operation that had gone wrong. Their plans had been confused! This individual who was killed had been involved in the trafficking of children for over twenty years…and then, by divine intervention, his trafficking ended with judgment.

The mercy of God, when accepted, allows us to avert the judgment of God. This is how God is both just and merciful.

PROLONGED MERCY, DELAYED JUDGMENT

> *"Behold, I am against you," says the* Lord *of hosts.*
>
> (Nahum 2:13 NKJV)

This terrible announcement was a long time coming. It was as if God kept delaying taking this position against the Assyrians just so there could be another opportunity for them to repent. But once God pronounced this judgment, it marked the end of the Assyrians.

The mercy of God is long, but the judgment of God is swift.

I shudder to think what grace the Assyrians must have resisted and what rebellion they must have insisted on to be in a state where God Himself declared that He was against them. I have seen this exact scenario play out in people's lives both inside and outside of the church.

Part of the Holy Spirit's role is to show us things to come. (See John 16:13.) This usually has been interpreted in a foretelling, prophetic way, and rightly so. However, the Spirit does not just give us words of personal prophecy for edification, exhortation, and comfort (see 1 Corinthians 14:3); His showing us things to come also includes giving warnings of any future judgments. *It is the mercy of God that He reveals future judgment.*

A final day of reckoning for sin is coming...but that day is not yet. This is *still* a day of salvation. As believers, this is our message as well as our lifestyle!

HABAKKUK

Moved from Despair to Worship

Habakkuk is a book examining how the prophet moved from utter despair to trust and worship, from complaining to confident expectation. Engulfed and overwhelmed by the corruption and violence he saw around him, Habakkuk concluded that, at a vital point in Judah's history, God had abandoned the people to the evil men around them—that He was not to be found anymore, anywhere, by anyone.

THE SPIRIT IS HOLY

> *But you are pure and cannot stand the sight of evil. Will you wink at their treachery? Should you be silent while the wicked swallow up people more righteous than they?* (Habakkuk 1:13 NLT)

The Holy Spirit is...holy! We must continue to remind ourselves of this vital truth. This means that the Spirit doesn't ever condone unholiness. The Holy Spirit doesn't "wink" at sin—sin grieves Him.

The Spirit will never lead any believer into any form of disobedience to God's Word. The Holy Spirit is also the Source of any righteous indignation we have against injustices.

The only reason the Holy Spirit is around sin is that He seeks to woo offenders into God's love and mercy, which are offered before the judgment of God is pronounced.

EAGER TO HEAR

> *I will stand my watch* [*"climb up to my watchtower"* NLT] *and set myself on the rampart, and watch to see what He will say to me, and what I will answer when I am corrected.* (Habakkuk 2:1 NKJV)

Habakkuk was so determined to have God answer him that he was even willing to climb up a *watchtower* to wait on God.

Rather than run *from* God, Habakkuk ran *to* God during that challenging time.

Something powerful happens when we "*incline* [our] *ear*" to hear what God has to say. (See, for example, Proverbs 4:20, various translations.) The Hebrew verb translated "*incline*," *natah* (*Strong's*, H5186), implies "to bow" or "to bend"—in other words, to be humble and lower ourselves so that we can hear. It is a powerful spiritual truth that proud people don't hear from anyone but themselves. Humility opens us to hear others and, most important, God. I have heard people pray that God would give them humility, or say that they are waiting for Him to make them humble. James 4:10, however, tells us to humble ourselves. It is much better and less painful for us to humble ourselves than to have God humble us!

HOW TO HANDLE THE WORD OF THE LORD

> *Then the* LORD *answered me and said: "Write the vision and make it plain on tablets, that he may run who reads it. For the vision is yet for an appointed time; but at the end it will speak, and it will not lie. Though it tarries, wait for it; because it will surely come, it will not tarry."* (Habakkuk 2:2–3 NKJV)

It requires skill and strength to hold on to the Word of the Lord. We know that the enemy aims to steal the Word once it is sown in us. (See Mark 4:15.) A word from the Lord can come to us either directly when we study and pray, when we hear the Word preached or taught, by the gifts of the Spirit, by dreams and visions, or by prophetic utterances.

God's instructions to Habakkuk to write the vision and make it plain so that it could be read speaks of how carefully we should handle the Word.

How we handle the Word will determine what we get out of it. I have seen that people can fall into one of two ditches when handling the Word. One ditch is overinterpreting the Word or forcing an interpretation of it; the other ditch is undervaluing, ignoring, or overlooking the Word.

I once knew of an older businessman who felt he had received a word that he was called to be a pastor. He was a regular member of a smaller church but had never been in a pastoral leadership role. After receiving that word, he started a home fellowship with about six people he knew from the church he attended. The actual pastor of the church was never informed about this. The businessman had all the participants in the home fellowship call him "pastor." Not long afterward, he started introducing himself as "pastor" and tried to get everyone else to call him that too. He said he wanted everyone calling him by that title because they were giving voice to his prophetic word. All the while, he remained a member of the church he had been going to and continued having meetings in his living room with the few people he invited from church. You can understand why this caused problems at the church he attended. After about three years of this, the man very suddenly fell ill and passed away. He never did get into a leadership position anywhere. He never did pastor a church or a fellowship.

It takes the wisdom of God to walk out a word from God. We cannot read too much into a word or force it to manifest in our life. We should also not *over-spiritualize* things. There are natural steps to be taken *even* when the Lord does speak. Counsel could be sought from mature, trusted voices. Usually, with a word from God, there is also an "appointed time." You may not step into the word that God gave you the very next morning! Then, of course, no word from God should cause anyone to act unethically or without love toward others. Wisdom is necessary for dealing with instructions from God. There is value in esteeming the Word of the Lord.

The second ditch—ignoring or overlooking a word from the Lord—can be the result of either familiarity or unfamiliarity with spiritual things. With regard to familiarity, some people are so used to having the manifestations of the Spirit in operation, with accompanying prophetic utterances, that those manifestations can seem commonplace to them. I have seen the presence of God come into a sanctuary, and some people are down front, crying, worshiping, and receiving ministry through the laying on of hands. Yet others are at the sides of the sanctuary or in the aisles talking and visiting with each other. They have allowed themselves to become so familiar with the presence of God that they no longer revere it.

Unfamiliarity, on the other hand, refers to people either not having been taught about the presence or, worse, having been trained by tradition and religion to ignore it. For the former, the remedy is teaching and training. For the latter, only a genuine hunger and desire for God can bring deliverance. Many Pharisees in Jesus's day were plagued with head-led traditions that had trained them to ignore heart-led revelations. They failed to recognize the presence of God while they were in the presence of Jesus!

THE DIFFERENCE MAKER

> *But the just shall live by his faith.* (Habakkuk 2:4 NKJV, KJV)

Applying the truth in this verse enabled Habakkuk to transition from the despair he expressed in chapter 1 to the victorious expectation he recorded in chapter 3 at the book's close. This phrase was later quoted in the New Testament letters of Romans and Hebrews.

Habakkuk found the bridge that leads away from despair and into victory: faith!

For the believer, faith is not an emotion, a religious belief system, tingly goosebumps, a message, or even a movement—it is a lifestyle.

Habakkuk discovered that the life of faith simply meant living beyond what his senses dictated by choosing to operate according to what God had promised. Faith is always and only based on what God has promised.

Faith is not blind. Faith chooses to look away from the circumstances and toward what God has said.

The believer is to live in a continual state of faith. Since this is how we are to live as believers, we need to ensure that our faith is protected, nourished, and engaged in all that we do.

Faith is the vehicle that will transport anyone from their "chapter 1" to their "chapter 3"!

FAITH FOR THE SPIRIT

Centuries later, writing to the Galatians, Paul taught that faith was the principle by which we receive the promised Holy Spirit; the "*blessing of Abraham*" comes upon us as a result of our belief in Jesus. (See Galatians 3:11–14, various translations.)

In showing Habakkuk that he needed to live by faith over his circumstances, the Holy Spirit was preparing the way for believers in the church to receive all that God had for them—not based on what they did or did not see but on what God had promised.

I love the idea that God could show Habakkuk something that, many years later, would also apply to us. Again, no word from the Spirit is limited to the one to whom it is originally spoken. The principles, if not the practice, of that word apply to everyone. *When the Spirit speaks, it creates tsunamis, tidal waves, and ripples in the Spirit realm that are felt for generations afterward.*

> *So shall My word be that goes forth from My mouth; it shall not return to Me void, but it shall accomplish what I please, and it shall prosper in the thing for which I sent it.* (Isaiah 55:11 NKJV)

When God speaks, He has the generations in mind. Part of what God intended when He spoke in the past was our application of His truths today in the "future-present." As a member of the eternal Godhead, the Spirit of God exists in eternity. This doesn't merely mean that God has an abundance of time but that He is outside of time. This is why, when the Spirit speaks, either through God's Word or by direct revelation, His words are fresh. Even if they were originally spoken centuries ago, they are still fresh to us. God lives and speaks in an everlasting "now"!

ZEPHANIAH

Faithful and Seeking

About a hundred years before God raised up the prophet Zephaniah, the ten tribes of Israel in the northern kingdom were conquered by the Assyrians. The southern kings started paying tribute to the Assyrians to avert a similar invasion of Judah.

This political alliance bore spiritually unholy fruit. Sorcerers and soothsayers were promoted and granted protection. Pagan altars were even erected in the temple. Child sacrifice and the worship of the Assyrians' mother goddess wormed their way into Judean society.

Zephaniah was sent as yet another extension of the grace and mercy of God to the people. His ministry to the southern kingdom arose during the time of Judah's boy king, Josiah, who ascended to the throne at age eight. When Josiah turned sixteen, he began zealously seeking God, and he later initiated a revival that broke forth among the people of God after the Book of the Law was found by Hilkiah the high priest while repairs were being made to the house of the Lord. Sadly, the lingering effects from the choices of the evil kings before Josiah had such a hold on Judah that it never recovered. (See 2 Chronicles 34.)

MERCY BEFORE JUDGMENT

> *Seek the LORD, all you meek of the earth, who have upheld His justice. Seek righteousness, seek humility. It may be that you will be hidden in the day of the LORD's anger.* (Zephaniah 2:3 NKJV)

Jesus explained that one of the Holy Spirit's functions is to seek out and convict those who are without God. (See John 16:8–11.) In the Old Testament, this work is seen through the sending of prophets who called the people to repentance. So, to reject the call to come back to God was to reject the call of the Holy Spirit Himself. This is important for us to remember when we seek to present the gospel to people and sometimes don't see immediate results: First, the rejection is not personal. And, second, as we see with all the Old Testament prophets, the Holy Spirit is persistent to repeatedly call for repentance. In this, He is faithful, even to those who don't believe.

The term *"the day of the LORD"* is used by other Old Testament prophets, but Zephaniah uses it extensively in the three chapters of his book. So, not only was the Holy Spirit faithful to warn and call the people in Zephaniah's time, but He also had a message for us living in our times. The Holy Spirit's offer to those who live in indifference and rebellion against God is consistent: come to God so that you can be *"hidden in the day of the LORD's anger"*!

It is the love of God in action to offer mercy before judgment. The Holy Spirit is on a continual mercy mission!

A PROMISE OF A PURE LANGUAGE

> *For then I will restore to the peoples a pure language, that they all may call on the name of the LORD, to serve Him with one accord.*
> (Zephaniah 3:9 NKJV)

"For then" signifies a shift in tone and content in what the Holy Spirit was saying through Zephaniah, moving from predictions of destruction to promises of peace and blessing.

The initial evidence that restoration and blessings were being released by God was a *"pure language."* Like the rest of God's Word, this verse has a multidimensional, multigenerational application and fulfillment. I believe there is and will be a fulfillment of this promise in Israel, in the world, and in the church. (See 1 Corinthians 10:32.)

In the decades leading up to the regathering of the nation of Israel in 1948 after the Jewish people had been scattered for two thousand years, there was a revival of the spoken and written Hebrew language. The Jews had also been able to retain the heart of their culture over those centuries. This is an often-understated miracle. My grandfather was originally from China. As a young man, he moved to Singapore, where he started a family from which I am descended. Yet, today, not only do I not speak any languages and dialects from China or Singapore, but I actually know very little about my grandfather's ancient heritage and culture. I know this is true for many others who were not birthed in the land of their ancestors or are no longer living there. The Jewish people, dispersed from their homeland under duress, were able to return after millennia and regain their cultural heritage and language!

The rest of Zephaniah 3:9 has not yet come to fruition in Israel, but, as with all other prophecies, this promise of God is unfolding gradually.

For the world, this verse will find fulfillment in our collective prophetic future when the earth is purged, all of creation is redeemed, and we are all under the direct rulership of the King!

In *The Amplified Bible, Classic Edition*, this verse reads, *"I will give to the people a clear and pure speech from pure lips."*

For the church, the restoration of *"clear and pure speech from pure lips"* began in the upper room on the day of Pentecost. (See Acts 2:4.) Not only did speaking in tongues restore the unity of language lost at the Tower of Babel (see Genesis 11:1–9), but it also restored our ability to speak directly to God in a heavenly language.

When we speak in tongues, we are speaking a pure, Spirit-empowered language. This shows again that what happened in the upper room was not a one-off oddity but rather a fulfillment of prophecy that originated in the mind of God.

The gift of speaking in tongues was not limited to those early disciples of Jesus but is an ongoing spiritual manifestation available for all of us.

The last part of Zephaniah 3:9 says, "*...to serve Him with one accord.*" We serve the Lord when we speak in the pure language of tongues because, when we do so, we prophetically speak forth the "*mysteries*" of God (see 1 Corinthians 14:2, various translations) on the earth and thus make room in the Spirit for those mysteries to be manifested in the earthly realm. To pray in tongues is to work with and serve God in Spirit-led prayer and proclamation. This is a crucial end-time ministry that enables the "sons and daughters" to prophesy. (See Acts 2:17.)

You may not ever travel to other nations to minister.

You may not ever occupy a pulpit in your hometown to preach.

However, you can serve God by speaking in the pure language of heaven!

HAGGAI

Always with Us

Haggai had the profile of a good pastor: he understood the people, had a word to uplift them into the things of God, and, most important, knew the mind of God.

Like all good pastors, Haggai was busy building the saints to build the house of God.

The people had returned to their homeland after the exile to rebuild the temple of the Lord, but they had given in to discouragement and stopped their work because they had listened to mockers. How important it is to guard our ears as we go about the Lord's service! The right words can encourage and spur us on, but the wrong words can dissuade and hinder us. The prophets Haggai and Zechariah co-labored to rally the people and saw the completion and dedication of the temple in five years.

A REASON FOR THE DROUGHT

> *"You looked for much, but indeed it came to little; and when you brought it home, I blew it away. Why?" says the* Lord *of hosts.*

> *"Because of My house that is in ruins, while every one of you runs to his own house. Therefore the heavens above you withhold the dew, and the earth withholds its fruit. For I called for a drought on the land and the mountains, on the grain and the new wine and the oil, on whatever the ground brings forth, on men and livestock, and on all the labor of your hands."* (Haggai 1:9–11 NKJV)

It is a divine principle that when we tend to God's house, He tends to ours! Of course, by "God's house," we mean that which is of concern to God.

Jesus reemphasized this principle in Matthew 6:33 (NKJV), telling us, *"But seek first the kingdom of God and His righteousness, and all these things shall be added to you."* When we put God first, He arranges or rearranges the rest. *It honors God when we put Him and His first, and God reciprocates that honor by honoring us.*

Just as darkness is the absence of light, the curse is simply the absence of the blessing. When the people chose to walk away from God's plans, they walked away from the blessings of God and into the darkness of the curse.

Serving God and having His plans in and for our lives does not cost us… it frees us.

I have met people who either knew God's plan for them but ran away from it or who never even bothered to give thought to the idea that God might have a plan for their life. They might have been successful in the ventures they were involved in, but there was always something inside them that knew there was more for them and that they were missing out on it. The "house of the Lord" worldwide needs building, and we all have an invitation from heaven to participate somehow in that building process. This does not mean that everyone needs to aspire to having a pulpit preaching ministry, but it does mean that all believers need to recognize that they individually have a specific role in the collective plan of God. There is a place for all of us!

GOD CALLS FOR A RESPONSE

> *Then Zerubbabel the son of Shealtiel, and Joshua the son of Jehozadak, the high priest, with all the remnant of the people, obeyed the voice of the LORD their God, and the words of Haggai the prophet, as the*

> *Lord their God had sent him; and the people feared the presence of the Lord.* (Haggai 1:12 NKJV)

The voice of the Lord came through *"the words of Haggai the prophet."* As New Testament believers, we have direct access to the leading of the Holy Spirit, but we should also avail ourselves of others whom God might send our way with a word from Him. Certainly, nothing anyone tells us that is contrary to the Word of God and does not edify or solidify what God has already told us is to be received. But God does anoint men and women who can deliver words on His behalf. Believers having access to prophetic voices is both a pattern we see in Scripture and a privilege.

One real result of any true prophetic word is that it produces a healthy, godly fear of the presence of the Lord. Genuine prophetic words will not cheapen the Lord's presence with casual familiarity but will always increase a sense of holy, reverent awe of God. When the Holy Spirit delivers a holy word, it carries a holy presence.

> *Then Haggai, the Lord's messenger, spoke the Lord's message to the people, saying, "I am with you, says the Lord."* (Haggai 1:13 NKJV)

When any prophetic word is accepted, its purpose is to usher God into that circumstance. Here, Haggai delivered a powerful declaration: God was with them! They were not alone in facing the needed construction and rebuilding. God has a prophetic word for every area of our life that needs rebuilding because He never intends for us to rebuild alone what the enemy has ransacked. God always wants to be with us as we rebuild because it takes His strength, which only comes from His presence, to restore what the enemy has sought to destroy.

Seek His voice, and you will find His presence!

> *So the Lord stirred up the spirit of Zerubbabel the son of Shealtiel, governor of Judah, and the spirit of Joshua the son of Jehozadak, the high priest, and the spirit of all the remnant of the people; and they came and worked on the house of the Lord of hosts, their God.*
> (Haggai 1:14, various translations)

It takes the Spirit of God to stir up the spirits of men to serve Him. God is Spirit, and, as His children, made in His image, we are also spirit.

The Spirit realm is the primary domain where God communicates with us and where we move with Him.

Sometimes, there are fundraising infomercials on late-night TV featuring orphans or others who need humanitarian assistance. While the organizations behind these infomercials may be valid, and doing valid work, as believers, we ought not to be moved to be involved just by what is being broadcast *alone*. We should be moved by the Spirit of God and not by what we see on TV. Now, God can speak to us by what we see on TV, but, again, what we see on TV alone does not establish a call from God. There must be clear direction from the Spirit, a witness in our spirit, to constitute a call from God.

The work of God can only be fulfilled with a call from God. And with a call from God, and *only* with a call from God, comes God's power to fulfill that call.

DO NOT FEAR!

> *According to the word that I covenanted with you when you came out of Egypt, so My Spirit remains among you; do not fear!*
>
> (Haggai 2:5 NKJV)

God's command not to fear is based on His Spirit being and remaining with us…and the Spirit's presence with us is *"according to the word"* that He has covenanted with us. Once more, we see that the Word of God and the Spirit of God work hand in hand.

When the people were surrounded by naysayers and enemies, the Spirit of God rose up to guide and protect them. They were roused by the Spirit's presence. However, this ongoing presence did not manifest, as evidenced by the absence of dew (see Haggai 1:10), until after the people obeyed God. Obedience opens us to the presence of God.

As believers, we always have the Spirit with us. Disobedience closes us off from the leading of the Spirit and shuts us out of the peace that can come only when we follow Him. I have noticed that the Spirit *always* leads us toward paths of peace. This sometimes involves our going through enemy territory; at other times, He leads us around it. But the Spirit's destination is always peace!

ZECHARIAH

A Wall of Fire

Together with Haggai, Zechariah was raised up to call for the completion of the temple's reconstruction. God raises up ministry partners—He calls no one to do anything alone.

The anointing is too weighty to be contained by any one person.

The call of God is too big to be answered by any one person.

It is always the enemy's plan to promote isolation and exclusivity among believers—especially for those who are in ministry.

The enemy seeks to puff up the individual. The Spirit of God seeks to build the body of Christ.

There is power in an individual flow, but a corporate flow allows for the full manifestation of the Spirit.

The Spirit of God also gave Zechariah some of the clearest and most uniquely insightful prophecies about the coming Messiah. Zechariah motivated the people to complete the temple by reminding them that the Messiah would one day rule from a restored temple in a restored city. (See Zechariah 9–14.)

A DIVINE "WRAPPING"

> *"For I," says the* Lord, *"will be a wall of fire all around her, and I will be the glory in her midst."* (Zechariah 2:5 NKJV)

The Spirit of God promised to wrap Himself around His people as *"a wall of fire."* This is not just a promise of protection for physical Jerusalem but also for all of us who are the spiritual building of God. (See 1 Peter 2:5.) Walls are built to keep some things out and other things in. God wraps His Spirit around us to keep the enemy off us and to keep His presence in us. There is a divine "wrapping" around you by the Spirit that the enemy cannot breach. The Spirit's wrapping around us preserves us from the dust and the rust of the world.

"...BUT BY MY SPIRIT"

> *So he answered and said to me: "This is the word of the* Lord *to Zerubbabel: 'Not by might nor by power, but by My Spirit,' says the* Lord *of hosts."* (Zechariah 4:6 NKJV)

This is the rallying call for all Spirit-led believers. The choice of how we go about living life is simple: it is either by our might and power or by the Spirit. No doubt, the Spirit will give us might and power for life—but He, and not the arm of flesh, must be the Source. This also tells me that might and power are available from natural sources, but God is offering us something higher. So then, what the Spirit has to offer must be more than what earthly might and power can offer us. The world has might and power available, but we have access to the Spirit!

I have seen many a child or grandchild coerced into going into the ministry because they had parents or grandparents who were in ministry. If such children and grandchildren succumb to that pressure, they'll have to do so without the anointing because the anointing only accompanies what we do in response to God. *By His Spirit, God anoints what we respond to when He calls.*

I have also seen children who have taken their parents' ministries far beyond what their parents ever did, but that was always and only because they heard and responded to God's call for themselves. God doesn't anoint those whom we call; He anoints those whom *He* calls!

A woman pastor of a successful church with various ministries and outreaches once asked if I would talk to her husband. I knew the whole family, and they all either were involved in the ministry or supported it in some way. Her husband had a good job working for the government, and he also administratively oversaw the ministry. But she wanted him to preach. She did a good job in the pulpit, but she felt that he ought to have a bigger role in preaching as well. I knew that, for many years, she had been after him to preach, but he was a quiet man and didn't quite like getting up in front of people. The few times she did get him to host or try preaching at a service, it was evident to all that he was not in his flow. However, she talked to me for quite a while, trying to convince me to try to convince him.

I finally reminded her that, before she was in the ministry, she was a schoolteacher with no aspirations for serving in ministry or ministry experience. Her love for the Lord prepared the way for her as she faithfully served in every position that opened to her. It was not a career plan but a service of love and obedience that had brought her to where she was. I told her, "It's the same for your husband. He loves the family, and he loves the Lord. He is faithful to serve in the capacity that he can—we must not maneuver him into areas that the anointing has not called him to. Leave him where he is. Only the Lord can call someone to preach." She reluctantly agreed. A few years later, the church needed more property. There was land available in the area where they were looking, but the local officials repeatedly blocked the sale until someone from the husband's governmental department intervened. The husband would not have had that work relationship—and the church would not have been able to obtain that property—if he had quit his job years earlier to preach. By His Spirit, God positions people to be in *all types of environments* to affect His plan.

It is not just what we would consider "ministry matters" for which there is an anointing. There is an anointing for every aspect of life because God, in His love, does not will us to live any part of our life just in our own strength. Man's might and power are insufficient for the life the believer is called to. Choose not to engage in any area of life according to natural might and power alone—choose to live a life by His Spirit!

HEARTS LIKE FLINT

> *Yes,* ***they made their hearts like flint, refusing to hear*** *the law and the words which the* Lord *of hosts had sent by His Spirit through the former prophets. Thus great wrath came from the* Lord *of hosts.*
> (Zechariah 7:12 NKJV)

I have found that no one ever fails to hear God because He hasn't spoken to them. People miss hearing God either because they don't recognize His voice when He speaks or because of their hardened heart.

Usually, people don't recognize God's voice because they were taught to religiously look for alternate "signs" besides the presence of peace and the finality of God's Word. They see outward conditions as more important than inward leading. Being trained to follow a sense of spiritual peace and God's Word as our final authority conditions us to hear clearly from God.

I have often pondered if part of God's anger at people's disobedience is mainly because they miss out on the blessings He has planned for them, which they would have experienced if they had obeyed. God is well able to raise up others who can pick up the slack of disobedience. *God's plans are not jeopardized by the disobedience of man!*

GRACE AND SUPPLICATION

> *And I will pour on the house of David and on the inhabitants of Jerusalem the Spirit of* ***grace and supplication****; then they will look on Me whom they pierced. Yes, they will mourn for Him as one mourns for his only son, and grieve for Him as one grieves for a firstborn.*
> (Zechariah 12:10 NKJV)

This description of the Spirit strengthens me. He is the Spirit of "*grace and supplication.*"

God mercifully gives us grace, freely and undeservedly. And supplication is prayer. True Spirit-led prayer is always full of grace. It is the grace of God that draws us to go to Him in prayer. The Spirit infuses us with grace so our prayers can be filled with grace. Grace-filled prayers bring God on the scene!

MALACHI

A Turning of Hearts

The prophet Malachi is not mentioned anywhere in the Scriptures other than in this book, but we can see that he had a great love for Judah and the temple. The abuses, the lukewarmness, and the deadness of religion among the people angered this prophet.

Malachi, meaning "my messenger," truly was a messenger of the Spirit! His zeal for an inward fire and an outward flame among God's people reflects the heart of God for all believers. Such an attitude goes beyond human determination. It can be birthed only by the Spirit because He is the Source of all good things.

SPIRIT-SENT MESSENGERS

"Behold, I send My messenger, and he will prepare the way before Me. And the Lord, whom you seek, will suddenly come to His temple, even the Messenger of the covenant, in whom you delight. Behold, He is coming," says the Lord *of hosts. "But who can endure the day of His*

> *coming? And who can stand when He appears? For He is like a refiner's fire and like launderers' soap."* (Malachi 3:1–2 NKJV)

The Spirit of God is always sending messengers who will prepare the way of the Lord. This prophecy foretold John the Baptist's ministry in preparing the way for the King but also a prophetic company that the Spirit would raise up to prepare the way for the kingdom. The latter happened on the day of Pentecost when the same Spirit who had spoken through Malachi about the sending of John the Baptist fell upon a hundred and twenty of Jesus's disciples in the upper room. As these disciples declared the things of God in heavenly languages, three thousand people were added to the church! (See Acts 2:41.) We in the present-day church can rightly trace our roots to those believers in the upper room in both our empowerment and our purpose. We are the Spirit's sent messengers!

The Spirt-fire that manifested on the day of Pentecost was the *holy* fire of the Spirit. It cannot be overstated that the Holy Spirit is...holy! This means that anyone He falls upon and fills is cloaked and endued with divine holiness. He is the *"refiner's fire,"* and we are what the fire is sent to refine. The Spirit is *"like launderers' soap,"* cleansing and "bleaching" (see Malachi 3:2 NLT) us. Those who carry a prophetic message must also allow the Spirit to keep them in the way of holiness. It is the standard of the Spirit for a holy message to come through a holy messenger.

"THE HEARTS OF THE FATHERS"

> *Behold, I will send you Elijah the prophet before the coming of the great and dreadful day of the* Lord. *And he will turn the hearts of the fathers to the children, and the hearts of the children to their fathers, lest I come and strike the earth with a curse.* (Malachi 4:5–6 NKJV)

Prophesying about John the Baptist heralding the beginning of the New Testament age and also about the New Testament age itself, the Spirit spoke of an anointing that would be sent, turning *"the hearts of the fathers to the children."* The birth of the church made room for those from the established faith of the patriarchs to meet and congregate on an equal footing with those who were from the gentile world. The Spirit woos us to unite at the cross so that He can be poured out upon us through the resurrection.

It has always struck me that it wasn't first "the hearts of the children to the fathers" but the other way around. This reflects the nature of our heavenly Father. His heart was turned to us before ours was turned to Him. But it also tells us that the New Testament era would usher in an end to a spiritually fatherless generation. The Spirit wants to end absentee spiritual fatherhood. When fathers are absent, community is affected. This is so in the natural realm, but it is also true in spiritual matters.

Today, every minister, as well as every believer, should have a core message to the world that the Father's love is reaching out, and a call for the "children" to respond and return to Him.

In the Old Testament, God had servants, but the New Testament is a revelation of sonship!

NEW TESTAMENT

PART ONE

THE HOLY SPIRIT IN THE GOSPELS AND ACTS

MATTHEW

Heavenly Fire, Heavenly Spirit

As we'll see with each of the four gospel accounts, the Spirit was specific in what He breathed on the individual human authors to record. They each presented a unique side of Jesus. There is specificity when the Spirit leads!

With over sixty references to the Old Testament, the gospel of Matthew bridges both Testaments beautifully. Matthew was a tax collector, and the Spirit led Matthew to systematically present Jesus as the Son of David, the King of the Jews, the Lion of the Tribe of Judah, and the Promised One who fulfilled the Old Testament prophecies of the Messiah.

Matthew was so sensitive to his Jewish audience that he referred to "the kingdom of heaven," whereas the other gospels spoke of "the kingdom of God." The Jews held the name of God in such high esteem that they did not want to use it in everyday speech. Matthew's opening genealogy traces Jesus's ancestry back to Father Abraham, and he cites Jewish customs without pausing to explain them. The Holy Spirit knows how to present what we need to hear in a way that we will hear it. The anointing is not offensive—except to rebellious hearts. The Holy Spirit lands like a gentle dove before He comes like a flash of lightning!

Matthew consolidated the teachings and the works of Jesus into five main groupings. This structure was common in Judaism and also mirrored the Torah, the first five books of the Hebrew Scriptures.

WITH CHILD BY THE HOLY SPIRIT

> *Now the birth of Jesus Christ was as follows: when His mother Mary had been betrothed to Joseph, before they came together she was found to be with child by the Holy Spirit.... But when he* [Joseph] *had considered this, behold, an angel of the Lord appeared to him in a dream, saying, "Joseph, son of David, do not be afraid to take Mary as your wife; for the Child who has been conceived in her is of the Holy Spirit."* (Matthew 1:18, 20 NASB95)

The Holy Spirit is the birthing agent of all God's promises. "*Conceived... of the Holy Spirit*" is God's will for all of us. Lean on the Holy Spirit to bring from conception to birth all the promises of God for your life. The Holy Spirit, as God, is the Essence of Life, and there can be no emptiness in your womb of promise with Him inside you!

THE HOLY SPIRIT AND FIRE

> *As for me, I baptize you with water for repentance, but He who is coming after me is mightier than I, and I am not fit to remove His sandals; He will baptize you with the Holy Spirit and fire.*
> (Matthew 3:11 NASB95)

We now live in an age in which this prophetic utterance by John the Baptist is being fulfilled. To be baptized means to be fully immersed, "dunked in"—and we are to be baptized with the Holy Spirit and fire!

The Holy Spirit and heavenly fire are inseparable. The filling empowerment of the Holy Spirit is a fire that can be seen and felt by everyone around you. You cannot hide the light and heat of fire. A believer filled with the Spirit is a walking testament of the presence of God.

THE HEAVENLY SPIRIT

> *After being baptized, Jesus came up immediately from the water; and behold, the heavens were opened, and he saw the Spirit of God descending as a dove and lighting on Him.* (Matthew 3:16 NASB95)

There are degrees of function to the Spirit's role in our life. The Spirit that sparked Jesus's conception now descended and lighted on Him. This speaks of the Spirit having various functions, various manifestations, in the life of Jesus. Obviously, Jesus, as the eternal Son of God, was Himself God and had access to all of the Holy Spirit without measure. (See John 3:34.) But, as an example for us, the Spirit's weight grew heavier on Jesus as He grew "*in wisdom and stature*" (Luke 2:52, various translations). *It is never about the Spirit's availability but only about our capacity.* Unwrapping the gift of the Holy Spirit requires our spiritual growth.

Paul taught that we can prophesy "*according to the proportion of* [our] *faith*" (Romans 12:6 NASB95, AMPC), and also that our faith can grow "*exceedingly*" (2 Thessalonians 1:3, various translations). So, since we prophesy in proportion to our faith, and our faith can grow, this means that our ability to prophesy can grow. We can grow in the Spirit and in spiritual things!

> *Then Jesus was led by the Spirit into the wilderness to be tempted by the devil.* (Matthew 4:1 NIV)

Here we see Jesus led by the Spirit to a full-on confrontation with the devil. The previous recorded event in Matthew was the Spirit's descending on Jesus at His baptism and the proclamation from heaven declaring Jesus to be the Father's beloved Son. (See Matthew 3:16–17.) The Father knew that even the devil couldn't shake Jesus off this pronouncement. The Spirit was taking Jesus a step toward the reversal of the effects of the fall of Adam in the garden of Eden. Jesus, as the Last Adam, was to be tempted in all points as we are and to show us the way to victory. (See Hebrews 4:15.)

This desert battle was orchestrated by the Spirit to give us a blueprint for how to respond when the enemy shows up. In each of the enemy's three challenges, Jesus's only response was to quote the Word. (See Matthew 4:4, 7, 10.) There is no victory over the enemy without the Word. The written

Word, quoted and spoken by us, contains the same power as the Word spoken by God. The Spirit *only* leads us to conclusive victories!

THE SPIRIT SPEAKS IN YOU

> *For it is not you who speak, but it is the Spirit of your Father who speaks in you.* (Matthew 10:20 NASB95)

What a comfort to know that, in times of pressure, when we don't know what to say or how to say it, the Spirit can speak for, in, and through us. We have access to the authority of the King, but we also have the Spirit of the Father. The King's authority deals with demons and disease, but the Spirit of the Father deals with opposers and oppressors. (See verses 17–19.)

CASTING OUT DEMONS

> *But if I cast out demons by the Spirit of God, then the kingdom of God has come upon you.* (Matthew 12:28 NASB95)

It takes the power of the Spirit to cast out demons. Demons are a reality of the spiritual realm. They are not a fragment of an ancient overactive imagination. Demons have not faded away in these modern times.

As I wrote earlier, believers cannot be possessed by demons, but they can be harassed or oppressed by them. Not every challenge in a believer's life is directly caused by demons, but if a believer doesn't stand on the promises of God and allows the pressure of a challenge to overwhelm them, then demons will capitalize on that entry point and magnify the challenge. The same is true when a believer allows their fleshly appetites to run away with them. Not every addiction is the result of a demon, but demons will take advantage of our runaway desires when we don't exercise wisdom and self-control.

Demons need to be cast out, but the *"old man"* (see, for example, Romans 6:6 NKJV, KJV), or the fleshly nature, needs to be brought under submission to our spirit.

The answer to demons is the same today as it was in New Testament times: demons must be restricted and cast out by the power of the Spirit.

BLASPHEMY!

> *Therefore I say to you, any sin and blasphemy shall be forgiven people, but blasphemy against the Spirit shall not be forgiven. Whoever speaks a word against the Son of Man, it shall be forgiven him; but whoever speaks against the Holy Spirit, it shall not be forgiven him, either in this age or in the age to come.* (Matthew 12:31–32 NASB95)

In the eternal purpose of the triune God, the Father conceived the plan of redemptive salvation, the Son fulfilled that plan, and the Spirit continually reaches out to the world, convicting people of their need for God's offer of salvation.

When someone who is not yet a believer blasphemes the Son, as Saul of Tarsus did (see 1 Timothy 1:12–14), the Spirit still has ground to work on him, leading him to repent and place his faith in the Son. However, when someone resists and blasphemes the Spirit Himself, then, like the Pharisees to whom Jesus was speaking in Matthew 12, they have turned away from the one divine channel that is ordained to bring them to repentance and salvation. Since they refuse the Messenger of redemption—the Holy Spirit—they also refuse redemption, and so "*it shall not be forgiven* [them]"; it cannot be forgiven them because they have refused redemption and forgiveness.

DISCIPLES OF THE FATHER, THE SON, AND THE HOLY SPIRIT

> *Go therefore and make disciples of all the nations, baptizing them in the name of the Father and the Son and the Holy Spirit.*
> (Matthew 28:19 NASB95)

After I was born again, I joined a charismatic church that had a big emphasis on world missions. That is something that has stayed with me my whole life. I always had the idea that missions outreach, especially in third-world nations, primarily meant presenting a John 3:16, salvation type of message—and maybe, if time allowed, some foundational biblical teachings. Yet, while I was preparing for and praying about a missions trip years ago, the Spirit asked me, "Is a disciple one who is discipled in the Word alone?" I didn't answer this question right away but pondered it for a while. I finally said, "No...a disciple is one who is discipled in both the

Word and the Spirit." This changed the way I saw missions and ministry. I saw that not only must we teach the Word, but we must also make room for encounters with the Holy Spirit. It is the Spirit who breathes life into the written Word. It is the Spirit who is the Guide and Counselor to the people to whom I minister. If all I did was to teach from an outline and not introduce the people to the Holy Spirit, then I was robbing them of a relationship with the Teacher—God Himself. Disciples are those who are baptized in the name of the Father, the Son, *and* the Holy Spirit!

MARK

Authority and Power

John Mark was the cousin of Barnabas (see Colossians 4:10) and a close associate of the older apostle Peter. When Peter was released from prison, it was to the home of Mark's mother that he went. (See Acts 12:12.) There are recurring references to Mark in the book of Acts. Mark was a young man who ran with the right crowd! It is proper for those who are older in the faith to make room for younger ones to have a place at the table so they can have access to the things of God.

Papias of Hierapolis was an early bishop and one of the Apostolic Fathers. About AD 40, he reported a statement by the apostle John indicating that Mark wrote down everything he remembered of Peter's teachings and recollections about Jesus, consolidating them into a single work. Moreover, approximately AD 150, Christian apologist and philosopher Justin Martyr called Mark's gospel "the memoirs of Peter." And, circa AD 185, bishop and theologian Irenaeus wrote that Mark was "the disciple and interpreter of Peter." Mark's gospel, therefore, seems to have drawn from Peter's life and experiences with Jesus.[9]

9. John MacArthur, "Introduction to Mark," *The MacArthur Study Bible*, NKJV, ed. John MacArthur (Nashville, TN: Thomas Nelson, 1997), Kindle edition.

Mirroring Peter's temperament, this gospel is short and to the point. It is light on details and heavy on deeds. The Greek word *eutheos*, usually translated as "*immediately*," occurs in Mark about forty times! In this gospel, there is no genealogy of Jesus, no account of the Savior's birth, and few references to the Old Testament. This suited the Roman audience, who were not interested in Jewish intricacies but were impressed by demonstrations of power. The book of Mark records more accounts of miracles than any of the other gospels.

Mark presents Jesus as the Suffering Servant (see Mark 10:45), showcasing Christ's human emotions and human side.

THE SAME SPIRIT

> [John said,] *"I baptized you with water; but He will baptize you with the Holy Spirit."… Immediately coming up out of the water, He saw the heavens opening, and the Spirit like a dove descending upon Him.… Immediately the Spirit impelled Him to go out into the wilderness.*
>
> (Mark 1:8, 10, 12 NASB95)

These accounts of Jesus's baptism and sojourn in the wilderness are almost identical to what we saw in Matthew's gospel. And we will see some mention of them again in the gospels of Luke and John. It is important to know that, because the Spirit inspired the writing of Scripture (see 2 Timothy 3:16), no details are included or repeated unintentionally. The Spirit purposefully wanted us to know and remember these details from the very beginning of Jesus's public ministry.

Jesus was "*the Lamb slain from the foundation of the world*" (Revelation 13:8 NKJV, KJV), but it was His continued obedience to the leading of the Spirit that brought that calling to fulfillment. The Spirit works with us in the same way. Our journey toward what the Spirit has called us to involves the sometimes slow unfolding of an ongoing series of events that will require our obedience at every step. He guides us one step at a time, and each step necessitates our yielding. We are successful in life as believers when we learn to yield to yielding!

ALL SINS WILL BE FORGIVEN

> *Truly I say to you, all sins shall be forgiven the sons of men, and whatever blasphemies they utter; but whoever blasphemes against the Holy*

> *Spirit never has forgiveness, but is guilty of an eternal sin.*
> (Mark 3:28–29 NASB95)

The contrast between *"all sins shall be forgiven"* and *"never has forgiveness"* is stark. This shows the vital role the Holy Spirit has in our salvation. *Jesus purchased salvation for us, and the Holy Spirit delivers it to us.* Again, when people refuse the delivery, they refuse the contents of the package. Accepting the ministry of the Holy Spirit will always lead us to the complete work of Jesus and His ability to save us.

The gentleness of the Spirit is treasured among the triune Godhead. The Father will forgive blasphemy against the Son but not against the Spirit. This is because the Spirit is meek and does not speak of Himself. (See John 16:13.) This shows an equality among the Trinity. *To be accepted by the Father, you must accept the person of the Son. To accept the person of the Son, you must accept the ministry of the Spirit. All three members of the Godhead are involved in our salvation.*

SPEAKING BY THE SPIRIT

> *David himself, speaking by the Holy Spirit, declared: "The Lord said to my Lord: Sit at my right hand until I put your enemies under your feet."* (Mark 12:36 NIV)

Jesus, quoting David from Psalm 110:1, stated that David's inspiration came from the Holy Spirit. This is the essence of the Bible: men speaking by the Holy Spirit. *The Bible consists of the verbalizations of the Spirit through man.* When we see the Bible in this way, we will prize and honor it above all other writings and recitations.

This is also what prophecy is: man speaking by the Holy Spirit. Since all believers have the Holy Spirit living inside them, all believers have the potential of flowing in prophecy at some level. Prophecy, man speaking by the Holy Spirit, is the will of God and the means by which heaven is ushered into the earthly realm.

SPIRIT CODE WORDS

Mark liberally used the words *authority* and *power.* This was code for the ministry and activity of the Holy Spirit!

> *They were amazed at His teaching; for He was teaching them as one having authority, and not as the scribes.* (Mark 1:22 NASB95)

It was not just Jesus's signs and wonders or even His bold statements that caught the people's attention. He taught with authority. Jesus taught with the anointing of the Holy Spirit. The learned scribes also taught but evidently without that force of authority. As deep and profound as Jesus's teachings were, the people noticed the authority by which they were delivered. Good teaching alone does not cause an impact of change in people. It shows people what is possible but does not deliver divine assistance to accomplish what is possible. These are the requirements for change to occur:

- An anointing must be upon the words.
- An anointing must be upon the one speaking those words.

It is the anointing alone that destroys yokes. (See Isaiah 10:27.)

It takes the Holy Spirit to communicate the truths of God to our spirit because spiritual things can only be discerned and digested with and by our spirit. (See 1 Corinthians 2:14.)

Sound motivational, inspiring speeches and teaching can inform and instruct the mind of man and can accomplish some good and bring some level of change. But because God is Spirit and we are spirit, God wants a deeper communication with us.

"*Deep calls to deep…*" (Psalm 42:7, various translations). It takes the "*deep*" of the Holy Spirit to call to the "*deep*" of our spirit.

The presence of the Holy Spirit ministering with, through, and on a person is tangible. That presence is not discerned just by good feelings or goose bumps. There is a calm authority that comes with His presence.

The authority that comes with the anointing renews our mind while illuminating, uplifting, and feeding our spirit.

> [The chief priests, the scribes, and the elders] *began saying to Him, "By what authority are You doing these things, or who gave You this authority to do these things?"* (Mark 11:28 NASB95, AMP)

The religious leaders' challenge against Jesus was an issue of authority, not doctrine. They understood that if they could shake Jesus's authority, then His teaching itself would not matter. This is still true today. The world has no lack of good teachers of every possible ism and ideology. But none of them can usher the Word of the Lord into the earthly realm and set people free. It takes the anointing to destroy the yoke!

AUTHORITY OVER DEMONS

> *They were all amazed, so that they debated among themselves, saying, "What is this? A new teaching with authority! He commands even the unclean spirits, and they obey Him."* (Mark 1:27 NASB95)

> *They came to Jesus and observed the man who had been demon-possessed sitting down, clothed and in his right mind, the very man who had had the "legion"; and they became frightened.*
> (Mark 5:15 NASB95)

> *And He said to her, "Because of this answer go; the demon has gone out of your daughter."* (Mark 7:29 NASB95)

One undeniable proof that Jesus's ministry was from God was His authority over demons. The religious leaders of that time taught and chastised the people, but the demons remained. Not so with the ministry of Jesus! The authority of the Holy Spirit equips us to confront the powers of the enemy head-on. People's misconceptions and misunderstandings about God can be corrected by the Word through Spirit-led teaching. But direct demonic influences must be dealt with before people can receive freedom. Deliverance is available as long as the anointing is available. Demons will always take advantage of bad doctrine to steal, kill, and destroy. (See John 10:10.) So, a lack of an understanding of God will always put us at a disadvantage—but the direct source of that lack is not always demonic.

Both teaching and deliverance require divine authority to bring people into freedom.

AUTHORITY OVER DEATH AND SICKNESS

> [Jesus said,] *Which is easier, to say to the paralytic, 'Your sins are forgiven'; or to say, 'Get up, and pick up your pallet and walk'? But so that*

> *you may know that the Son of Man has authority on earth to forgive sins"—He said to the paralytic, "I say to you, get up, pick up your pallet and go home." And he got up and immediately picked up the pallet and went out in the sight of everyone, so that they were all amazed and were glorifying God, saying, "We have never seen anything like this."*
> (Mark 2:9–12 NASB95)

Jesus, as the "*last Adam*" (1 Corinthians 15:45, various translations), came to remove what the first Adam had, through sin, caused to come into the world, namely, separation from God, sickness, and death. "*The Son of God came to destroy the works of the devil*" (1 John 3:8 NLT). This was what Jesus was anointed to do. The "*works of the devil*" are the same "yoke" that the anointing destroys.

> *Taking the child by the hand, He said to her, "Talitha kum!" (which translated means, "Little girl, I say to you, get up!"). Immediately the girl got up and began to walk, for she was twelve years old. And immediately they were completely astounded.* (Mark 5:41–42 NASB95)

Death is the end result of sickness and will be the last enemy to be destroyed. (See 1 Corinthians 15:26.) Knowing that Jesus has authority over sickness leads us to understand that Jesus also has authority over death. The Spirit of God is a life-giving Spirit. Just as light dispels darkness, so the Spirit of life displaces the spirit of death!

ACCESS TO ANOINTING AND AUTHORITY

> *These signs will accompany those who have believed: in My name they will cast out demons, they will speak with new tongues; they will pick up serpents, and if they drink any deadly poison, it will not hurt them; they will lay hands on the sick, and they will recover.*
> (Mark 16:17–18 NASB95)

The anointing and the authority that were manifested in the ministry of Jesus were not meant to end with His ascension. Jesus authorized those who believed in Him to continue His ministry in both the same purpose and power. We could not do this without also having the same Spirit in us!

LUKE

The Worldwide Ministry of the Spirit

This gospel and the book of Acts are a two-volume account penned by Luke, a gentile medical doctor. (See Colossians 4:14.) With his medical background, Luke uses markedly different language from the other gospel writers when recording healings and other medical issues. Luke was also a frequent companion of Paul on his travels.

Luke presents Jesus as the Son of Man and therefore traces Jesus's genealogy, through Mary, all the way back to Adam. Perhaps because he himself was a gentile, Luke presented the gospel to be all-encompassing of nationalities. He portrayed Jesus as a worldwide Savior of mankind, not just the foretold Jewish deliverer.

True to his observant professional training, Luke includes many features omitted by Matthew and Mark. Of the twenty miracles recorded in this book, six are found nowhere else in the Gospels. Eighteen parables are also exclusively recorded in Luke. The Emmaus road account, details of the resurrection, and obstetrical observations of the virgin birth all make the book of Luke a uniquely insightful gospel account. Additionally, the Lord's prayer is found only in Luke and Matthew.

Luke has much to say about the Holy Spirit, so it's no surprise that he also has much to say about prayer. There are seven recorded occasions where we see Jesus in prayer. With more than fifteen references to the Holy Spirit in this book, the Spirit's activity in the lives of Jesus and the disciples is clearly chronicled.

THE SPIRIT PREPARES THE WAY

Beyond the movement of the Spirit on the prophets of the Old Testament, we see the Spirit actively moving on people in the New Testament in preparation for the imminent arrival of Jesus. Not only were there Old Testament prophetic utterances heralding Jesus's coming, but a Spirit-filled community of sorts was raised up to actually surround Jesus at His arrival. God wants to move us past the day of the lone prophet or minister, past even prophetic communities, and into the day of prophetic families. The call of God comes to individuals, but it takes a multiplicity of anointings to birth and walk out those calls. As I talked about previously, the Lord showed me that no one is ever called alone. For every person the Spirit calls, others are called to bring and add their supply to that call. As we run our race, others are able to run as well!

JOHN THE BAPTIST

> *For he will be great in the sight of the Lord; and he will drink no wine or liquor, and he will be filled with the Holy Spirit while yet in his mother's* [Elizabeth's] *womb.* (Luke 1:15 NASB95)

Everything in Scripture before the birth of Jesus prepares for His arrival and ministry. It took John being *"filled with the Holy Spirit while yet in his mother's womb"* to fulfill his call to be a trumpet for Jesus's first coming. John's arrival and ministry were partly in fulfillment of Malachi's prophecy about the coming Messiah. (See Malachi 3:1). So, there were others prophesying about John's ministry so he could prophesy about Jesus's ministry. *No call is singular.*

If it took such a level of Spirit activity and anointing on John, before he was even born, to prepare him for his ministry at Jesus's first coming, I have often wondered how many more babies in wombs the Spirit will be filling to anoint so they can be prepared for their place in the declaration of Jesus's second coming! John was at least thirty years old before he began ministering. This means the anointing he received in the womb to fulfill his call lay dormant for thirty years before it manifested in fullness. *The anointing falls on you today to prepare you for your tomorrow!* Evidently, God has no qualms about anointing and calling a baby in the womb. This was also the case with Jacob and Esau when God told their mother, Rebekah, *"Two nations are in your womb"* (Genesis 25:23). No one is ever too young to receive from the Spirit.

Elizabeth's womb did not only nurture John, but it also nurtured the anointing on him. The Spirit is not just looking for rooms for the anointing—He is looking for wombs for the anointing!

Later, during the in-between time before the full manifestation of his calling, John nurtured the anointing by his adherence to the Nazirite lifestyle (see Numbers 6:2–21) that he was called to (see Luke 1:15). To receive a call from God is an undeserved *gift,* and it is just the beginning of the journey. It takes diligence to *grow* into where the anointing wants to take us. Can someone walk away from a call? Samson certainly did. But his rejection of that call didn't cause God to revoke the call. The call simply went into sleep mode and reawakened once Samson realigned himself with God.

"For God's gifts and his call can never be withdrawn" (Romans 11:29 NLT).

MARY

> *The angel answered and said to her, "The Holy Spirit will come upon you, and the power of the Most High will overshadow you; and for that reason the holy Child shall be called the Son of God."*
>
> (Luke 1:35 NASB95)

The primary thing that the Holy Spirit gives birth to is prophetic promise.

Mary was chosen and brought into the prophetic promise of the Messiah's coming.

The Holy Spirit moves upon us so that we are on the pathway of prophetic promise.

The Holy Spirit plucks us from obscurity and puts us in places of prominence.

The Holy Spirit plants the seed of the prophetic word in the womb of our spirit so that conception can take place.

The Holy Spirit plants the promises of God in us so that a birth of manifestation can come.

I have often pondered the simple faith that Mary must have had to receive something she had *not* been praying to receive. Like most devout Jews, Mary had a fervent expectation and hope of the Messiah's coming. But she received above and beyond what she could ask for or think. (See Ephesians 3:20.)

Just as the Holy Spirit overshadowed Mary so she could conceive the Child of Promise, the Holy Spirit indwells and overflows from us so we can conceive the promises of the Father.

Jesus Christ, the Anointed One, was born to destroy the works of the enemy. Likewise, the anointing of the Holy Spirit seeks to be "birthed" or manifested through us so that the works of the enemy around us can be destroyed.

Jesus's sending the Holy Spirit to dwell in each of us is above and beyond what anyone in the Old Testament could even have hoped for. Again, in the Old Testament, only the prophet, king, and priest had the Holy Spirit temporarily *upon* them, but today, in the New Testament era, we have the Holy Spirit *in* us. *We live in an age of an overflow of the Spirit!*

> *And Mary said, "Behold, the bondslave of the Lord; may it be done to me according to your word." And the angel departed from her.*
>
> (Luke 1:38 NASB95)

Clearly, Mary was not just devoted and expectant, but she was also willingly obedient. Our willingness and obedience give the Holy Spirit room to work.

> *If you are willing and obedient, you will eat the good things of the land.* (Isaiah 1:19 NIV)

Willingness speaks of the heart, and obedience speaks of the head. The heart—or the spirit—because it is the core depth of man, the place from which we respond to God. The head, because we cannot be obedient to what we do not know. It is possible to be obedient without being willing, but that doesn't qualify us to *"eat the good things of the land."*

Obedient is what servants and hirelings are. Willing is what sons are.

It is one thing to know what to do, and another thing to want to do it. We can be willing, desiring to be led, but we can only be obedient after God shows us what to do.

ELIZABETH

> *When Elizabeth heard Mary's greeting, the baby leaped in her womb; and Elizabeth was filled with the Holy Spirit.* (Luke 1:41 NASB95)

What we hear can cause our spirit to leap for joy and victory or slump with doubt and heaviness.

It is a blessing to be like Elizabeth and have good news brought to us, but we should also aim to be like Mary and bring words that cause the spirits of others to rejoice.

Through Mary's greeting, the Holy Spirit touched two generations: baby John and Elizabeth. And the reach of an anointed "greeting" can affect more than just the immediate hearers.

Elizabeth was the recipient of answered prayer. She and her husband, Zacharias, had prayed for a child. We know that Zacharias, while serving in the temple, had a surprise visit from the angel Gabriel, announcing John's conception and birth. We also know that Zacharias initially reacted in such doubt and unbelief that Gabriel caused him to lose the ability to speak for a season so that his words would not hinder and undo the miracle that God was about to bring forth. It was about a week later that he was able to go home after his temple duties. We do not have a record of Elizabeth's immediate response to what her husband encountered, but we do know she did conceive as Gabriel had declared. (See Luke 1:5–25.)

The doubt of others does not have to stop *us* from receiving God's promises. You might have an unbelieving spouse or relatives who put you down every time you try to believe God for something, but, again, the unbelief of others *does not* have to stop you from believing and receiving!

ZACHARIAS

> *And his father Zacharias was filled with the Holy Spirit, and prophesied, saying....* (Luke 1:67 NASB95, NKJV)

What a beautiful picture of redemption. Zacharias, who just months earlier had had to be struck dumb by Gabriel, was now filled with the Spirit; and the Spirit spoke through a tongue that once had spoken in doubt and unbelief! God can take an unbelieving tongue or heart or life and make it new so that it is fit for the Master's use. I have known people who used to spew the foulest of language. It seemed like they could hardly start or finish a sentence without swearing. But then they were born again and encountered the Word and the Spirit, and their life and their mouth alike were turned around. Praising and prophesying replaced cursing and swearing.

Prophesying is an overflow of and a yielding to the Holy Spirit. Prophecy doesn't come from our mind. It comes from the Spirit, through us. Like Zacharias's, may our tongues be loosed so we can prophesy the plans of God for our generation!

SIMEON AND ANNA

> *And there was a man in Jerusalem whose name was Simeon; and this man was righteous and devout, looking for the consolation of Israel; and the Holy Spirit was upon him. And it had been revealed to him by the Holy Spirit that he would not see death before he had seen the Lord's Christ.* (Luke 2:25–26 NASB95)

> *And there was a prophetess, Anna the daughter of Phanuel, of the tribe of Asher. She was advanced in years and had lived with her husband seven years after her marriage.* (Luke 2:36 NASB95)

Simeon and Anna had the privilege of peering into the dawn of the unfolding new covenant. Both of them had such a relationship with the Spirit that it was revealed to them, in specificity, where and when they could get a glimpse of the Messiah. It was even revealed which specific

Child, out of the other children present that day at the temple, was the Messiah. When the Spirit speaks, He will be specific. It may not be the complete sentence we want to hear, but He may give us a word or a phrase that, if we obey it, will lead us to the next word or phrase in the complete sentence. God does not give vague instructions. This passage encourages me greatly to hear with prophetic accuracy. We should not settle for generic, dime-a-dozen prophetic words!

Since Simeon and Anna, under the old covenant, could attain such an intimate level of being led by the Holy Spirit, how much more should we, past Calvary, who have the Holy Spirit living within us, have an even higher expectation for the Spirit to lead us toward encounters with Jesus?

The leading of the Spirit always brings us to a revelation of Jesus because He is the answer to everything!

Anna served God *"night and day with fastings and prayers"* (verse 37 NASB95, AMP). She was a prayerful woman. We can also assume that Simeon, being *"righteous and devout,"* was a prayerful man. Prayer tunes us to the leading of the Spirit.

I believe that in the era in which God has ordained for us to live, a company of Simeons and Annas will be raised up who are hungry for God and will be divinely led by the Spirit to specific encounters with Jesus!

THE SPIRIT IN THE LIFE OF JESUS

As our example, Jesus operated on the earth as a Man anointed by the Spirit of God. If Jesus walked in the supernatural only because He was divine, then that would have left us out. Yet all believers are given the same authority to do the same works He did. (See, for example, Mark 16:17–18.) The way the Spirit moved in the life of Jesus is a pattern for how He will move in our lives.

> *And Jesus kept increasing in wisdom and stature, and in favor with God and men.* (Luke 2:52 NASB95, AMP)

The progression in the life of Jesus was both spiritual—*"wisdom"*—and natural—*"stature"*—with God and with man. Part of that growth was the increase of the Spirit's moving in His life.

At the start of Jesus's public ministry, the Spirit's first move was to come *upon* Jesus gently like a dove at His baptism. (See Luke 3:22.)

Second, the Spirit *led* Jesus into a confrontation with the devil in the wilderness. (See Luke 4:1.)

After Jesus's victory over the wilderness temptations, He made His way back to Galilee *"in the power of the Spirit"* (Luke 4:14, various translations).

It was only after this that Jesus declared that the Spirit was *upon* Him to preach and minister and that the prophecy He quoted from Isaiah 61:1–2 was fulfilled in Him. (See Luke 4:16–21.) The evidence of this prophetic fulfillment was Jesus's immediate ministry with *demonstrations of power and might* (see Luke 4:31–44) that continued for the whole of His ministry.

Thus, this was the progression of the Spirit in Jesus's life:

1. The Spirit came upon Jesus, ministering to Him personally.
2. The Spirit led Jesus.
3. Jesus was filled with the power of the Spirit.
4. The Spirit came upon Jesus again, this time for public ministry.
5. Jesus began ministering in demonstrations of power.

The Holy Spirit works with us in the same progression.

Our walk with God starts with the Holy Spirit coming upon us, ministering to us personally. At Jesus's baptism, immediately after the Holy Spirit descended gently (like a dove) on Him, the Father announced from heaven, *"You are My beloved Son, in You I am well-pleased"* (Luke 3:22 NASB95). Here you see all members of the Trinity present!

This announcement was made *before* Jesus did any miraculous works. *Our Father's pleasure with us is not based on what we do but on the condition of our heart.* Jesus's obedience and humility to be baptized by John pleased the Father. Obedience and humility are of great value in the Spirit realm.

Works—what we do in service to God, outside of maintaining an obedient heart—are not what our Father is looking for. He is after our heart, not our hands. This does not mean that what we do or don't do is of no significance. Rather, it means that if our heart is right, right actions will certainly be forthcoming. Our actions alone don't prove our heart, but our heart can certainly be proven by our actions.

Of course, Jesus always was, and is, the eternal Son of God. So the Spirit was simply, reassuringly affirming who Jesus already was. For the rest of us, our *initial* encounter with the Holy Spirit is *always* a call toward unmerited sonship. The Holy Spirit's interaction with all of humanity is for the purpose of bringing people to the Father. (See Ephesians 1:5.) The Holy Spirit woos us to sonship before we are saved and reveals our sonship after we are born again!

The Spirit led Jesus in response to Jesus's act of obedience. Again, obedience opens us up to the leading of the Spirit. Being led by God requires our obedience because whenever God leads, our willingness to obey is necessary for us to move forward in His leading. So, an obedient heart is a prerequisite to being led by the Spirit of God. As the saying goes, "You cannot drive a parked car!" The Holy Spirit cannot lead us if we have already decided what we want to do before we hear from Him. Having an openness and a willingness to yield to going in a different direction are necessary to be a candidate for the leading of the Spirit.

For example, believing for a move of the Spirit in revival and awakening is meaningless unless we are also prepared to yield to Spirit-led changes in our lifestyle and schedule.

To be led by the Spirit means being willing to put aside what, when, how, and with whom we usually do what we usually do.

To be led by the Spirit means being open to the *un*-usual!

To be led, we must be lead-able!

The Spirit was faithful to see that Jesus was *not* led into the wilderness until *after* He had first been *"filled with the Holy Spirit"* (Luke 4:1 NKJV). God never wills that we encounter the enemy with an empty tank! Jesus was *not* led to the wilderness facing an uncertain future—His victory was assured by virtue of the filling of the Spirit. As I mentioned previously, Jesus was led by the Spirit into the wilderness to demonstrate to us how to have victory over the enemy.

While in the wilderness, Jesus responded to each of the devil's three temptations by speaking the written Word of God. (See Luke 4:2–13.)

The Spirit in Jesus drew the Word out of Jesus because the Word and the Spirit *always* work together. That is how Jesus handled the direct assault of the enemy: being filled with the Holy Spirit and speaking the Word of God. Speaking the Word and giving the Word priority is a characteristic of a Spirit-filled life.

Being filled with the power of the Spirit always follows being led by the Spirit. Whenever God leads, He also supplies the power to follow that leading and to occupy the places to which He leads us. God does not lead us to places that our natural self can sustain. He does not need to. It takes the strength of God to do the things of God. The power of God in operation in the life of the believer is not optional; it is essential if we are to live as believers.

The filling of the Spirit follows the emptying of ourselves. The act of emptying ourselves is the essence of obedience. We empty ourselves of our "lesser," and God fills us with Himself, the Greater! God could not fill us with Himself without also filling us with His power because His presence and His power go together. There is no powerless presence of God! The power of the Spirit filled Jesus *before* His public ministry. *Jesus Himself had no public ministry before the Spirit came upon Him in power.* Later, Jesus would leave corresponding instructions with His disciples. (See Luke 24:49.) Like Him, they were not to start a largescale public ministry until after the Spirit came upon them. (See Acts 1:8.) This is the divine blueprint: *encounters with the Spirit before expeditions to the masses.*

The power of the Spirit flowing in the life of Jesus sustained Him personally and enabled Him publicly. The Spirit of God gives us abilities for ministry *and* also gives us longevity in our personal walk with God.

The public ministry of Jesus was really a demonstration of the will of the Father for mankind on earth. God wants to meet us supernaturally in this natural realm. That level of life and ministry is not attainable in our own strength. It requires an infusion of God Himself. This is the function of the Holy Spirit. He is the infusion of God in us! It takes God in us to express God through us.

Once more, Jesus's public ministry *started only after* the Holy Spirit's outpouring on and overflowing from Him. This was heaven's blueprint for Jesus, and it is heaven's blueprint for us.

THE SPIRIT OF PRAYER

One main way in which the Holy Spirit, as our Helper, assists us is by both inspiring us to pray and praying through us. (See Romans 8:26.)

> *It was at this time that He went off to the mountain to pray, and He spent the whole night in prayer to God.* (Luke 6:12 NASB95)

> *And it happened that while He was praying alone, the disciples were with Him, and He questioned them, saying, "Who do the people say that I am?"... Some eight days after these sayings, He took along Peter and John and James, and went up on the mountain to pray.*
> (Luke 9:18, 28 NASB95)

Luke records Jesus praying at critical junctures of His ministry. The Spirit who birthed Jesus's public ministry was now also guiding Him on the necessary and vital steps to take. The Holy Spirit as our Guide stays with us all the way. One manner in which the Holy Spirit guides us is in prompting us to pray. *The fruit of ministry is always the result of the ministry of prayer.* It takes Spirit-led prayer to have Spirit-led results.

First, in Jesus's calling of the twelve disciples, and then later, in His prodding them toward a revelation of His divinity and the subsequent declaration of the building of the church, prior prayer was made by Him through the unction of the Spirit. In both these accounts, the lives of the disciples, by being called by Jesus—and also our lives today, by being called into the church that Jesus was and is building—were changed by the prayers that Jesus prayed. *The Spirit leads us to seed prayer so that we can harvest revelation.*

When we let the Spirit lead us to prayer, not only will our lives be changed, but also many others will be called into His plans!

THE SPIRIT OF JOY

> *The seventy returned with joy, saying, "Lord, even the demons are subject to us in Your name."... At that very time He rejoiced greatly in the Holy Spirit.* (Luke 10:17, 21 NASB95)

Fittingly, for a biblical book with so many references to the Holy Spirit, Luke describes the joy of the Lord in Jesus and the believers. He uses five different Greek words for joy and uses them twice as many times as are used in the other gospels.

Joy, in thanksgiving to God, is the natural response of the believer who has experienced the power and liberty of the Spirit. Just as we laugh and rejoice when we celebrate joyful events in the natural, there are dimensions in the Spirit where we laugh and rejoice at the victory we have in Jesus. I have seen people yield to the Spirit in prayer and weep holy tears in intercession for souls. I have personally experienced this as well. I have also experienced and seen where the gift of special faith was in manifestation and things were said and done with a holy boldness that would not be normally expressed or carried out. Why should we not also be able to rejoice in the Spirit with holy laughter? Anything expressed under the influence of the *Holy* Spirit is *holy* by definition, And there is power in anything holy!

JOHN

A Personal Love

The apostle John was a fisherman. He was the brother of James and was likely a cousin of Jesus. Together with James and Peter, John was part of Jesus's inner circle. He is commonly known as "the disciple whom Jesus loved," and we quickly note that this phrase or a similar one is *found only in John's own gospel.* (See John 13:23; 19:26; 20:2; 21:7, 20.) So, we see that John deeply personalized the love Jesus had for him. It is *important* to know that God loves the whole world, but it is *powerful* to know that, in the whole world, God loves you—specifically you! It is one thing to know that God has a plan for humanity, but it is another thing to know that God has a plan for you. It is good to know that the Bible is God's Word, but it is personally impactful to know that the Bible is God's Word to you.

John's gospel stands out from those of Matthew, Mark, and Luke (which are known as the Synoptic Gospels for their similar structure and content) not only for the outline John uses but also for its exclusive content. John uniquely includes Jesus's seven "I am" statements, lengthy and weighty discourses, and seven "sign" miracles, five of which are not found in any other gospel account.

And, more than the author of any other gospel, John extensively writes of Jesus talking about the Holy Spirit and records Jesus as saying, *"My sheep hear My voice"* (John 10:27 NASB95, NKJV). I believe that the voice of the Holy Spirit led John to personalize Jesus's love so much that, as far as John was concerned, he, John, was Jesus's favorite disciple. The Holy Spirit is God to and in us *personally*. The Holy Spirit makes the written Word come alive and applies it to us!

Knowing the love Jesus had for him undoubtedly sustained John through the many persecutions and trials he faced as the last surviving original apostle. Knowing the love of God is a stabilizing factor through the storms of life.

SPIRIT-BAPTIZED

> *John testified saying, "I have seen the Spirit descending as a dove out of heaven, and He remained upon Him. I did not recognize Him, but He who sent me to baptize in water said to me, 'He upon whom you see the Spirit descending and remaining upon Him, this is the One who baptizes in the Holy Spirit.' I myself have seen, and have testified that this is the Son of God."* (John 1:32–34 NASB95)

God had told John the Baptist that the messianic sign to him would be that of the Spirit Himself. So when he saw the Spirit, like a dove, descending and remaining on Jesus, it convinced him of Jesus's messiahship. *The Spirit is a divine sign that points to Jesus.* He is still pointing people to Jesus today. (See, for example, John 16:14–15.) Again, it is only the Holy Spirit who can reveal Jesus to anyone because the things of God are spiritually discerned. (See 1 Corinthians 2:14.) Never underestimate the ministry of the Spirit to present and confirm Jesus as the Lamb of God through the simple preaching of the gospel! Preaching is not primarily an intellectual endeavor but a spiritual one. Preaching and teaching might include facts and figures, arguments and explanations, but it takes the Holy Spirit to speak to the hearts of people.

Perhaps, besides recognizing that Jesus was the Son of God that takes away the sin of the world, John the Baptist's other great revelation was that Jesus would "baptize in the Holy Spirit."

In addition to water baptism, there are two baptisms that the Holy Spirit is intimately involved in. The first is when we receive Jesus as the Lamb of God and are born again, and the Holy Spirit baptizes us *into* the body of Christ. Paul taught that *"in one Spirit we were all baptized into one body"* (1 Corinthians 12:13 ESV). This is the baptism *of* the Holy Spirit and is the *only* baptism that will save you.

The second—and this is what John the Baptist was referring to by the inspiration of the Spirit—is when, *after* the Holy Spirit baptizes us into the body of Christ, Jesus then baptizes us, His body, into the Holy Spirit. This is the baptism *with* the Holy Spirit. Just as with water baptism, where we are baptized *with* or *in* water, in this baptism, we are baptized *with* or *in* the Holy Spirit. In baptism by immersion, we are submerged in water, and when we are baptized with the Spirit, we are literally submerged in the Spirit!

The baptism *of* the Holy Spirit is for eternal life. The baptism *with* the Spirit is for power. (See Acts 1:8.) This is the baptism *"with the Holy Spirit and fire"* (Matthew 3:11, various translations) that sets believers ablaze with the power of God. We see this first fulfilled in the upper room in Acts 2:3–4.

SPIRIT-BORN

> *Jesus answered, "Truly, truly, I say to you, unless one is born of water and the Spirit he cannot enter into the kingdom of God. That which is born of the flesh is flesh, and that which is born of the Spirit is spirit.... The wind blows where it wishes and you hear the sound of it, but do not know where it comes from and where it is going; so is everyone who is born of the Spirit."* (John 3:5–6, 8 NASB95)

At creation, God proclaimed that everything would produce after its own kind. (See Genesis 1:11–12.) Now, we see Jesus expanding this principle to include the spiritual nature of man.

Throughout the Old Testament, water was a symbol of refreshing, renewal, and cleansing. Ezekiel prophesied of a time when God would *"sprinkle clean water on you...cleanse you...give you a new heart and put a new spirit in you...put my Spirit in you"* (Ezekiel 36:25–27 NIV). The new birth is necessary because it cleanses us in our inner being, our spirit-man. Once more, we are reminded that other religions of the world seek to cleanse adherents by outward rituals, rules, regulations, dos and don'ts—but only Jesus offers a deeper cleanse of a true renewal. Having such a refurbishment of our inner being is the only way we can host the Holy Spirit Himself *in* us. *The blood cleansed us so the Spirit could fill us!* God did not intend for us to be cleansed and empty. This explains why the Spirit was only *on* but not *in* anyone in the Old Testament. Those individuals were not renewed in their spirit-man because the blood of the Lamb had not yet been shed for the world.

> *Do not be amazed that I said to you, "You must be born again."*
> (John 3:7 NASB95)

Found multiple times in the New Testament, the Greek word *anothen* (*Strong's*, H509), translated here and in Galatians 4:9 (NKJV) as *"again,"* is also rendered in various translations as *"from the top"* (see, for example, John 19:23), *"from above"* (see, for example, James 1:17), and "from the (very) first; from the (very) beginning" (see, for example, Luke 1:3). In contrast to our first and natural birth on the earth below, we are now born *"from above," "from the top."* So, our first birth is lower than our second birth because it is of an earthly, physical, temporal origin, and the latter is from a heavenly, spiritual, eternal origin.

Jesus said, *"You must…."* This was not a suggestion but a command if anyone wanted to see the kingdom of God. Being born again, in and by the Spirit, is the beginning of our entry into and acquisition of all that the kingdom of God has for us! *It takes the Spirit to get us into the Spirit.*

LIVING WATER IN SPIRIT AND TRUTH

> *Jesus answered and said to her, "If you knew the gift of God, and who it is who says to you, 'Give Me a drink,' you would have asked Him, and He would have given you living water…. But whoever drinks of the water that I will give him shall never thirst; but the water that I will give him will become in him a well of water springing up to eternal life."*
> (John 4:10, 14 NASB95)

In the arid, desert environment of Palestine, societal life centered around the availability of water. Meeting a Samaritan women at a well, Jesus made an astonishing statement: He offered living water that, when received, would be transformed into a *"well of water."* So, the living water, the work of the Spirit in salvation, when received, bubbles up in a person and becomes a well of water from within! With a well of living water inside them, the believer no longer needs to be thirsty as they walk through the dry places in life.

The Spirit of God is the flow of life, the flow of living water, from within the believer.

Well water is hidden within the well until and unless it is purposely drawn out. Similarly, the life of God in the believer, together with the gifts and callings of God, lies dormant until we intentionally *"stir up the gift of God which is in* [us]" (2 Timothy 1:6 NKJV). We primarily stir up the things of God in us by *"building* [ourselves] *up...praying in the Holy Spirit"* (Jude 1:20, various translations), hearing and receiving the Word of the Lord (see Romans 10:17), and doing what we hear (see James 1:22).

> *But an hour is coming, and now is, when the true worshipers will worship the Father in spirit and truth; for such people the Father seeks to be His worshipers. God is spirit, and those who worship Him must worship in spirit and truth.* (John 4:23–24 NASB95)

In the same conversation with the Samaritan woman, Jesus went on to explain that the Father was seeking *true* worshipers, implying that, up to that point, no true worship had been offered. This is a shocking statement when you consider that, throughout the Old Testament, many people had been faithfully and fervently worshiping God. Although their worship was accepted by God, it was not true worship in the highest possible sense because none of those worshiping were doing so from a born-again, recreated spirit, since no one was born again under the old covenant. Because man is primarily a spiritual being, true worship—worship from and with our true nature—would be worship from and by our spirit-man. Before the shed blood of Jesus, no man's spirit was cleansed, and therefore none could approach God directly, spirit to Spirit. Second Samuel 6:14 (various translations) records that *"David danced before the LORD with **all his might.**"*

David didn't dance in the spirit. He danced with his might, his strength. The Lord accepted this worship because it was offered to the fullest extent that David could have worshiped. But, all that time, in the Old Testament, God was seeking those who could worship in spirit and in truth, and no one was found able to do so until people could be born again, and the church was born.

To worship God *"in spirit"* means that the worship sincerely originates from our core, our spirit. It is worship that is not mechanical or legalistic. This does not mean that traditional or liturgical styles of worship are unacceptable, but it does mean that any physical postures or symbolic actions we take must be infused with heart. People can be legalistic even with more contemporary forms of worship. Clapping, shouting, moving about, or even waving banners doesn't mean anything unless we do it because we are moved by the majesty of God.

"In spirit" could also be interpreted as a reference to the Holy Spirit. Paul said in Philippians 3:3 (NLT), *"For we who worship by the Spirit of God are the ones who are truly circumcised."* True worship is by the Spirit, in the spirit, through our spirit!

When I hear people talk about how they want to return to Old Testament forms of worship, I always wonder, "Do they know that it is only under the new covenant that we have the potential to be the true worshipers God is looking for?"

The other element of genuine worship is its being done *"in truth."* I have seen believers who seem to prefer to "worship in spirit" but don't appear to be very concerned about truth. They seem to think that focusing on truth has the potential to quench the Spirit. Apparently, they determine the success of their worship by the thrills, chills, and goose bumps they experience.

Worship must not be emotionless. As believers, our emotions are to be aroused by the truth of God's Word. Yet I would be just as cautious about believers who are heavy on emotion with no love for truth as I am about believers who emphasize truth but will not let it affect their emotions!

Emotions without truth lead to shallowness.

Truth without emotions leads to decay.

Emotions with truth lead to worship.

THE RIVER OF THE SPIRIT

> *Now on the last day, the great day of the feast, Jesus stood and cried out, saying, "If anyone is thirsty, let him come to Me and drink. He who believes in Me, as the Scripture said, 'From his innermost being will flow rivers of living water.'" But this He spoke of the Spirit, whom those who believed in Him were to receive; for the Spirit was not yet given, because Jesus was not yet glorified.* (John 7:37–39 NASB95)

At the end of the dry season in Israel (which usually occurred in September or October), Jesus went to the Feast of Tabernacles in Jerusalem. On the last day of Tabernacles, the Jews participated in a ceremony in which a priest would fill a large pitcher with water at the Pool of Siloam and would then carry it to the temple and symbolically pour that water on the altar. As he did so, he would pray for an early autumn rain.

It was in this setting that Jesus made a prophetic pronouncement that involves us today. The soon-coming Holy Spirit would be like a *river*, flowing from the hearts of believers.

As we saw in John 4, when Jesus talked to the Samaritan woman, He offered her salvation, a drink of eternally thirst-quenching living water that would be a "*fountain*" (verse 14 NKJV), a "*well*" (KJV, NASB95), or a "*spring*" (various translations) of living water. Here, speaking of the Holy Spirit, Jesus said we would receive "*rivers of living water.*"

With salvation, we receive a well; and with the Holy Spirit, we receive a river!

Well water has no current or flow. I mentioned earlier that a well contains hidden water. No one sees that water unless it's intentionally drawn out. It's there whenever you need it as long as you draw it out.

Wells dispense water by the bucketful. Many people in a community could drink from a well, but they would have to wait in line for the bucket to come back up as each person took their turn.

A river, on the other hand, is water that is in the open for all to see and access. Rivers have a strength, a current, a flow. They also contain fish and other life forms. Rivers can supply water to entire villages and their livestock. Nobody needs to wait in line for a bucket; they can all partake of the water at the same time.

Wells quench the thirst of individuals, while rivers quench the thirst of communities.

Some people have stayed around the well of salvation, not going any further, but God is inviting us to the river of the Spirit. You can drink from a well, but you can submerge your entire being and go swimming in a river. I believe that Christ wants His body to jump in the river of His Spirit!

INTRODUCING THE PARACLETE

> *I will ask the Father, and He will give you another Helper, that He may be with you forever; that is the Spirit of truth, whom the world cannot receive, because it does not see Him or know Him, but you know Him because He abides with you and will be in you. I will not leave you as orphans; I will come to you.* (John 14:16–18 NASB95)

In an exclusive, lengthy, three-chapter discourse (John 14–16), Jesus introduced *"another Helper"* whom the disciples had not imagined they would ever need. They had, rightly, considered Jesus to be the sum of all things divine. Their understanding of the plan of God saw no need for anything or anyone else. They assumed that Jesus would wrap up what He had started by personally ushering the reign of God into all aspects of earthly life.

Then Jesus told them that besides having Him, they would have *"another Helper,"* whom He would ask the Father to send them.

The Amplified Bible expands on the word *"Helper"* in John 14:16 to include the meanings of *"Comforter, Advocate, Intercessor—Counselor, Strengthener, Standby."*

Here is what *Vine's Complete Expository Dictionary* says about the Greek word for this term (*Strong's*, 3875):

> *paraklētos*..., lit., "called to one's side," i.e., to one's aid, is primarily a verbal adjective, and suggests the capability or adaptability for giving aid. It was used in a court of justice to denote a legal assistant, counsel for the defense, an advocate; then, generally, one who pleads another's cause, an intercessor, advocate, as in 1 John 2:1, of the Lord Jesus. In the widest sense, it signifies a "succorer, comforter." Christ was this to His disciples, by the implication of

> His word "another (*allos*, "another of the same sort," not *heteros*, "different") Comforter," when speaking of the Holy Spirit, John 14:16. In 14:26; 15:26; 16:7 He calls Him "the Comforter."[10]

I was once led to take time to ponder and meditate on each of the seven descriptive terms for the Holy Spirit found in the *Amplified Bible*. It greatly shifted the way I saw the Holy Spirit. He is not just a force or an impression. He is, tangibly, God Himself, sent to live in me and to help me. What a help He is! What help is available to us as believers!

When we realize that God's plans for us are bigger than what we could possibly fathom, that the life we are called to live as believers is impossible in our own strength, and that the plan of God requires the power of God... we have a *Helper*.

When we are troubled and distressed...we have a *Comforter*.

When we are accused by other people, the enemy, or even our own conflicting thoughts...we have an *Advocate*.

When we are in need of help that can come only by divine mediation... we have an *Intercessor*.

When we are lost, confused, and seeking direction...we have a *Counselor*.

When we feel beaten down by circumstances and exhausted by life... we have a *Strengthener*.

When life seems uncertain and we are not sure if our finite resources are sufficient to see us through...we have a Faithful One who is always on *standby*.

TEACHER AND TESTIFIER

> *But the Helper, the Holy Spirit, whom the Father will send in My name, He will teach you all things,* ***and bring to your remembrance all that I said to you.*** (John 14:26 NASB95)

---

10. W. E. Vine, Merrill F. Unger, and William White, Jr., *Vine's Complete Expository Dictionary of Old and New Testament Words* (Nashville, TN: Thomas Nelson Publishers, 1996), New Testament, 111.

> *When the Helper comes, whom I will send to you from the Father, that is the Spirit of truth who proceeds from the Father,* ***He will testify about Me.*** (John 15:26 NASB95)

The Spirit will *always* agree with and amplify what the Word of God has already said. There are no "new" revelations—meaning, in addition to the truths already established in the Word—birthed by the Spirit of God. And there are certainly no contrary revelations—meaning, those that go against both the spirit and the text of Scripture—birthed by the Spirit of God.

Many people get excited that the Holy Spirit is a Revealer, but they forget that He is also a Teacher! What a joy it is for me to have the Holy Spirit walk me through the Word of God. I have had visions, dreams, and many other supernatural leadings and encounters, but some of the most profoundly intimate moments I have enjoyed with God have been when the Holy Spirit brought light to me, and the Word came alive for me. *Being Spirit-led includes being Spirit-taught.*

THE MINISTRY OF THE HOLY SPIRIT

> *But I tell you the truth, it is to your advantage that I go away; for if I do not go away, the Helper will not come to you; but if I go, I will send Him to you. And He, when He comes, will convict the world concerning sin and righteousness and judgment; concerning sin, because they do not believe in Me; and concerning righteousness, because I go to the Father and you no longer see Me; and concerning judgment, because the ruler of this world has been judged.* (John 16:7–11 NASB95)

The Holy Spirit is an apostolically *Sent One*. He is sent by Jesus *and* the Father on a specific mission.

The Holy Spirit is not just a Comforter; He is also a Convicter.

The Holy Spirit convicts the world of sin (singular, not plural). As I expressed previously, since the only sin that separates mankind from God is the sin of not believing in Jesus, the Holy Spirit convicts people of their need for Jesus.

With us believers, the Holy Spirit convicts us *not of sin but of righteousness*—not our own righteousness but the righteousness that is ours by virtue of Jesus. Jesus told His disciples (and us), *"I go to the Father and you no longer see Me."* But He sent us the Helper in His temporary absence from the earth. The Holy Spirit is ever ready to remind us of what Jesus has already purchased for us, which is *"that we might become the righteousness of God in Him"* (2 Corinthians 5:21 NKJV); and when we don't live up to that standard of righteousness, the Spirit convicts us "upward" from unrighteousness—our position of having fallen short—to our seated position in Christ of righteousness. *The Holy Spirit convicts us; He does not condemn us!*

The Holy Spirit convicts the world of its false judgment of who Jesus is and of Satan as a completely defeated and eternally condemned foe. The world is under Satan's control, and so it can't make righteous judgments. The Holy Spirit thus judges Satan for originating the world system and for promoting that system.

> *I have many more things to say to you, but you cannot bear them now. But when He, the Spirit of truth, comes, He will guide you into all the truth; for He will not speak on His own initiative, but whatever He hears, He will speak; and He will disclose to you what is to come. He will glorify Me, for He will take of Mine and will disclose it to you. All things that the Father has are Mine; therefore I said that He takes of Mine and will disclose it to you.* (John 16:12–15 NASB95)

As great and exciting as it would have been to walk with Jesus as the initial disciples did, there were things that Jesus wanted to say to us and teach us that we could receive only after His ascension. We are not in a disadvantaged, lesser position today than the early disciples were. Actually, we are in a position to see, do, and be more than they saw, did, and were! Not only do we have the fullness of Scripture and the maturing of the fivefold ministry offices, but we also have the benefits of the ripening of revelation found in the Epistles. The Epistles are the teachings of Jesus, revealed by the Holy Spirit, that could be brought forth only after He sat down at the right hand of the Father.

All of Scripture is for everyone, but not all of Scripture is written to everyone. The Epistles were written *specifically* to the church. They were revealed by the Holy Spirit for the church age in which we live. In the Gospel, Jesus demonstrated the "what." In the Epistles, the Holy Spirit explained the "why." Thus, the Epistles are the continuation of Jesus's teaching through the ministry of the Holy Spirit.

As Jesus did, not only does the Holy Spirit teach us through the written Word, but He also helps us by guiding us into all truth and telling us of things to come.

The Spirit explained it to me in this way: "I'll guide you to which paths to take and warn you about where the potholes are!"

Not only is the Holy Spirit apostolically sent, but He is also prophetically oriented. The Holy Spirit points to Jesus and reveals the mind of God; this is the essence of prophetic ministry.

THE BREATH OF JESUS

> *So Jesus said to them again, "Peace be with you; as the Father has sent Me, I also send you." And when He had said this, He breathed on them and said to them, "Receive the Holy Spirit."*
>
> (John 20:21–22 NASB95)

Just as *"the* LORD *God formed the man from the dust of the ground…* [and] *breathed the breath of life into the man's nostrils, and the man became a living person"* (Genesis 2:7 NLT), so now Jesus breathes life into the body He formed and purchased—the church. It takes the breath of God, the Holy Spirit, to bring life because He is a life-giving Spirit!

In bestowing the Holy Spirit, Jesus was making both a proclamation of blessing and a pledge that He would do as He had promised: send the Spirit so that His followers would not be left as orphans and so that they would receive the fullness of the Spirit. The outward manifestation of this proclamation would be seen some forty days later on the day of Pentecost. (See Acts 1:8; 2:1–4.)

Part of the reason the disciples were recipients of the Holy Spirit was that Jesus had a mission for them. They were sent by Jesus, just as Jesus had been sent by the Father. This meant they had the same mission—and that would mean they would need the same empowerment to accomplish their mission. The Holy Spirit surging through Jesus was what propelled His ministry, and Jesus was promising His disciples the same surge of the Spirit. *We have the same Spirit today.* We, too, are sent as the disciples were sent, and they, in turn, were sent as Jesus was sent…in the power of the Spirit. God intends for the whole world to see the phenomenon of His presence through us!

ACTS

Jesus Continues His Ministry

The book of Acts has rightly been called "The Acts of the Holy Spirit" by some people because it is like a screenshot of what it means to live as a believer in the power of the Spirit.

In this book, Luke continues his *"orderly account"* (Luke 1:3, various translations) to Theophilus of the life and ministry of Jesus; but, this time, he reports about what Jesus continued doing after His ascension through the lives of the apostles—mainly Peter and then Paul and others. The book of Acts is a peek into the initial unfolding of the Great Commission. (See Matthew 28:19–20.) Although primarily not a doctrinal treatise, this book provides important historical insight into the infancy of the church that is found nowhere else. Luke does not portray the Holy Spirit theoretically; rather, he reports on the Holy Spirit filling believers and being received by them; on His falling, coming upon, and being poured out on various people. These terms, in essence, describe Jesus's promise to baptize believers with the Holy Spirit.

Acts is a book of transitions: from the old covenant to the new covenant; from Israel being God's main witness to the world to the church being God's mouthpiece; and, vitally, from the outpouring of the Spirit on

Jesus at His baptism in water to the outpouring of the Spirit on believers through their baptism of fire at Pentecost.

Regarding the structure of the book, Acts 13 is a transitional chapter, as Paul replaces Peter as the central figure.

The Holy Spirit is found in all aspects of Acts. We will not be able to review every verse that mentions Him, but we will look at enough passages to get a grasp of the Spirit's activity in the infant church.

A PROMISE REPEATED

> *...until the day when He was taken up to heaven, after He had by the Holy Spirit given orders to the apostles whom He had chosen.... He said to them, "....but you will receive power when the Holy Spirit has come upon you; and you shall be My witnesses both in Jerusalem, and in all Judea and Samaria, and even to the remotest part of the earth."*
>
> (Acts 1:2, 7–8 NASB95)

Luke mentioned the Holy Spirit right from the start, setting the theme and the tone of his second book. We could say that the Old Testament was the season of God the Father, the Gospels were the season of Jesus the Son, and the book of Acts was the season of the Holy Spirit. Of course, each member of the Trinity was involved in all three "seasons," but, individually, They seemed to have more prominence in a particular season. Beginning with Acts, we see the Holy Spirit openly and actively functioning in and through the church. As I expressed earlier, the Epistles are simply the continued teachings of Jesus to His disciples through the Holy Spirit.

The promise that Jesus first made in Luke 24:48–49 is repeated in the above passage. It signifies an unbroken continuation from the Gospels and underscores the role that the Holy Spirit would now assume. Luke was unashamed to put the Holy Spirit front and center of the start and growth of the church.

A RUSHING WIND

> *When the day of Pentecost had come, they were all together in one place. And suddenly there came from heaven a noise like a violent rushing wind, and it filled the whole house where they were sitting. And there appeared to them tongues as of fire distributing themselves, and*

> *they rested on each one of them. And they were all filled with the Holy Spirit and began to speak with other tongues, as the Spirit was giving them utterance.* (Acts 2:1–4 NASB95)

There are settings and environments that are "Spirit friendly," that invite and make room for the move of the Holy Spirit. It is in those settings that the Spirit can do His deepest work. Unity of focus and purpose, together with prayer and worship, is always an element in those environments. Each time believers gather, it is necessary for them to know that God has a specific purpose for that gathering. It takes the leading of the Spirit of God to know what the purpose of each gathering is. The Spirit desires a variety of meetings because there are a variety of purposes to be accomplished in the Spirit. Expecting the leading of the Holy Spirit is part of our setting the stage for the Spirit to move! Ritualistic meetings, where we simply gather to go through the motions in the same way we did at the previous meeting, don't honor the Spirit of God.

I'm not saying that we should forgo having a preplanned order to our services, but we should be willing to set aside the preplanned order if it seems that the Spirit is leading in a different direction. I have been in meetings where a spirit of prayer fell on those who had gathered, and all we did was pray during the whole service. In other services, spontaneous worship arose, and it seemed like all we could do was fall on our faces in adoration. I have also been in services where the joy of the Lord bubbled up over everyone, and all we did was laugh and get drunk in the Spirit. The list could go on. There are as many variables as there are expressions of the Spirit.

Of course, there also have been many services where there was straight teaching and preaching following the preliminaries and worship portion of the service. But, even in such meetings, we have to allow the Spirit to guide all aspects of the service. For us preachers, that might mean we're willing to depart from our notes and go in the direction that we feel is suddenly tugging at us. *Each time we gather, the main thing that the Holy Spirit is trying to teach us is to trust in Him more than we trust in our own abilities.* This means we must be willing to give up our illusion of having control and yield to His leading. It is only in environments where the Spirit is welcomed that He manifests and speaks.

In the church at Antioch, the consecration of ministering to the Lord, prayer, and fasting opened the way for the Spirit to speak and separate

Barnabas and Saul (Paul) for their first missionary journey. (See Acts 13:1–3.) It was *"being sent out by the Holy Spirit"* (Acts 13:4, various translations) that empowered them to encounter the opposition of witchcraft through Elymas the sorcerer. (See verses 6–11.) *The power of God is always found in the sending of God.* We must have more environments where we make room for the Spirit to speak!

Environments matter for the moving of the Spirit. This does *not* mean that the Spirit can move only where believers are present, but it does mean that the Spirit seeks hungry hearts.

The "suddenly" that fell upon the one hundred and twenty disciples on the day of Pentecost was not really sudden, in a sense, because the believers were waiting expectantly, having gathered by Jesus's instruction to be endued from heaven. (See Luke 24:49.) They did not know whom or what to expect. Nor did they know when to expect this *"power from on high"* (verse 49, various translations), but they were obedient to what they knew. *The "suddenlies" from heaven are always a result of our "obedientlies."*

Just as there was a sound that *"filled the whole house,"* there were also individual tongues of fire that sat on each of the believers. There is a corporate aspect as well as an individual aspect to the flow of the Spirit. We need them both. The corporate wind lights the individual flame, and the individual flames come together to be fanned into a fire in the corporate wind.

I've heard some people say that the church is not the building, and that since we all have the same Holy Spirit, we don't need any corporate gatherings; all we need to do is bring our Bible to a quiet spot, and the Holy Spirit can teach us individually and directly. It is true that the church is not a building, but a building can be the place where the church gathers. It is true that the Holy Spirit can teach us personally and directly. But it is a grave mistake to think that since the Holy Spirit can and does do that, we don't need to be involved in corporate gatherings. Why deprive ourselves of either the corporate or the individual flow? God offers and intends us to partake of both!

AN OVERFLOW FOR US TODAY

> *But Peter, taking his stand with the eleven, raised his voice and declared to them: "Men of Judea and all you who live in Jerusalem, let this be known to you and give heed to my words."* (Acts 2:14 NASB95)

What happened on the day of Pentecost was nothing short of a tsunami of the Spirit! Peter, who just a short while earlier had come back to Jesus after denying Him, was now promoted by the Spirit to deliver the first public address of the church. The acceptance of God doesn't take long! He doesn't put us on probation before He takes us back. Once we turn, or return, our heart to Him, He fully accepts and restores us.

The phrase *"Peter, taking his stand with the eleven..."* shows us that the unity the disciples had before the Spirit fell on them continued afterward as well. There was no jostling for position to be the leader who would represent the church to a captive audience but rather a Spirit-led, united front. Recognizing the anointing on Peter for the occasion, the other disciples stood with him publicly and in spirit to allow for the corporate anointing to flow. The outpouring of the Spirit is not just a manifestation of power but also the manifestation of love and unity.

What happened in the upper room was not a straitlaced, formal gathering. The one hundred and twenty believers were so rowdy that the crowd could only assume they were drunk! (See Acts 2:13, 15.) Drunk people are uncoordinated; they often stumble around and fall over. The believers' behavior went beyond the usual clapping and singing that we are accustomed to in our modern-day services. In the natural, it looked like chaos. *Many times, what looks like chaos in the natural is order in the Spirit, and what looks like order in the natural is chaos in the Spirit!*

Of course, Peter did not have to defend the disciples' sobriety every time they gathered. What happened in the upper room is *not* the prescribed order of service every time believers gather. But it would be equally wrong to say that such manifestations no longer take place today and to make no room for them if the Spirit starts stirring in that way. The flow of the Spirit requires that we stay out of the ditch on either side of the spectrum.

THE SPIRIT'S ORDER OF SERVICE

> *But this is what was spoken of through the prophet Joel.*
>
> (Acts 2:16 NASB95)

After such a spectacularly monumental happening, many a minister would have been tempted to preach by simply testifying about and retelling what had just happened. That would not have been wrong, but for this very first sermon of the church, the Holy Spirit, I believe, was setting a standard for how the Word and the Spirit are to function in a gathering. If we who are hungry for the Spirit to move are not careful, we'll fall into the ditch of basing our ministry solely on manifestations. Certainly, the Spirit *always* desires to manifest His presence, yet *the manifestations of the Spirit are not a substitute for the Word of God but a complement to it.* As I have been expressing, true manifestations will point to and be supported by the Word. Rather than have Peter camp at the awe-inspiring outpouring, the Holy Spirit led him to verify and expound on the manifestations by referring to the prophet Joel, to the higher measure of God's Word. The Spirit used the Word to verify what the Spirit Himself had just done. This is a pattern for ministry and for growth in spiritual things. The Word is milk by which we can grow. (See 1 Peter 2:2.)

The Word confirms the Spirit, and the Spirit confirms the Word.

POUR OUT OF...

> *And it shall come to pass in the last days, says God, that I will pour out of My Spirit on all flesh; your sons and your daughters shall prophesy, your young men shall see visions, your old men shall dream dreams. And on My menservants and on My maidservants I will pour out My Spirit in those days; and they shall prophesy.* (Acts 2:17–18 NKJV)

The Word identifies three groups of people on the earth: the Jews, those with the old covenant; the gentiles, those with no covenant; and the church, those with the new covenant. (See 1 Corinthians 10:32.) God communicates with and ministers to each group differently. You could almost say that God speaks the same message but in a different language to each group. For the Jews, the Spirit reminds them that He is not finished with the covenant He has with them. For the gentiles, He invites them to covenant with Him. For the church, He shows us all that our covenant includes.

When the Spirit fell upon the disciples in the upper room, fulfilling Joel's prophecy, the "*last days*" scripturally began. We have been in the last days for two thousand years! Some believers get caught up in "end-time frenzy" and try to interpret the Bible by what's happening in the world instead of interpreting what's happening in the world by the Bible. They become overly concerned with "*wars and rumors of wars*" (Matthew 24:6, various translations). Those are signs of the times, but they are primarily not signs to the church. In quoting Joel, Peter said that, in the last days, God will pour out of His Spirit. That's the primary sign we in the church need to be looking at. We are not to get caught up in the doom and gloom that the world peddles. We are to be looking at the movement of the Spirit.

People often use the expression "God poured out His Spirit" when talking about Pentecost, but this would imply that it was a specific, one-time event. I like the wording in Acts 2:17, which says that God will pour *out of* His Spirit, so that every outpouring is simply *out of* His Spirit, and since God's Spirit is infinite and boundless, there can be a multiplicity of outpourings. There was an outpouring for the disciples in the upper room, but there is also an outpouring for us today!

The immediate effect of the Spirit's outpouring was that sons and daughters would prophesy—speak forth under divine inspiration—and young and old men would have visions and dreams. What had typically been reserved for a select few in the Old Testament could now gush forth from everyone in the body of Christ. Speaking, prophesying, and seeing visions and dreams are all descriptive of prophetic functions. This doesn't mean that every believer is now a prophet but that every believer, because they have a prophetic Spirit within them, can be moved by the Spirit into realms of prophecy. God made a prophetic declaration over us—*"and they shall prophesy"*—so that we would make prophetic declarations!

Peter closes his message with a call to repentance and an offer for people to *"receive the gift of the Holy Spirit"* (Acts 2:38, various translations). From the day of Pentecost, this has been the message of the church to the whole world. To *"receive the gift of the Holy Spirit"* is to have God Himself!

WHAT DO YOU HAVE?

> *But Peter said, "I do not possess silver and gold, but what I do have I give to you: In the name of Jesus Christ the Nazarene—walk!"*
>
> (Acts 3:6 NASB95)

Receiving the Holy Spirit is not just a religious experience. It would have taken more than silver and gold to help the lame man in this account from Acts 3. He needed the life of God to flow to him. After Peter's sudden Spirit-given ability to share Jesus, as he did in Acts 2, the other immediate benefit of the upper room experience for him was that now he had something to give: the power of God. The baptism in the Spirit is a baptism of power!

We have the same Spirit who was upon Peter, who had the same Spirit who was upon Jesus. This means we have the same Spirit of power. In another example, the Holy Spirit in Peter responded to the death of a woman named Dorcas (also called Tabitha; see Acts 9:40) in an identical way that Jesus responded to the death of Jairus's daughter (see, for example, Mark 5:40–41).

As I have pondered this truth, I have learned to reread Acts 10:38 (NASB95): "*You know of Jesus of Nazareth, how God anointed Him with the Holy Spirit and with power, and how He went about doing good and healing all who were oppressed by the devil, for God was with Him.*" That is what the Holy Spirit did through Jesus, and that is what He wants to do through us!

THE SPIRIT GUARDS THE CHURCH

> *But a man named Ananias, with his wife Sapphira, sold a piece of property, and kept back some of the price for himself, with his wife's full knowledge, and bringing a portion of it, he laid it at the apostles' feet. But Peter said, "Ananias, why has Satan filled your heart to lie to the Holy Spirit and to keep back some of the price of the land? While it remained unsold, did it not remain your own? And after it was sold, was it not under your control? Why is it that you have conceived this deed in your heart? You have not lied to men but to God."*
>
> (Acts 5:1–4 NASB95)

When Ananias and Sapphira saw the honor that was being given to those who had been led by the Spirit to sacrificially give to the church, they sold land and decided to lie about the amount they were donating. They made it seem like they had presented the whole amount when they actually had presented only a part of it. They were under no obligation to give any of the amount but decided to give some of it out of hypocrisy and dishonesty. Unlike the others who had selflessly given, they had given out of deceitful ambition, and, in doing so, they "*lie*[d] *to the Holy Spirit...lied...to God.*"

Peter, operating in the gifts of the discerning of spirits and the word of knowledge (see 1 Corinthians 12:8, 10) confronted the couple and emphatically equated their lying to the Holy Spirit as lying to God. This, again, shows us that the Holy Spirit was seen by the early church as equal to God.

In some circles, there has been some debate as to whether Ananias and Sapphira were believers. If they were not, since Satan had filled their heart, God was protecting the infant church from the pollution of satanic political jockeying. If they were, the Holy Spirit must have also dealt with them in some way before this happened because such a major power grab, such a level of blatant dishonesty, could not have been their first venture into deceit for position. It must have been their normal lifestyle and not just a spur-of-the-moment decision because Satan could not have instantly filled their hearts. This must have been something they were knowingly, continually yielding to. The guidance of the Holy Spirit keeps believers safely in the will of God. Since we are all growing in our ability to hear and obey the Spirit, it is not our yielding perfectly, but our having a heart of submission, that keeps us in His plans. The enemy is not able to jump on any believer he chooses. (See 1 Peter 5:8–9.) If he could, he'd have devoured everyone already! The Holy Spirit can keep us safe—and He can keep the church safe.

STEPHEN: FULL OF FAITH AND THE HOLY SPIRIT

I have always thought that Stephen, the first martyr of the church, had an admirable scriptural resume. He was chosen to serve because he was *"full of the Spirit and of wisdom"* (Acts 6:3, various translations). This means that *before* he was officially serving the church, he was *already* living a life full of the Spirit and walking in wisdom. A mother once came to me asking if her son, who was in his thirties, could travel and work in the ministry with me because he had been running with the wrong crowd and hadn't ever been able to keep a job or be a regular attender of church. This is the mistaken view some have of the ministry: "We'll send you the worst and hope for the best!" Ministry is not for the "perfect," because then no one could ever be in ministry, but it is also not for those who are running away from life. The church must always be for the healing, restoration, and building up of broken lives everywhere, but unless people are already living strong and walking in the Word to an extent, they are not ready to enter into a more public ministry.

Luke wrote that Stephen was a man *"full of faith and of the Holy Spirit"* (Acts 6:5, various translations). He then reaffirmed, *"And Stephen, full of grace and power, was performing great wonders and signs among the people"* (Acts 6:8

NASB95). So Stephen was full of the Spirit, wisdom, and faith, and he had a ministry of signs and wonders. Faith deals with the unseen, and wisdom with the seen. Life on earth, as God intends it for us, would be unbalanced if we were capable only in one realm and not in the other. The Holy Spirit empowers us for both the seen and the unseen. We can have faith for the things we don't yet see and wisdom for the things we do see. To have faith is to live in the reality of what God has promised, and to have wisdom is to be able to deal with things in life as God sees them. To be full of the Holy Spirit is to have both faith and wisdom. Stephen's being full of the Holy Spirit also means the Spirit could flow through him to proclaim the gospel and help others; thus, Stephen was "*full of...power* [and] *was performing great wonders and signs among the people.*" Being full inside enables you to flow outside.

The same Spirit who lived in Stephen was also working on the crowds to whom he was ministering. When the angry mob rose up against Stephen, he preached to them, saying, "*You...are always resisting the Holy Spirit; you are doing just as your fathers did*" (Acts 7:51 NASB95). The Spirit had been faithful to court God's people toward His grace and mercy—but they had generationally resisted Him. They resisted the Holy Spirit but clung to their traditions and, in doing so, made the gospel and the power of God of no effect. *Again, the Holy Spirit seeks our cooperation more than our abilities.*

Even as the mob encircled Stephen, he remained "*full of the Holy Spirit.*" In His faithfulness, God opened Stephen's eyes so that he "*gazed intently into heaven and saw the glory of God, and Jesus standing at the right hand of God*" (Acts 7:55 NASB95). Stephen was not just full of the Spirit, but, true to his being full of the Spirit, he was also full of love! Echoing Jesus on the cross, he cried out, "*Lord, do not hold this sin against them!*" (Acts 7:60 NASB95; see also Luke 23:34). *The power of the Spirit is also manifested as the love of the Spirit.* Standing between the seen and the unseen realms, Stephen bore witness to Jesus and peacefully "*fell asleep*" (verse 60, various translations). What a glorious way to enter heaven!

SIMON SEES...

The Holy Spirit may be unseen, but, many times, His works and His presence are highly visible. After the apostle Philip preached in Samaria (see Acts 8:5), Peter and John were sent from Jerusalem to strengthen the revival there (see Acts 8:14–15). The Samaritans had received Jesus and seen miraculous works under Philip's ministry but had not received the fullness of the Spirit. As Peter and John laid hands on them, they "*were receiving the Holy Spirit*" (Acts 8:17 NASB95). Simon, a sorcerer who had been baptized under Philip's ministry, saw the effects of Peter and John's laying hands on the people and offered them money so that he would be able to do the same. (See verses 18–19.) Based on previous accounts of others who received the Holy Spirit, the Samaritans must have started speaking in tongues. It could not have been just a matter of Peter and John's laying hands on them and imparting a silent blessing because the result was tangible enough that Simon offered money to be able to do it as well. With his background in sorcery, "buying" spiritual power and manifestations may have been common to him. Today, the practice of buying spiritual rank or making a profit from holy things is called *simony*. Simon repented after he was immediately and harshly rebuked by Peter. (See Acts 8:20–23.)

I have heard some ministers imply that if they made room for the power of God to manifest in public in their services, it would scare off unbelievers and new believers. I always tell them that if Simon had been in some of those services, he wouldn't ever have bothered offering money for what he saw! Once more, the power of God cannot be forced or put on as a show, but it also should not be kept hidden in the back room.

RECEIVING THE SPIRIT...AFTER BELIEVING

> *So Ananias departed and entered the house, and after laying his hands on him said, "Brother Saul, the Lord Jesus, who appeared to you on the road by which you were coming, has sent me so that you may regain your sight and be filled with the Holy Spirit." And immediately there fell from his eyes something like scales, and he regained his sight, and he got up and was baptized.* (Acts 9:17–18 NASB95)

> *It happened that while Apollos was at Corinth, Paul passed through the upper country and came to Ephesus, and found some disciples. He said to them, "Did you receive the Holy Spirit when you believed?"*
> (Acts 19:1–2 NASB95)

In both these passages—the conversion of Saul, who later became known as Paul and wrote many of the Epistles, and Paul's interaction with the believers at the key city of Ephesus—we see a familiar cycle: people encountered Jesus, and then, afterward, they encountered the Holy Spirit. It takes the Holy Spirit for us to encounter Jesus, but after the Spirit introduces us to Jesus, He wants us to know Him as well! As we saw when we looked at John's gospel, the Spirit baptizes us into Christ, and then Jesus baptizes us in the Holy Spirit. These are two separate encounters, without a definite set time between them. The baptism in the Spirit can take place *anytime after* a person is born again. *Don't stop at the cross—move on to Pentecost!*

Unlike what occurred in the upper room and later in Acts 10—when Peter preached to the first gentile converts of the church, and the Holy Spirit fell on the believers directly—the Holy Spirit moved on Paul and the Ephesian believers through the laying on of hands. Believers' laying hands on others so that they can receive the Holy Spirit is part of the overflow of the rivers of living water flowing out from those believers. (See John 7:38.)

By his own admission, Paul frequently spoke in tongues. (See 1 Corinthians 14:18). In addition to the experience of the Ephesian believers on whom Paul laid hands for receiving the Spirit (see Acts 19:6), we see that in the upper room at Pentecost, and when Peter preached to the gentile converts, including Cornelius and his household (see Acts 10:44–46), the believers spoke in tongues when they received the Holy Spirit. So, we can surmise that Paul started speaking in tongues when Ananias laid hands on him. Despite what God had told him about Paul, Ananias could not have known the international, generational impact that Paul was going to have. Even today, we are recipients of Paul's ministry. Once, when I was getting ready to lay hands on a roomful of people, the Lord said to me, "There are callings and giftings in that room that you don't know about." I have often gone back to that statement when I have laid hands on others. It is the plan of God that the Spirit should overflow from one believer to another and, in doing so, spark another whole flow. *The laying on of hands can be used by God to spark the deposits of the Spirit in others!*

It is significant that God had Ananias, "*a certain disciple*" (Acts 9:10 NKJV)—not a known leader or an original apostle—go and lay hands on Saul. Thank God for recognizable prominent leaders in the body of Christ, but God also needs and moves through "certain disciples." Many people want to be a Peter, a John, or a James, but we should be just as eager to be an Ananias.

Jesus received the Spirit at His baptism in order to pour out the Spirit at Pentecost so that we, in turn, could pour out the Spirit on others. We see Paul receiving the Holy Spirit as Ananias laid hands on him, and then we see the Ephesian believers receiving the Holy Spirit as Paul laid hands on them. There is but one stream of the Spirit in the church, and it traces back to Jesus!

THE GUIDE IN THE CHURCH

The early church, which was comprised primarily of Jewish believers, kept the doors open wide to gentiles after the Spirit confirmed the gentiles' acceptance by filling them with the evidence of speaking in tongues when Peter preached to them. (See Acts 10:44–47.) Jesus's command to *"go into all the world and preach the gospel to every creature"* (Mark 16:15 NKJV) was not fully understood by His disciples until the Spirit demonstrated it and confirmed it for them.

These gentile believers were never law-keeping Jews to begin with, and some Pharisees and other believers started saying that they needed to keep the law of Moses and be circumcised in order to be saved. *"Paul and Barnabas had great dissension and debate with them"* (Acts 15:2 NASB95). It was determined that Paul and Barnabas needed to go to Jerusalem *"to the apostles and elders"* (verse 2, various translations) to seek clarity.

Doctrinal disputes and discussions within the church can be unpleasant but can actually be heathy if they are conducted with brotherly love, making room for the Holy Spirit to be our Guide and Teacher.

At the council in Jerusalem, Peter reiterated that God had accepted the gentiles and, as proof, had freely bestowed the Holy Spirit on them. The early church saw the Holy Spirit as the seal of salvation! In the end, *"it seemed good to the Holy Spirit"* (Acts 15:28, various translations), and the council decided that outside of abstaining from food offered to idols, blood, and sexual immorality, the gentile believers were free of all other obligations. So we see that the Holy Spirit was involved in shaping the doctrine and practice of the church. The council didn't just debate, argue, and vote—they let the Holy Spirit lead the way. The Holy Spirit was fulfilling His role as Teacher!

THE LEADING OF THE SPIRIT

As zealous as we should be to participate in the preaching of the gospel, I have learned that, as an individual, I cannot reach the world, but collectively, we, the body, can. Callings and anointings are specific to locations and functions. The power of God is in the "sendings" of God. There is always an accompanying anointing on both those whom the Spirits sends and where He sends them. Paul's desire was to evangelize the Roman province of Asia, but he and his team were *"forbidden by the Holy Spirit to speak the word in Asia"* (Acts 16:6 NASB95). Then Paul tried Bithynia and was again forbidden by the Spirit of Jesus. (See verse 7.) Luke associated the Holy Spirit with the Spirit of Jesus, affirming that the Son and the Spirit are divine and coequal.

In this instance with Paul, nothing dramatic was mentioned—no dreams, visions, or angelic messages. It simply says that the Spirit "forbade" Paul and his companions. The leading of the Spirit is not always loud. Then, to direct Paul to Macedonia, the Holy Spirit spoke to him in a night vision! The Spirit cannot be pigeonholed into certain channels of communication.

The same silent leading of the Spirit caused Paul to be *"greatly annoyed"* (Acts 16:18 NASB95) by the fortune-telling girl. Evidently, it was *"many days"* (verse 18) before Paul knew why he was annoyed and confronted the demons. Many times, the Spirit will speak to us through our spirit by either a sense of peace or a lack of peace. If a situation or person causes any internal agitation for seemingly no reason, that's a sign not to proceed until God gives clarity.

ACTS 29

The book of Acts ends abruptly in chapter 28 with the word *"unhindered"* (verse 31 NASB95). Acts is an unfinished book. It is still being written today by the believers of Jesus who are led by the Holy Spirit—unhindered by political, social, or geographical constraints!

PART TWO

THE HOLY SPIRIT IN THE PAULINE EPISTLES

ROMANS

Impartations and Empowerments

Romans has been called one of the most important theological documents in Christianity. It is fittingly positioned after Acts, where the gentiles were openly ushered into the church. Paul made three missionary journeys through most of the Mediterranean world, and he was largely responsible for the gospel being preached throughout the Roman Empire. In this book, Paul teaches how the gospel includes both Jews and gentiles. Romans weaves the Jews and the gentiles together into righteous sonship offered through faith in Christ.

IMPARTATIONS FROM THE SPIRIT

What Paul expressed as a desire *"to see you so that I may impart some spiritual gift to you, that you may be established"* (Romans 1:11 NASB95) was really the heart of the Spirit in His ongoing ministry to the church. *Impartations are a function of the Spirit.* I love the fact that, in a real way, the Spirit meets us today in the Epistles, teaching us new-creation truths and imparting to us spiritual endowments and manifestations. This ministry of the Spirit, expressed through Paul and the other early leaders, continues today through the fivefold ministries (see Ephesians 4:11) that the Spirit has raised up throughout the earth. The Spirit is *still* seeing, imparting to, and establishing us.

Impartations come *from* the Spirit and by His ongoing ministry through men and women on whom the anointing rests. *It takes an anointing to impart the anointing.*

The impartations of the Spirit are not just outward manifestations of "*signs and wonders, through the power of the Spirit of God*" (Romans 15:19 NIV) but also *initially* inward deposits of love (see Romans 5:5; 15:30) and of "*righteousness, peace and joy in the Holy Spirit*" (Romans 14:17 NIV). The Spirit works in us today so that "*the God of hope* [may] *fill* [us] *with all joy and peace as* [we] *trust in him, so that* [we] *may overflow with hope by the power of the Holy Spirit*" (Romans 15:13 NIV). The Spirit works quietly and deeply within us so that He can manifest loudly through us!

I have received indirect impartations from ministers whom I have never met but whose books and messages I have studied and whom I have financially partnered with and prayed for. I have also received direct impartations from ministers whom I knew personally and had the honor of ministering with and serving.

Impartations are one of the Spirit's ways of adding to our spiritual arsenal.

EMPOWERED TO SERVE

Here is what I wrote about spiritual gifts in my book *Releasing the Miraculous*:

> In Romans 12:6–8, we see that the Father gave the Church seven gifts:
>
> > "*Having then gifts differing according to the grace that is given to us, let us use them: if prophecy, let us prophesy in proportion to our faith; or ministry, let us use it in our ministering; he who teaches, in teaching; he who exhorts, in exhortation; he who gives, with liberality; he who leads, with diligence; he who shows mercy, with cheerfulness.*" [NKJV]
>
> In Ephesians 4:11, we see Jesus giving the Church five gifts:

> *"And he gave some, apostles; and some, prophets; and some, evangelists; and some, pastors and teachers"* (KJV).

> In First Corinthians 12:8–10, we see the Spirit giving the Church nine gifts:

> *"For to one is given the word of wisdom through the Spirit, to another the word of knowledge through the same Spirit, to another faith by the same Spirit, to another gifts of healings by the same Spirit, to another the working of miracles, to another prophecy, to another discerning of spirits, to another different kinds of tongues, to another the interpretation of tongues."* [NKJV]

> As believers, we belong to a gift-giving family!

> The gifts of the Father mentioned in Romans 12 are primarily for the strengthening of the local church.

> The gifts of Jesus mentioned in Ephesians are for the local church, the Body of Christ at large, and the world in general.

> The gifts of the Spirit mentioned in First Corinthians 12 are for both the local church and the world.[11]

The seven gifts listed in Romans 12 are foundational, motivational, and serving manifestations. A believer's gifts form part of their spiritual makeup and seemingly flow out seamlessly through their personality. Although these "gifts of the Father" are not the 1 Corinthians 12 "gifts of the Spirit," it takes the Holy Spirit to deposit, develop, and display them through the life of a believer. It takes the Holy Spirit to manifest *anything* from God to and through us. The anointing of the Spirit on the life of the believer is always necessary to manifest any aspect of God's nature or power. *The Holy Spirit is always the Activator of anything God has for us!*

As I indicated, in these manifestations, the Spirit deposits the Father's gifts in us so deeply—often through our personality and character traits—that they seem part of our everyday expressions of life and service. These manifestations are one of the ways in which the Spirit involves Himself in our natural makeup. Because these gifts are so intricately a part of our personality, their spiritual root can be overlooked. If we do not yield these

11. James Tan, *Releasing the Miraculous* (Shippensburg, PA: Harrison House Publishers, 2020), 22–23.

"personality gifts" to the Spirit so He can develop them in us, they can appear to be an aberration in our personality. For example, those who have the gift of leading can many times come across as "bossy" if they don't allow the personality of the Spirit (see Galatians 5:22–23) to be developed within their spirit. Similarly, those who are gifted to give must develop wisdom so that they don't abuse their giving or use it to control others. *Each gift requires growth.*

THE EIGHTH CHAPTER OF ROMANS

I have basked in Romans 8 for years! It is *so rich* in Spirit-sonship theology.

When walking in the Spirit, the believer, the one who is in Christ Jesus, has *"no condemnation"* because *"the law of the Spirit of life in Christ Jesus"* makes us free from *"the law of sin and of death"* (Romans 8:1–2 NASB95).

It is the Holy Spirit who activates the benefits of the Sonship sacrifice of Jesus in the life of believers. To be a son or daughter of God is to live in *"the law of the Spirit of life in Christ Jesus"*; it is to be set free from *"the law of sin and of death."*

The blood of Jesus opened the way to life, and the Spirit transported us to that life. I once asked the Spirit what it meant to "walk in the Spirit." He showed me that it was simply to walk in His ways over mine. When we choose faith over fear, we are walking in the Spirit. When we choose love over hate, we are walking in the Spirit. Walking in the Spirit means choosing to live in God's precepts over our own preferences.

Verses 5–8 tell us that setting our minds on the things of the Spirit elevates us to live in the Spirit. We can have the very thoughts of God! Actually, we *must* have the thoughts of God if we are to live in the Spirit.

Here's why having our minds renewed, tuned to God's mind, is important: God's actions are a results of God's thoughts. Our actions are a result of our thoughts. God's actions and reactions in and through us are a result of God's thoughts being manifested in and through us.

Man's thoughts come from the carnal mind, which leads to death. God's thoughts originate from the spiritual mind, the mind of the Spirit, which leads to life and peace. (See verse 6.) This is the mind that God offers us: His very own!

Our soul consists of our will, emotions, intellect, memory, and imagination. We see how the Spirit wants to be imbued into the various aspects of our soul.

We should not restrict the Spirit's activity in our life to our spirit in salvation and to our body in healing or protection. We are a three-part being! We are a spirit, we have a soul, and we live in a body. We need to allow the Holy Spirit to work in all three parts of our makeup.

THE SPIRIT IN US...AND US IN THE SPIRIT!

> *However, you are not **in the flesh** but **in the Spirit**, if indeed the Spirit of God dwells in you.* (Romans 8:9 NASB95)

I think that many Spirit-filled believers have often confused being "*in the Spirit*" with participating in a particularly anointed service where the Spirit was in manifestation or with a personally impacting experience with the Lord. These believers tend to equate being in the Spirit with ecstatic spiritual encounters. For sure, there are anointed services and ecstatic experiences to be had in the Spirit, but the Spirit realm is not a revolving door where we are sometimes in the Spirit but most times out. There are times when we are more aware of the Spirit and yielded to Him, but, scripturally, as far as God is concerned, all believers are in the Spirit all the time because all believers have the Spirit dwelling in them to some measure. God sees us as seated in heavenly places in Christ. (See Ephesians 2:6.)

How could we have the Spirit *in us* but then not *be in* the Spirit?

How much more "in the Spirit" can we get than being seated with Christ in the heavenlies?

These are God's thoughts that the Spirit offers us!

Rather than wait for an occasion so we can say we were in the Spirit, we need to let the Spirit help us to develop an awareness that we are in the Spirit all the time—and that, because we are, we have access to all that is in the heavenly realm.

Maintaining my thought life in accordance with Romans 8:9 has helped me to stand in faith and see many a mountain move out of my way!

THE SPIRIT GIVES LIFE TO GOD'S CHILDREN

> *And if the Spirit of him who raised Jesus from the dead is living in you, he who raised Christ from the dead will also give life to your mortal bodies because of his Spirit who lives in you.* (Romans 8:11 NIV)

Continuing the same thought of the indwelling Spirit in the life of a believer, we now see that the Spirit gives life to our mortal physical body. *The only kind of life that the Holy Spirit can give us is the God-kind of life because that is the only kind He has.* This means that *both* divine healing and divine health are available. Healing is good, but health is better! Receiving healing today is simply a corrective manifestation back toward God's original intent for our earthly body. Walking in divine heath is a preview of our future heavenly state. Obviously, in this fallen earth and atmosphere, there is a limit to our time in our current physical body, but since we are spiritual beings, with the Holy Spirit living inside us, we are able to tap into the Spirit realm.

> *For those who are led by the Spirit of God are the children of God. The Spirit you received does not make you slaves, so that you live in fear again; rather, the Spirit you received brought about your adoption to sonship. And by him we cry, "Abba, Father." The Spirit himself testifies with our spirit that we are God's children.* (Romans 8:14–16 NIV)

The way we receive anything from the Holy Spirit is by His leading us back to what is rightly ours as children of God. The Holy Spirit in us is the Spirit of adoption because He dwells only in God's children. The Holy Spirit is *always* leading us to, reminding us about, and revealing to us our sonship because our sonship is the basis for everything that God has for us. While the Holy Spirit certainly can and does communicate clearly and sometimes loudly through external and demonstrative means, His primary means of communication with us is by gently "testifying with our spirit." This means He communicates internally for the simple scriptural fact that that is where He dwells! As believers, we need to learn to "look inside" because that is where our Helper is.

The Holy Spirit points us to our sonship—not to our sins. This does not mean that He condones wrongdoing in our life or that He leaves us to continue in sin but that He brings us back to our true identity and reminds us that, because we are God's children, sin is beneath us; we are from a higher realm.

Reminding us of our sonship is no "minor" ministry because creation is eagerly awaiting our revealing! (See Romans 8:19.)

THE INTERCESSOR

> *In the same way, the Spirit helps us in our weakness. We do not know what we ought to pray for, but the Spirit himself intercedes for us through wordless groans. And he who searches our hearts knows the mind of the Spirit, because the Spirit intercedes for God's people in accordance with the will of God.* (Romans 8:26–27 NIV)

True intercession, like everything else in our life, is not birthed out of good intentions or out of observing a need but by the Spirit of God working in us. Intercession is standing in the stead of another and presenting their case before God. In a place of true intercession, the Holy Spirit prays with and through us in bringing forth the plans of God on the earth. Because intercession involves peoples and places besides ourselves, it is the Spirit alone who knows the true situation, and so He alone knows what truly needs to be prayed about. Too many times, well-meaning believers have prayed according to their limited knowledge of situations, and however well-intended those prayers may be, they fall short because they originate from sense knowledge. The Helper seeks to assist the church in what is arguably our most important function on earth: prayer!

There are times in intercession when mere words cannot convey the intensity of the spiritual exchange taking place. The most that our physical body can do in that situation is to groan under the weight of it. There is genuine groaning in the Spirit, just as there is genuine laughing, weeping, and singing in the Spirit. Actually, many emotions and reactions that we have in the natural are also possible in the Spirit because the natural man is only a reflection of the deeper spirit-man. Groaning in the Spirit, like true intercession, is not birthed by our will but by our yielding. Just as a woman necessarily groans in the birthing process, intercession, because it is a part of birthing the plans of God on the earth, can sometimes become so intense that groaning is the only possible response. It is only *after* Spirit-led intercession that *"all things work together for good"* (verse 28, various translations).

THE SPIRIT IS ALL OVER ROMANS

You can see why I said I have basked in Romans 8! Actually, there is much of the Holy Spirit to see in this book. I am sorely tempted to agree with Martin Luther, who wrote in his commentary on Romans that this letter is truly the most important piece of the New Testament.

1 CORINTHIANS

Concerning Spirituals...

This book of Scripture is known for Paul's listing of spiritual gifts and manifestations of the Holy Spirit through believers (chapters 12 and 14), and for the "love chapter" (chapter 13), which is a mainstay Scripture reading at weddings around the world.

Of course, the Holy Spirit is the Source of both gifts and love. And both are interdependent. The love of God meets and ministers to mankind through spiritual gifts, and spiritual gifts work best from a position of love.

In writing this epistle, Paul was resolving doctrinal and practical problems that had arisen within the church at Corinth. Typical of apostolic ministry, Paul first established the church and then continued a relationship with it after his departure. Hearing disturbing reports about moral and spiritual misconduct within the Corinthian church while he was at Ephesus, he started a series of correspondences with the congregation. Of Paul's three letters to this church, two have been preserved. What we know in our Bible as 1 Corinthians is actually Paul's second letter to these believers.

PREACHING DEEP THINGS

> *My message and my preaching were not with wise and persuasive words, but with a demonstration of the Spirit's power.... These are the things God has revealed to us by his Spirit. The Spirit searches all things, even the deep things of God. For who knows a person's thoughts except their own spirit within them? In the same way no one knows the thoughts of God except the Spirit of God. What we have received is not the spirit of the world, but the Spirit who is from God, so that we may understand what God has freely given us.*
>
> (1 Corinthians 2:4, 10–12 NIV)

Ministry in general and teaching and preaching in particular are operations of the Spirit that occur through the spirit of the one ministering to the spirits of the ones receiving the ministry. Ministry is a spiritual transaction, meant to produce, at least initially, spiritual results.

In His ministry, the Spirit searches and reveals the deep things of God. We can see "*deep things*" in two ways, both of which I believe are applicable to us as believers. First, in contrast to man's wisdom, the things of God are deep. A motivational speaker or a college professor might impart facts and information, but that type of communication alone does not have the power to change someone's heart toward the things of God. The deep things of God touch people in their deepest core, their spirit-man. Second, it is only the Spirit Himself who can lead us toward the deep things of God. This implies that there are degrees to the things of God and that it takes His leading and guidance for us to get from the milk to the meat of His ways. The Spirit can take a verse that we think we know, that we have studied and perhaps have even taught to others, and show us aspects of it that make what we used to know about it seem shallow! God's will is for us to receive His "*deep things.*"

KNOWING SPIRITUALS

> *Now concerning spiritual* **gifts**, *brethren, I do not want you to be ignorant.* (1 Corinthians 12:1 NKJV)

In many translations of the Bible, the word "*gifts*" in this verse is italicized in the otherwise Roman text of the Bibles. That's because this word was not in the original Greek but was added by the translators for clarity. So we could read this verse as, "Now concerning spirituals,...I do not want you to be ignorant."

This is a great truth. We can choose *not* to be ignorant of spiritual things. This means we can learn about spiritual manifestations and thus flow better with them. And, since we are told not to be ignorant, we can say that ignorance about spiritual things is often a choice. Both the Word and the Spirit are available to teach and train us in the matters and ways of God. The ways of God are available to be found by those who seek to find them!

> *Therefore I want you to know that no one who is speaking by the Spirit of God says, "Jesus be cursed," and no one can say, "Jesus is Lord," except by the Holy Spirit.* (1 Corinthians 12:3 NIV)

Our initiation into spiritual things started with our acknowledgment of Jesus as Lord, and this was not the result of a decision we made; rather, it was our response to the unseen wooing of the Holy Spirit. There are many different avenues by which we might have come to a saving knowledge of Jesus; but, behind it all, it was the Spirit Himself empowering us to call on Jesus as Lord. So we see that the Holy Spirit was vitally and intricately involved in our life even before we identified ourselves as believers. It takes the Holy Spirit for us to see Jesus for who He is.

ONE SPIRIT

> *There are different kinds* ["*diversities*" NKJV] *of gifts, but the same Spirit distributes them.... For we were all baptized by one Spirit so as to form one body—whether Jews or Gentiles, slave or free—and we were all given the one Spirit to drink.* (1 Corinthians 12:4, 13 NIV)

The Holy Spirit is diversely unified. There is no aspect of our life as believers that the Holy Spirit is not actively initiating and in which He is not empowering us. As a member of the Godhead, the Spirit is our All in All. Part of our "not being ignorant" of spiritual things is knowing that our reliance on the Holy Spirit is more necessary than we know!

Not only was Paul writing to teach us the diversity of spiritual operations, but he was also showing us that while the body of Christ is multifaceted in scope and range of expression, there is really only one Holy Spirit who knits the whole body together; it is He who empowers each part of the body to function in the way that they do to the extent that they yield to Him and allow Him to. Because the Corinthian church did not understand this, there were schisms among them. (See 1 Corinthians 1:10–13.) True unity in the body starts with our recognizing that we are woven together by one Spirit. Without an understanding of the Spirit's active but varied function in each part of the body, all efforts toward unity can stem only from the soulish intentions of man. The body of Christ is a spiritual organism before it is anything else, and any attempt to try to redefine it otherwise will fall short of God's best.

NINE DISTINCT MANIFESTATIONS

I have written extensively about the nine gifts of the Spirit listed in 1 Corinthians 12:7–11 in my book *Releasing the Miraculous: Walking in All Nine Gifts of the Holy Spirit*. Each gift deserves a deeper look than I can afford to get into here. It is vital to remember that like everything else that is initiated by the Spirit, these manifestations are spiritual in nature and not just "natural" talents. Thus, the gifts of different kinds of tongues and the interpretation of tongues do not refer to just the ability to learn and speak different languages. Neither do the gifts of the word of wisdom and the word of knowledge apply to someone who is academically inclined or street-smart. Of course, I am not saying that being able to learn languages or being book smart or street-smart is not profitable but simply that those are not the spiritual manifestations listed here.

As believers, we err any time we make something spiritual natural, and something natural spiritual.

We are told in no uncertain terms that *"the manifestation of the Spirit is given for the common good"* (1 Corinthians 12:7 NIV). Many a segment of the body of Christ suffers loss and deficit because they have stifled these manifestations. The things of the Spirit are for our good, if we allow them to be!

2 CORINTHIANS

Guarantee of Life

Not only did Paul's initial epistles to the Corinthians not resolve the issues this church was facing, but opposition to Paul's apostleship was intensified. He attempted a trip to Corinth (see 2 Corinthians 12:14) but was met with even more hostility. This epistle, written after Paul returned to Ephesus, was a firm assertion of his apostolic office and authority.

OUR GUARANTEE

> *Now it is God who makes both us and you stand firm in Christ. He anointed us, set his seal of ownership on us, and put his Spirit in our hearts as a deposit, guaranteeing what is to come.*
>
> (2 Corinthians 1:21–22 NIV)

The Spirit, who was given to live in us as believers, is a deposit or guarantee of our eternity with God. Since the eternal Spirit now lives in us, we have His eternal wellspring from which to draw! The Spirit is our guarantee of both eternal life and all the benefits of eternal life. The Spirit in us is God's seal that our healing, deliverance, provision, and protection are guaranteed. The Spirit seals us to God and guarantees that God's life flows through us today. The enemy cannot claim any part of us because God has already sealed us to Himself by His Spirit.

Paul continued his theme of the Spirit's being the guarantee of our eternal state with God when he wrote that we are not naked but have the promise of being clothed with a heavenly dwelling. (See 2 Corinthians 5:2.) The Spirit is our *"deposit, guaranteeing"* (2 Corinthians 5:5 NIV) that we are more than this temporal body! Just as *"deep calls to deep"* (Psalm 42:7, various translations), so also the eternal Spirit in us calls to eternity.

MINISTERS OF LIFE

> *He has made us competent as ministers of a new covenant—not of the letter but of the Spirit; for the letter kills, but the Spirit gives life.*
> (2 Corinthians 3:6 NIV)

One sure way to identify Spirit-led ministers is this: they bring us into and remind us of the new covenant. New-covenant ministry centers on the finished work of Jesus and our being seated in heavenly places with Him. New-covenant ministry reminds us of who we are in Christ and what is available to us because we are! This does not mean that we ignore or dismiss the Old Testament Scriptures, but it does mean that we read and study the thirty-nine books of the Old Testament through the filter of the New Testament. The Spirit gives life through the ministry of new-covenant ministers because it is only in the new covenant, through the sacrifice of Jesus, that true life is made available to us.

The Word of God must be present *"not of the letter but of the Spirit."* Religiously rigid preaching produces death. When man interprets the Word through his own intellectual lenses and prejudices, not making room for the Spirit to breathe life on his understanding, the result is always legalistic. Legalism makes no room for the Spirit. Legalism stands firmly on its own set of rules and regulations, by which it judges everyone else. And, invariably, those whom legalism judges fall short. The judgment of legalism is always death, alienation from God. Legalism says, "Strain upward to my standards, and, possibly, God may accept you." The Spirit always points us to the finished work of Jesus so that we may see His perfection instead of looking at our imperfection. The Spirit gives life!

> *Now the Lord is the Spirit, and where the Spirit of the Lord is, there is freedom.* (2 Corinthians 3:17 NIV, ESV)

The contrast between the letter of the law and the Spirit is the contrast between bondage and freedom. The fruit of new-covenant ministry is freedom! I have learned to look for a sense of freedom and lightness whenever I attend a gathering where the Word has been shared.

THE COMMUNION OF THE SPIRIT

> *The grace of the Lord Jesus Christ, and the love of God, and the communion of the Holy Spirit be with you all. Amen.*
> (2 Corinthians 13:14 NKJV)

Paul closed this epistle by speaking grace, love, and communion over the Corinthians. Just as we have received the grace of Jesus and the love of the Father, we can have the communion of the Spirit. And if we can have the communion of the Spirit, then we can also have communion *with* the Spirit. If believers are untaught in the Word, they may see the Father and Jesus as more tangible and "real" than the Holy Spirit. But just as we can relate to the Father and to Jesus, we can relate to and have communion with the Holy Spirit.

By learning about the Holy Spirit, as we have in this book, we have in a real way started strengthening our communion with Him. The "communion of the Holy Spirit" includes communication with and from Him. The more we know about Him, the better we will be at recognizing and trusting Him when He communicates with us. The Holy Spirit has actually been seeking communion with us all our life. Part of that communication is that He gives us a desire to study Him and to know Him more—again, as we have been doing here. We are not just studying to know Him, but we are studying because He has drawn us to Him. And as we yield to His drawing us to study Him, we are not left to our own devices because He is actively involved in teaching us. In communing with Him, we know Him. In knowing Him, we have life!

GALATIANS

Freedom from Foolishness

Galatia was not a city but a region, so this is a unique epistle because it is not addressed to a specific church but to a group of churches.

This letter shows Paul in his apostolic element. A rogue group of legalists, called the Judaizers, had infiltrated the churches and taught that believers were still under certain Old Testament laws. These Judaizers did not outwardly deny faith in Jesus, but they did insist that faith in Jesus alone was not sufficient. To that faith, they added the observance of elements of the Mosaic law. And in doing so, they rendered the sacrifice of Jesus incomplete.

This so upset and grieved Paul that he used the strongest possible language found in any of his epistles to condemn them. (See Galatians 1:6–9.) It is telling that Paul did not use such strong language when he confronted the immorality in Corinth. Certainly, this did not mean that Paul tolerated immorality. He clearly classified it as sin. (See 1 Corinthians 6:18.) But Paul was swift to ensure that the Galatians knew in no uncertain terms that what the Judaizers were promoting was a clear departure from the faith. The Judaizers were not just believers who were living in sin—they were not believers, and they and their message were accursed, period. (See Galatians 1:8–9.) Attempting to lead believers back to an observance of the law pitted the Judaizers contrary to the liberty that the Spirit brings.

THE SPIRIT IS FREELY GIVEN

> *I would like to learn just one thing from you: Did you receive the Spirit by the works of the law, or by believing what you heard? Are you so foolish? After beginning by means of the Spirit, are you now trying to finish by means of the flesh?... So again I ask, does God give you his Spirit and work miracles among you by the works of the law, or by your believing what you heard?* (Galatians 3:2–3, 5 NIV)

Continuing his theme of keeping the sacrifice of Jesus complete, free from obligations to the Mosaic law, Paul went on to emphasize that the Spirit, accepted by faith, was given freely. We receive the Spirit, who is the seal of our salvation, through our faith and not by any work of the law. We can *learn* to collaborate with the Holy Spirit, but we cannot *earn* being inhabited by the Holy Spirit!

We did not receive the Holy Spirit by our own merit, and we do not keep Him by our merit. The Spirit is received by us in the same way that salvation is offered to us: by grace, through faith. (See Ephesians 2:8.)

As I mentioned previously in *Seeing the Spirit*, some believers view the Holy Spirit as flighty and temperamental, as if He hurriedly flutters off anytime they do anything that displeases Him. If the Holy Spirit left us every time we made a mistake, then no one would ever have the Holy Spirit! The only reason we can even turn back to God after we have strayed is that He draws us (see John 6:44), and since the Holy Spirit is, functionally, the Hand of God, it is the Holy Spirit Himself who draws us back to God. We could not come to God without the ministry of the Holy Spirit. Paul reminded the Galatians that just as it took the Holy Spirit for us to initially see Jesus, it takes the Holy Spirit for us to go on seeing Jesus. *We are blind without the Holy Spirit!* He is the light by which we see everything about God.

WALKING AND BEING FRUITFUL IN THE SPIRIT

> *So I say, walk by the Spirit, and you will not gratify the desires of the flesh. For the flesh desires what is contrary to the Spirit, and the Spirit what is contrary to the flesh. They are in conflict with each other, so that you are not to do whatever you want. But if you are led by the Spirit, you are not under the law.... But the fruit of the Spirit is love, joy, peace, forbearance, kindness, goodness, faithfulness, gentleness and self-control. Against such things there is no law. Those who belong to Christ Jesus have crucified the flesh with its passions and desires. Since we live by the Spirit, let us keep in step with the Spirit.*
>
> (Galatians 5:16–18, 22–25 NIV)

Remember, we don't "*walk by the Spirit*" only when we laugh, dance, run around the room, fall prostrate, or are overcome at a particularly anointed service. We may do all those things *in response to* the Spirit, but walking in the Spirit is not an event as much as it is a lifestyle for the believer. *The fruit of the Spirit is the manifestation of God's qualities and exemplifies the way He would have us live life.* The fruit of the Spirit is heaven's response to life on earth.

Walking in the Spirit is, once more, as simple as choosing *not* to live by the actions and reactions of our "natural" self. This is where it begins. There are realms and demonstrable manifestations of the Spirit available for and through those who walk and progress in the Spirit. But it must be understood that walking in the Spirit is *not* just a spiritual, heavenly state that has no earthly consequences. We ought to stop excusing believers who are rude or pushy or belligerent when quoting Scripture, calling them "prophetic" or saying that their behavior stems from their "calling and anointing." Regardless of what gifts and callings they may have, we in the Spirit-filled community need to place as high a value on character and stability as we do on gifts and anointings. The anointing does not cause behavioral abnormalities! Rather, it is an undisciplined, unrenewed mind—it is not walking in the Spirit, not bearing the fruit of the Spirit—that produces unstable believers. Rather than make excuses for such believers, we should allow and expect discipleship and growth from them!

EPHESIANS

Prayers from the Spirit

Part of Paul's series of epistles that he wrote from prison, Ephesians is a revelation of God's plan for the church: to have the body, comprised of both Jewish and gentile believers, equipped and matured to express Christ on earth.

A SPIRIT-LED PRAYER

As he did in his epistle to the Galatians, Paul spoke in this letter of the Spirit as the seal and guarantee of our salvation. (See Ephesians 1:13–14.) So we see that this was a recurring theme by the Spirit. It is important that we know we are sealed and have the Spirit as our deposit or guarantee of all that the Father has for us!

An aspect of the Spirit's ministry that we saw in Romans 8:26 is that the Spirit makes intercession through us. Intercession is one form of prayer. As our Helper, the Spirit assists us in all forms of prayer.

> *For this reason, ever since I heard about your faith in the Lord Jesus and your love for all God's people, I have not stopped giving thanks*

> *for you, remembering you in my prayers. I keep asking that the God of our Lord Jesus Christ, the glorious Father, may give you the Spirit of wisdom and revelation, so that you may know him better. I pray that the eyes of your heart may be enlightened in order that you may know the hope to which he has called you, the riches of his glorious inheritance in his holy people, and his incomparably great power for us who believe. That power is the same as the mighty strength he exerted when he raised Christ from the dead and seated him at his right hand in the heavenly realms, far above all rule and authority, power and dominion, and every name that is invoked, not only in the present age but also in the one to come. And God placed all things under his feet and appointed him to be head over everything for the church, which is his body, the fullness of him who fills everything in every way.*
>
> (Ephesians 1:15–23 NIV)

This is a powerful, Spirit-inspired prayer that Paul did "not stop" praying for the Ephesians. There are other such Spirit-inspired prayers for the church in Ephesians 3:14–19 and Colossians 1:9–12.

The Spirit can inspire and instruct us in prayers that need to be prayed repeatedly over people and situations. I am not referring to the prayer of faith, which we mainly pray for ourselves, that we believe we receive after we have prayed once. (See, for example, Mark 11:24.) Paul's prayer in Ephesians 1 was one that he repeatedly prayed. If Paul could pray this prayer continually for the Ephesians, we can pray this prayer regularly for ourselves and others as well. These Spirit-led prayers were recorded for us for that very reason!

Paul prayed that the Ephesians would receive "*the Spirit of wisdom and revelation*" so that they might know the Father better. This does not refer to an additional "Spirit of wisdom" outside of the Holy Spirit but rather to an amplification of the Spirit's functional ministry to us. Just as we pray for the will of God, such as healing, to be received and made manifest in the lives of believers, we can pray for the functions of the Holy Spirit—such as Teacher, Guide, and Revealer—to be hungered for and amplified in the lives of believers. Prayer is our asking on earth so that heaven will make an entrance into this realm. Similarly, this prayer that Paul was inspired to pray asks that the ministry of the Spirit would have an entrance into the lives of believers. *The ministry of the Holy Spirit, in its layered, manifold fullness, is unfolded in our lives through prayer.*

Evidently, *"the eyes of* [our] *heart"* require enlightening or illuminating, being flooded with light. Without light, we are in the dark and cannot see. The Holy Spirit can bring light to various areas of our life so that we don't stumble about in the dark.

I have often thought that this prayer in Ephesians is so rich in theology and in truths about the reality of what it means to be in Christ that our hearts need enlightening to comprehend it! This is why I often pray this prayer over myself.

GRIEVING THE SPIRIT

> *And do not grieve the Holy Spirit of God, with whom you were sealed for the day of redemption.* (Ephesians 4:30 NIV)

The fact that the Spirit can be grieved implies that He has emotions and a personality, which implies that He is a Person. Again, the Holy Spirit is more than a gust of wind or a warm glow. Knowing that the Holy Spirit is a Person allows us to relate to Him in a way that we could never do if we saw Him as just an impersonal force. The Holy Spirit can be known by us personally because He is a Person!

Ephesians 4:25–32 is not a complete list of telltale signs of a lifestyle that is ungodlike, but it is a descriptive checklist of it. Paul's admonition to the Ephesians was simple: *"Follow God's example, therefore, as dearly loved children"* (Ephesians 5:1 NIV).

This might sound like a simple enough exhortation, but how do we follow God's example?

FILLED WITH THE SPIRIT, FILLED WITH GOD

There is a side of man-made religion that seeks to be like God. And like all attempts of man-made religion, it fails. Paul's admonition to follow God's example means that, first, it is possible for believers to follow the example of God; and, second, like everything else God asks of us, it will require supernatural empowerment to accomplish. Third, God, in His faithfulness, always freely supplies that supernatural empowerment before we know we have need of it. God supplied Jesus as *"the Lamb slain from the foundation of the world"* (Revelation 13:8 NKJV, KJV) before any of us were even around to know we needed a Savior. In the same way, Jesus preempted the disciples' need of power to be His witnesses before they even realized their powerlessness without the Spirit.

So, since we are invited to follow God's example, we can safely know that God has provision for us to enable us to do this.

In Ephesians 5:18–19 (NKJV), Paul prescribes, *"And do not be drunk with wine, in which is dissipation; but be filled with the Spirit, speaking to one another in psalms and hymns and spiritual songs, singing and making melody in your heart to the Lord."* As we read in Acts 19:1–7, through Paul's ministry, the believers at Ephesus had first encountered the filling of the Spirit and speaking in tongues. Yet here in Ephesians 5, Paul repeated the invitation to be filled with the Spirit. *We must keep in mind that more than one filling of the Spirit is available to us. God does not intend for us to live today with yesterday's filling.* Each day requires a fresh filling of the Spirit!

In the original language, Paul's admonition to *"be filled"* carries the idea of an ongoing occurrence, not a onetime event. Paul was telling the Ephesians to "be being filled" continually with the Spirit.

The chapter and verse divisions in the Bible were put in place sometime in the thirteenth century. So, really, Paul's correspondence to the Ephesians was just one continuous letter. In warning the believers not to grieve the Spirit, Paul had, among other things, previously instructed them to speak the truth, to not lie (see Ephesians 4:25), and to *"not let any unwholesome talk come out of* [their] *mouths, but only what is helpful for building others up according to their needs"* (verse 29 NIV). Three of his instructions had to do with words. We can grieve the Holy Spirit with our words.

Then, in the instructions he listed when he encouraged the Ephesians to follow God's example, Paul said, *"Nor should there be obscenity, foolish talk or coarse joking, which are out of place, but rather thanksgiving"* (Ephesians 5:4 NIV). Again, we see the importance that the Holy Spirit, through Paul, placed on words.

So, not surprisingly, in wanting them to *be being filled* with the Spirit, Paul told them to be sober, *"speaking to one another in psalms and hymns and spiritual songs."* Part of being filled with the Spirit is not just our speaking in tongues but our speaking in a godly way—period.

As it was with the Ephesians, our ability to follow God's example and to speak in psalms, hymns, and spiritual songs is polluted and hindered when we allow the *"unwholesome talk"* that Paul warned about. Granted, guarding the words that we speak was not the only precaution that Paul listed, but words were vital enough that Paul mentioned them throughout this epistle in relation to grieving the Spirit and following God's example.

Once more, speaking in tongues, as the Ephesians experienced in Acts 19, was just our initial encounter with the fullness of the Spirit. As we live life, we need to allow our Spirit-fullness to be maintained and refilled by continually speaking in tongues and yielding our tongue to the Spirit. We are not to be drunk with wine, but we are to be drunk with the Spirit!

The *"psalms"* that Paul mentioned here are not just the one hundred and fifty psalms in the Old Testament but spiritual poems that may not always rhyme but can be sung or spoken out. *"Hymns"* are songs of praise and worship that remind us of and are directed to God. *"Spiritual songs"* are songs that are birthed by the Spirit and that contain a revelatory element of the Word and of spiritual demonstrations.

The practice of speaking or singing psalms, hymns, and spiritual songs is not confined to those who have musical training. These are spiritual operations and do not depend on our natural abilities. Those who are musically capable may in fact sing psalms, hymns, and spiritual songs; but even those, like myself, who have no musical ability can receive psalms by the Spirit. You can speak or recite hymns and spiritual songs even if you don't sing well!

Speaking out or singing such utterances as we receive them in the Spirit is necessary to maintain a flow of the Spirit in our life.

Following God's example requires that we be full of the Spirit *and* "be being filled" with the Spirit!

HOW TO WIELD THE SWORD

> *Take...the sword of the Spirit, which is the word of God. And pray in the Spirit on all occasions with all kinds of prayers and requests.*
>
> (Ephesians 6:17–18 NIV)

The sword of the Spirit is the Word of God, but words are dormant unless they are spoken. If words are not spoken, they are only thoughts or musings. Words are only words after someone speaks them. Speaking the Word is exactly what we saw Jesus do in His wilderness encounter with Satan. Each time He was tempted, Jesus spoke the Word and banished the devil. So again, the sword of the Spirit is not wielded by thoughts. You cannot battle the fiery darts of the enemy just by thinking good thoughts. You have to counter those darts by speaking the Word. The way you tame your thoughts—both natural thoughts and the ones that the enemy tries to plant in you—is by speaking the Word out loud.

Prayer also involves words. When I was a kid, I used to hear people ask others to pray for an "unspoken prayer request." I have found that an "unspoken prayer request" can also be called an "unanswered prayer request"! When Jesus's disciples asked Him to teach them to pray, He responded with, "*When you pray,* ***say****...*" (Luke 11:2, various translations). You are not praying if you are not saying. You cannot agree with or add your faith to anything unspoken by others because it is unknown.

The sword of the Spirit and prayer involve Spirit-inspired words!

PHILIPPIANS

Fellowship and Unity

Paul established the Philippian church during his second missionary journey. (See Acts 16:12–40.) He likely wrote this letter during his first Roman imprisonment to acknowledge the Philippians' partnership with and financial generosity toward him. The Philippian believers retained a missionary zeal and were firm supporters of Paul's ministry. They enjoyed a special relationship with him that the other churches did not seem to have.

A SUPPLY FOR ALL SEASONS

> *For I know that through your prayers and God's provision of the Spirit of Jesus Christ what has happened to me will turn out for my deliverance.* (Philippians 1:19 NIV)

Despite Paul's imprisonment, this was a joyful letter. Paul understood that the prayers of this partner church and the provision of the Spirit would bring him safely through to the deliverance that he needed.

The "*Spirit of Jesus Christ*" is the Holy Spirit. When we have the Holy Spirit, we have the Spirit of Jesus. *The ministry of the Spirit today is the continuation of the ministry of Jesus through us.* Just as the Holy Spirit empowered the Man Jesus, the Holy Spirit empowers us.

The Philippians' prayers for Paul were especially potent because of their partnership with him. In praying for him, they were not just paying dutiful lip service. They received from his ministry but were also invested, practically and spiritually, in it. It was this connection, in both the natural and spiritual realms, that Paul knew could secure his deliverance in prayer. Prayer is a spiritual connection to God, primarily, *but also* to those for whom we are praying or from whom we are receiving prayer. Prayer is based on connections. Our prayers have the greatest effect when they are directed to or received from those to whom we have a covenantal connection. In intercession, there are times when the Spirit of God will connect you to people whom you have never met or don't know, and prompt you to pray for them. Prayer is a way by which the Spirit brings provision through the body to peoples and places.

There is a provision of the Spirit for every imprisonment in which the enemy tries to entrap us!

UNITY: FELLOWSHIP AND WORSHIP

In the book of Philippians, Paul wrote about the joy of fellowship and unity in ministry. Not only did he share this fellowship and unity with the Philippian church, but he also wanted the members there to experience it among themselves.

> *Therefore if there is any consolation in Christ, if any comfort of love, if any fellowship of the Spirit, if any affection and mercy, fulfill my joy by being like-minded, having the same love, being of one accord, of one mind.* (Philippians 2:1–2 NKJV)

> *For it is we who are the circumcision, we who serve God by his Spirit, who boast in Christ Jesus, and who put no confidence in the flesh.*
> (Philippians 3:3 NIV)

Paul recognized that joy came from fellowship with Jesus before it came from fellowship among the believers in the church. The *"fellowship of the Spirit,"* the unity that brings believers together corporately, is really possible only when believers fellowship with the Spirit individually. Unity within the body of Christ is not birthed just by good intentions. It is a result of a conviction from the Spirit that comes only from fellowship with the Spirit.

I once hosted a ministers' gathering in a particular region with some pastors to whose congregations I had been ministering. I had been led by the Lord to return to that region regularly, and a few pastors and churches had gathered together to support the meetings, believing for God to move in that area. At the ministers' luncheon, we talked about what we sensed the Spirit birthing in that region and how we had collectively agreed to come together on a regular basis to seek God and make space for the Spirit to move. After I had addressed the room, we opened the floor for the ministers to ask questions and make comments. One of the visiting ministers, who had not attended any of the previous meetings, spoke up and said, "I get that we are gathering when Dr. Tan is here, and God seems to be moving in birthing unity in this region among us. I don't understand why we haven't gathered before this. We need to gather regularly outside of these meetings!" He continued in that fashion, berating the group. Yet not only did he never come back to the meetings, but he never got together with any of the other ministers! You see, he had only an intellectual concept of unity. He had neither a word from the Lord nor the anointing to initiate it. And, sadly, he did not have the humility of heart to see what God was birthing and to join in with it. Maybe he saw the need in his natural mind, but he did not spend enough time with God to hear the Spirit instruct him regarding his part in it.

For believers, unity across denominational, cultural, and racial lines is a result of an internal posture of heart before God before it is manifested as an outward gathering.

Again, the *"fellowship of the Spirit"* comes from fellowship with the Spirit.

Someone who has such a heart posture of humility also, *always*, has a worshipful heart. *When we worship God in the Spirit, we hear God in the*

Spirit. Worship in the Spirit individually is a precursor to worship in the Spirit collectively. The truth is that there is only one body of Christ. It takes the Spirit to enable us to see this!

COLOSSIANS

More Prayers from the Spirit

Paul never visited the city of Colossae, but the church there was birthed as a result of his time in Ephesus. (See Acts 19:1–10; 20:31.) Epaphras, who likely founded the church (see Colossians 1:6–8; 4:12–13), sought help from Paul because false teaching had crept into the congregation.

LOVE IN THE SPIRIT

Epaphras…told us of your love in the Spirit. (Colossians 1:7–8 NIV)

This is the singular direct reference to the Holy Spirit in this epistle. Interestingly, a congregation struggling with doctrine and the deity of Christ still retained a love and respect for Paul. This was crucial because it was their relationship with Paul and the level of respect they had for him that allowed Paul the inspiration from the Spirit to write this correspondence that they needed. *God can use the relationships that we honor to honor us!*

All churches, ministries, and individual believers run into times when they need a mature, mentoring voice to speak into their lives. The church in Colossae had that voice in Paul, a man whom they had not met but had a relationship with through Epaphras. *The relationships with others that we have allow us access to the anointings that they have access to.* The Holy Spirit flows through relationships because the anointing is transferable. We need to ensure that we have qualified leaders like Epaphras in our lives. Among other things, what qualified Epaphras was that he had leaders like Paul in his life. The Spirit once instructed me in this way: "Only follow leaders who follow after other leaders!"

PAUL'S COLOSSIAN PRAYERS

> ***For this reason, since the day we heard about you, we have not stopped praying for you.*** *We continually ask God to fill you with the knowledge of his will through all the wisdom and understanding that the Spirit gives.* (Colossians 1:9 NIV)

The *"reason"* for Paul's prayers was that he had heard about the Colossians' faith, their love for God's people (see Colossians 1:4), and their *"love in the Spirit"* (verse 8). There are doorways that can open up Spirit-led prayers for us. This is a major benefit of the Spirit's ministry in our lives.

Paul's prayer in verses 9–14 resembles the prayers he prayed for the Ephesians both in content and in the frequency in which the prayer was prayed. Again, the Spirit inspired Paul to pray that God would fill the Colossians *"with the knowledge of his will through all the wisdom and understanding that the Spirit gives."* Wisdom and understanding from the Spirit are synonymous with the Holy Spirit's activity in the life of a believer. I have found that it is always right to pray for wisdom and understanding—for myself and for those to whom I minister!

1 THESSALONIANS

Joy Amid Suffering

Paul established a major church in Thessalonica. It was comprised of both Jews and gentiles, and the believers' faith was renowned. (See 1 Thessalonians 1:6–7.)

Initially in Philippi and later in Berea, the Jewish leaders and Roman officials were incensed by Paul's ministry, under which the three cities of Philippi, Thessalonica, and Berea were marked by the flame of the Spirit as well as by fierce persecution.

THE GOSPEL BRINGS JOY

> *Our gospel came to you not simply with words but also with power, with the Holy Spirit and deep conviction. You know how we lived among you for your sake. You became imitators of us and of the Lord, for you welcomed the message in the midst of severe suffering with the joy given by the Holy Spirit.* (1 Thessalonians 1:5–6 NIV)

Paul never preached the gospel just on the basis of his academic background. He also did so empowered by the Holy Spirit. The apostle was a formidable academic, but his identity as a minister was based on the leading and power of the Spirit. Presenting such a message, through such a messenger, produces believers who can endure suffering with the joy of the Holy Spirit. The Thessalonians were steadfast believers who were not swayed by the opposing winds of public opinion.

"The joy given by the Holy Spirit." The Holy Spirit imbues difficult situations with ease and joy! He is a Spirit of faith and therefore of joy. Faith is not a pained tolerance of the discomforts of life. Faith charges life with joy because faith is always victorious.

GOD GIVES YOU HIS SPIRIT

> *Therefore, anyone who rejects this instruction does not reject a human being but God, the very God who gives you his Holy Spirit.*
>
> (1 Thessalonians 4:8 NIV)

Leading up to his speaking about the return of the Lord (see 1 Thessalonians 4:13–5:11), Paul exhorted the Thessalonians about the importance of a life of purity. To the extent that a believer rejects holiness, they reject the Holy Spirit's work in their life. This does not mean that the Spirit rejects or abandons them, but when a believer chooses immorality, indulging in their fleshly senses, they dull their senses to the Spirit. Whatever "sense" we feed and indulge in dominates us. I have learned that focusing on one sense will drown out the others.

We have an invitation to choose the Spirit because the Spirit has already chosen us!

CHOOSE NOT TO QUENCH THE SPIRIT

> *Do not quench the Spirit.*
>
> (1 Thessalonians 5:19, various translations)

I always pause when I read this verse and think about what an awesome responsibility I have—that I can choose *not* to quench the Spirit of God! What a powerful image of the Spirit's gentle authority. To think that God the Holy Spirit would humble Himself to allow for the possibility that we, His creation, mere human beings, might "quench the Spirit"! This humility mirrors that of Jesus, *"who, being in very nature God, did not consider equality with God something to be used to his own advantage; rather, he made himself nothing by taking the very nature of a servant, being made in human likeness"* (Philippians 2:6–7 NIV).

As I wrote in an earlier study, God is so strong that He can afford to be gentle!

Thus, the manifestations of the Spirit are never forced on us—they are offered to us. I have met individuals who either thought that the Holy Spirit would "make" them speak in tongues or that, once they did, they would lose all control. Those are not the actions of the Holy Spirit.

It is not so much our actions that quench the Spirit as it is our choices. Our actions are always and only a result of our intentions, and God values our heart posture much more than our natural mind can comprehend. Jesus spoke out against a religious mindset's natural inclination toward settling for the formality of action over the substance of heart. (See Matthew 5:21–30.)

A Spirit-filled believer who speaks in tongues and lifts their hands during a worship service but whose mind and heart are not set on God is *not* more spiritually advanced than an earnest believer of heartfelt faith who attends a traditional church where the manifestations of the Spirit are not encouraged and flowing.

It is not just when a believer *"treat*[s] *prophecies with contempt"* (1 Thessalonians 5:20 NIV) that the Spirit is quenched; He is also quenched when a believer says, "Thus saith the Lord" when He hasn't said anything! The first ends up shutting the Spirit off, while the second makes up voices or, worse, follows demonic voices, and follows them as if they were the voice of the Holy Spirit.

Staying in a place of pliability before God, being yielded to Him, is how we keep the flame of the Spirit burning bright!

2 THESSALONIANS

Sanctified by the Spirit

Similar in language and theme—the return of the Lord—to 1 Thessalonians, Paul's second epistle to the believers in Thessalonica was likely written a few weeks after his initial correspondence to them.

First Thessalonians dealt with the question of whether the death of loved ones meant that they had missed the Lord's return. (See 1 Thessalonians 4:14–18.) In 2 Thessalonians, Paul encouraged the believers to stay steadfast in the face of persecution and hardship but, most important, not to have a lax, improper attitude toward Christ's coming. While they had withstood persecution from outside the church, they also had to withstand erroneous doctrine from within the church.

The Spirit who strengthened this church against persecution could also protect and correct it against the poison of bad doctrine, which ironically came into the church either *"by a prophecy or by word of mouth or by letter"* (2 Thessalonians 2:2 NIV)—meaning that there were either forged letters proclaiming these false doctrines or that prophetic utterances, incorrectly ascribed to the Holy Spirit, had been given to promulgate these ideas. The assault of the enemy had an open door through the people's lack of understanding of the Word and their not recognizing the voice of the true Spirit. The answer for us today is the same as it was then: we need to know the Word of God so we can recognize the voice of the Spirit! The Word and the Spirit work hand in hand for our growth and protection.

SET ASIDE FOR A SPECIAL PURPOSE

> *But we ought always to thank God for you, brothers and sisters loved by the Lord, because God chose you as firstfruits to be saved through the sanctifying work of the Spirit and through belief in the truth.*
>
> (2 Thessalonians 2:13 NIV)

Our salvation and our sanctification are a result of the ministry of the Spirit. Again, this points to the fact that while the Spirit may be the least seen and understood of the Trinity by some believers, His work in and on our behalf is tirelessly ongoing. We can depend on the faithful Spirit to save and sanctify us.

To be sanctified simply means to be set aside for a special purpose, to have one's life repositioned to be of use to God. The Holy Spirit positions and repositions us into the plan and places that God has for us. We need not strive to get into God's plan for us. In order to get into God's plan, we need to depend on the Spirit, yielding to Him and moving as He leads.

Today, in the midst of an environment that is increasingly hostile to the church and that has an abundance of scripturally lite, self-gratifying ideologies masquerading as true teaching and preaching, we must lean in for the guidance of the Spirit!

1 TIMOTHY

Spiritual Sons and Daughters

Timothy was the son of Eunice, who, together with her mother, Lois, was fruit from Paul and Barnabas's ministry in Lystra, a city of Lycaonia in Asia Minor. Even though he was raised and instructed in Judaism, Timothy's gentile father did not allow him to be circumcised.

Timothy represents a very important relationship and ministry pattern in the life of Paul. Every one of us needs a Paul above us, leading us; a Barnabas beside us, encouraging us; and a Timothy below us, whom we are raising up.

Paul's paternal relationship with Timothy gave him the spiritual authority to write to him to teach and encourage him. Paul was not just an instructor to Timothy. He was a spiritual father.

Whenever I read Paul's letters to Timothy, I am reminded that part of the purpose of all my spiritual growth and maturity is to produce spiritual sons and daughters, disciples of Jesus. This is the true purpose of the Spirit in and through us: in us, to enable us to be disciples; and through us, to enable us to make disciples.

The Lord once told me that the reason we don't see more sons and daughters in the ministry is that there is a lack of spiritual fathers. Just as families in the natural suffer when there are absentee parents, so the spiritual family lacks when we don't have fathers and mothers in the faith.

A spiritual father or mother is one whose walk with the Lord has been established by length of time and depth of relationship with the Word and the Spirit, and who has a heart big enough to selflessly embrace a younger or less mature believer.

The ongoing ministry of the Spirit is seen in the *"petitions, prayers,* [and] *intercession"* that Paul exhorted *"be made for all people"* (1 Timothy 2:1 NIV). From Paul's previous epistles, we know that such prayers are made through the Spirit's aid. (See, for example, Romans 8:26.) We need to be exhorted and reminded to pray Spirit-led prayers so we don't forget to do so and revert to soulish prayers. Spirit-led prayers point us to and produce God's desires. Soul-led prayers might be vehemently prayed, but they are made out of biased preferences.

In praying for *"all those in authority"* (verse 2), the primary goal is that a peaceful and quiet life be afforded to everyone, because it is in such an environment that the gospel is most easily proclaimed. (See verses 3–4.)

"THE SPIRIT EXPRESSLY SAYS"

> *Now the Spirit expressly says that in latter times some will depart from the faith, giving heed to deceiving spirits and doctrines of demons.*
> (1 Timothy 4:1 NKJV)

Not only does the Spirit bring us exhortation and edification, but He can also bring us warnings. Timothy was not specifically instructed to pray against those who were giving heed to deception and doctrines of demons, but he also undoubtedly knew that he had authority over demons. Regardless, as the warning declares, *"some will depart from the faith."* Intercessory prayer can and should always be made for people who are being deceived. Such prayer frees people from demonic influences, but this does not remove a person's ability or right to decide. Those who depart from the faith will "give heed to" deceiving spirits. They could just as easily decide not to give heed! Entertaining vain imaginations and pondering doubts that question God's Word and His faithfulness will soon lead to an attempt by one's human reasoning to "deconstruct" the spiritual nature of the things of God. Those who go down that path invariably never really constructed the fundamentals of the Word or the Spirit within themselves to begin with. I have often wondered how someone could deconstruct something that they had not first constructed. The enemy always offers deception. The people of God must learn to not accept his offer!

IMPARTATIONS THROUGH THE LAYING ON OF HANDS

> *Do not neglect your gift, which was given you through prophecy when the body of elders laid their hands on you.* (1 Timothy 4:14 NIV)

We can receive the infilling of the Spirit and the gifts of the Spirit through prophecy, the laying on of hands, or both. Through the laying on of hands, a *charisma*, a grace gift of the Spirit, was deposited into Timothy, and this gift equipped him for the ministry God had ordained for him.

Impartations are a spiritual reality because one way the Spirit flows into our life is through others in the body of Christ. I have laid hands on thousands of people around the world and seen this result firsthand. I have also been the grateful recipient of having hands laid on me. As much as I believe in impartations and the laying on of hands, I am cautious about whom I allow to lay hands on me. Or rather, it's *because* I believe in impartations and the laying on of hands that I don't want just anybody laying their hands on me. I make sure that those who lay hands on me have something in God that I want and need!

2 TIMOTHY

Stirred Up

Second Timothy is a tender, pointed letter from Paul to Timothy, written toward the end of Paul's life. Paul only had Luke with him at the time he wrote this letter, and he desired to see both Timothy and Mark. (See 2 Timothy 4:9–11.) Although Paul wanted Timothy to come and see him, his main concern was for the church and safeguarding the ministry.

STIR UP THE GIFT

> *That is why I would remind you to stir up (rekindle the embers of, fan the flame of, and keep burning) the [gracious] gift of God, [the inner fire] that is in you by means of the laying on of my hands.*
>
> (2 Timothy 1:6 AMPC)

It is a grievous mistake to assume that just because God wills us to have something and gives it to us, it will automatically take root in our life and bear fruit. What God gives and deposits in us can lie dormant if we neglect it.

If Timothy needed to be reminded to stir up the gift he had inside him, we would do well to do the same. I have told God that it is my intention that no gift He gives me will go "unstirred" and underutilized. The gifts God gives us contain all the supernatural supply we need for life and ministry.

We can stir up the gifts of God within us by staying in a faith-filled environment, keeping our faith active, being attentive to the promptings of the Spirit, and praying much in tongues. It makes scriptural sense that just as spiritual gifts can be deposited in us, the laying on of hands can stir up dormant deposits within us.

A SOUND MIND

> *For God hath not given us the spirit of fear; but of power, and of love, and of a sound mind.* (2 Timothy 1:7 KJV)

The Holy Spirit, in contrast to a spirit of fear, produces "*power,*" "*love,*" and "*a sound mind.*" There is no room for fear in our life when we walk in power, love, and a sound mind—all of which are available to us through the Spirit in us!

I especially love the fact that a sound mind is an aspect of the Spirit's dwelling in us. As believers, we should not be "scatterbrained" or unsociably quirky! A sound mind makes sound decisions, and sound decisions make for a stable life. From the very many media channels available to us, we have access to a peek into all kinds of lives through "reality TV": from people who hoard piles of trash at home to people who compulsively and excessively overeat. While there is obviously demonic activity involved in such compulsion, the seat of that bondage is an unsound mind. *But a sound mind closes the door to the enemy.*

Outside of a sound mind, power and love have no means of expression. The Spirit of God is the fount of a sound mind. I also believe that a sound mind is a testimony to the world. The ability to have clear, calm, precise thoughts, mirroring the thoughts of God, is both a defense against the enemy and a guide through life.

The alternative to having what is, in essence, a description of the mind of God, is having a "*spirit of fear.*" A spirit of fear acts and reacts irrationally by God's standard and in contradiction to God's Word. In a very real way, the spirit of fear is the carnal mind in action, while the sound mind is the renewed mind. (See Romans 12:2.)

God has *not* given us a spirit of fear—instead, what He has given us is power, love, and a sound mind. Just as a spirit of fear cannot be "earned" but must be allowed into someone's life, power, love, and a sound mind cannot be earned but must be received freely from the grace of God by faith.

STRENGTH TO KEEP

> *Guard and keep [with the greatest care] the precious and excellently adapted [Truth] which has been entrusted [to you], by the [help of the] Holy Spirit Who makes His home in us.* (2 Timothy 1:14 AMPC)

The things God gives and deposits in us can be received and retained only by the Holy Spirit. This is just how good God is! Not only is He the One who gives to us, but He is also the One who enables us to keep what He gives. He is truly the Beginning and the End.

Dead religion is the enemy of revelation—and it is always the result when revelation is received from the Spirit but is then attempted to be understood, processed, and maintained by the mind of man and the arm of flesh. We see this outcome in some sectors of mainline Protestant denominations today. They have strayed so far from the truths that their founders received by revelation, and that their denominations began with in a burst of the Spirit, that if their founders were alive today, they would not even recognize them.

It takes the Spirit to keep what the Spirit gives us because the arm of flesh cannot hold on to what the Spirit offers us!

TITUS

Regeneration and Renewal

Titus was Greek and another of Paul's spiritual sons. He was trusted by Paul and hand-delivered the epistle that we know as 2 Corinthians to the Corinthian church.

As Paul did with Timothy, he encouraged and instructed Titus in leading the churches of which he had oversight. Specifically, Paul wrote to Titus about organization, doctrine, and works that showcased the work of the Spirit. Titus was instructed to ordain elders in every city, similar to the way in which prophets, kings, and priests were consecrated and ordained in the Old Testament.

The act of ordaining ministers to the work of God alone is an indication of the Spirit's ministry. It takes the Spirit to call and empower someone to leadership in the church, it takes the Spirit for us to recognize that they are called, and it takes the Spirit to establish them as an elder. Ministry is a Spirit-inspired, Spirit-led, and Spirit-sustained activity!

SPIRIT-LED CORRECTION

Immediately after Titus appointed elders (see Titus 1:5), Paul wanted the elders to bring correction to the Cretans (see verses 10–16.) The Cretans were an admittedly unruly group of people who were *"liars, evil brutes, lazy gluttons"* (verse 12 NIV). It has always struck me that before Paul sought to bring correction to the Cretans, he told Titus to appoint elders. *It takes Spirit-led leadership to bring needed Spirit-led correction.*

It is the anointing of the Spirit that breaks the yoke of bondage. The Cretans did not just make mistakes in their lifestyle choices, but their whole culture and societal orientation were of continual unsoundness. They did not just make the occasional slips in behavior—they were bound by a cycle of depravity so that *"both their minds and consciences* [were] *corrupted"* (verse 15 NIV). Paul knew they would not be set free with just a well-intentioned, stern rebuke. It would take elders, appointed by the Spirit, flowing in the anointing of that position, to bring correction to them.

The ills of society are the results of the choices of unregenerate man. It takes more than just good policies to rectify the problems of society. It takes elders in the city, raised and anointed by the Spirit, to break the cycle of generational degradation with which the enemy has shackled cultures. It takes the church rising up in the power of the Spirit to confront the prevailing spirits of bondage.

William and Catherine Booth, founders of the Salvation Army, are examples of elders raised up by God to confront alcoholism, immorality, and the neglect of the family. What they originally birthed in the East End of London eventually spread to become an international work. They went beyond what politicians or social reformers were able to accomplish—not just righting the wrongs of society but righting the wrongs of the hearts of man with the gospel.

I see English parliamentarian William Wilberforce as another example of an elder who was raised up by God to confront a society that had forsaken God. Driven by his biblical beliefs, Wilberforce roared against slavery and contributed to the abolition of the slave trade.

It takes men and women called and anointed by the Spirit to bring a course correction to any society that hell has bound!

NOT OUR WORKS BUT HIS

> *He saved us, not on the basis of deeds which we have done in righteousness, but according to His mercy, by the washing of regeneration and renewing by the Holy Spirit.* (Titus 3:5 NASB95)

The Lord once showed me that I had learned to depend on Him to do the work of the ministry, but if I wanted to run my race to its completion, then I also had to learn to depend on Him to regenerate and renew me. Not learning to do this is the cause of what is commonly called burnout and fatigue. Regardless of our zeal and good intentions, human effort will get us only so far in the things of God. *It takes the Spirit to walk in the Spirit. He is both the Source and the Strength of our walk with Him.* What is begun in the Spirit must also be maintained by the Spirit.

The work of the ministry and, in fact, any aspect of our life as believers can be sustained only by having an ongoing walk with the Spirit. We who are Spirit-born must be Spirit-nourished. Trust in the Spirit's ability to regenerate and renew you!

PHILEMON

Embraced in God

Philemon was a wealthy slave owner who had likely been born again under Paul's ministry in Colossae. One of his slaves, Onesimus, had run away after engaging in theft of, or having caused some damage to, Philemon's property. In Rome, Onesimus came in contact with Paul while the apostle was imprisoned, and he was led to Christ.

This epistle was written from Paul's Spirit-led desire to see true reconciliation and a reordering of the relationship between slave owner and runaway slave, now both equally redeemed brothers in the Lord (see Galatians 3:28) and both equally responsible for their actions (see Ephesians 6:5–9). Through the Spirit, there could be forgiveness and acceptance.

The Spirit's aim in this epistle was to have Philemon wholly embrace Onesimus as a brother in Christ. This is the standard of all true Christian unity—that, at the foot of the cross, all mankind was found equally in need of a Savior; that, at the empty tomb, all mankind was equally offered a resurrection; and that, in the upper room, all mankind was equally offered a fresh encounter with the Spirit!

In this letter, we see that the body of Christ is truly one, *"accepted in the Beloved"* (Ephesians 1:6 NKJV).

The inward working of the Spirit in the life and character of a believer is seen throughout the book of Philemon. The ability to seek and grant forgiveness, to see others as God sees them, and to reconcile with others—these are all attributes of the life of a believer indwelled by the Spirit.

PART THREE

THE HOLY SPIRIT IN THE GENERAL EPISTLES AND REVELATION

HEBREWS

Better Than!

Although the human author of Hebrews is unnamed, it is believed by some scholars that this book was authored by Paul. Written to strengthen wavering Jewish believers, Hebrews is rich in doctrine; it declares the overwhelming superiority of Jesus over all that was offered under the old covenant. Jesus is contrasted with and found better than the prophets, angels, Moses, Joshua, and all of ritualistic Judaism.

Hebrews points to Jesus as—simply—better! (See, for example, Hebrews 12:24.) Part of the better covenant we have in the New Testament is that we have a better High Priest in the person of Jesus. (See Hebrews 4:14–16.) In Old Testament times, the high priest was a symbolic type of a mediator between God and man. In the New Testament era, we have the Son of God Himself as our Mediator.

THE WITNESS OF GIFTS

> *God also testifying with them, both by signs and wonders and by various miracles and by gifts of the Holy Spirit according to His own will.*
>
> (Hebrews 2:4 NASB95)

In the natural, we understand that no gift is without some form of outward evidence. If someone were to give you a gift of a new car, you would have physical evidence of that car. Similarly, the gifts of the Spirit come with outward evidence. "*Signs and wonders and…various miracles*" all point to some practical, physical tangibility. Even if a miracle was one of an inward nature, such as peace or freedom from depression, there would still be some outward, external evidence of it.

There is an aspect of the things of the Spirit that testifies to those around us. Receiving the Spirit Himself as a gift is not a silent, secret event. The new birth is an inward work that has outward fruit. We ought to be recognizable to others as believers even when we are not talking to people about Jesus or offering to pray for them. The Light in us ought to shine through us!

So, being a witness is not just something we do but what we are. We are not just to be witnessing, but we are to be witnesses. This is the function of the Spirit in our lives. He empowers us to be witnesses for Jesus. (See Acts 1:8.)

This was especially important for the Hebrew believers to remember because they were tempted to go back to Judaism due to the persecution they were facing. Believers can depend on the Holy Spirit to enable them to stand for the things of God in a world that is set against God.

THE SPIRIT SAYS!

Even though the author of Hebrews twice proclaims that the new covenant is better (see Hebrews 7:22; 8:6), before he quotes the Old Testament, he references the Holy Spirit as the One who did the speaking (see Hebrews 3:7–11; 10:15–17). This immediately demonstrates that it is the same Spirit who inspired both Testaments. As we have repeatedly seen in this book, there is but one Holy Spirit!

Since the Spirit inspired the Old Testament as well as the New Testament, we are not to prefer one Testament over the other in our approach to it as the Word of God. However, because of the progressive nature of revelation and God's plan of redemption, it is important to know that the Spirit had to speak in increments of revelation leading up to the appearing of the Messiah and then again after the completeness of Calvary.

In other words, there were things the Spirit could not reveal fully in the Old Testament before Jesus came, and there were things the followers of Jesus in the Gospels could not grasp until after Jesus ascended and was seated at the right hand of God. (See, for example, Hebrews 1:3; 12:2.) This is why reading and studying all the Epistles (Romans to Jude) and especially Paul's letters are crucial to our growth and development as believers. The New Testament epistles bring the Old Testament Scriptures into perspective and clarity. The Gospels point to Jesus as the Lamb prophesied about in the Old Testament. The Epistles reveal the heavenly inner workings of our redemption that are not revealed anywhere else. In a very real way, the Epistles are the "advanced teachings" of Jesus that He was not able to tell the disciples about while He lived among them. (See John 16:12–14.)

THE TEACHER TEACHES

> *The Holy Spirit is signifying this, that the way into the holy place has not yet been disclosed while the outer tabernacle is still standing.*
>
> (Hebrews 9:8 NASB95)

Not only is the Spirit the Divine Author of Scripture, but He is also the Divine Interpreter of spiritual truth. Since He is the Author of both Testaments, He seamlessly ties them together to show us how "the New is in the Old concealed, and the Old is in the New revealed," as famously expressed by Saint Augustine.[12]

The interpretation and comprehension of the Word go beyond our mental and intellectual capacities. It takes the Spirit to illuminate the Word to us.

Until the Holy Spirit illuminated the Old Testament practices and articles in the light of Jesus and His completed work, for most people, the Old Testament was shrouded in practices with unknown principles. It took the Holy Spirit, inspiring the New Testament writings, to illuminate the Old Testament writings. The Word is the best commentary on the Word because the Spirit is the Author of the Word!

---

12. Augustine discusses this idea in several places in his writings. See "Reference for This 'New Is in the Old Concealed' Quote That Is Attributed to Augustine?" Christianity, Stack Exchange, https://christianity.stackexchange.com/questions/68916/reference-for-this-new-is-in-the-old-concealed-quote-that-is-attributed-to-aug.

PART AND PARCEL OF OUR SALVATION

> *For in the case of those who have once been enlightened and have tasted of the heavenly gift and have been made partakers of the Holy Spirit....* (Hebrews 6:4 NASB95)

Calling on Jesus as Lord and Savior, being born again, opens us up to being made "*partakers of the Holy Spirit.*" Just as we need to continually look to Jesus as the "*author and finisher of our faith*" (Hebrews 12:2 NKJV, KJV), we do not partake of the Holy Spirit only once, at our spiritual rebirth, but we need to continually partake of and from the Spirit. It is the ministry of the Spirit to make Jesus real to us. We see Jesus as we partake of the Spirit!

When we partake of the Spirit, we partake of His power and His personality. And since there is perfect consistency within the Trinity, that also means we partake of God the Father and Jesus the Son's power and personality!

> *How much more will the blood of Christ, who through the eternal Spirit offered Himself without blemish to God, cleanse your conscience from dead works to serve the living God?* (Hebrews 9:14 NASB95)

Traditionally and rightly, Jesus is the focus when we talk about Calvary, but it is important to remember that it was "*through the eternal Spirit*" that Jesus's sacrifice was made. So again, we see that the Spirit was not dormant in any aspect of our redemption.

LONG-SUFFERING AND MERCIFUL

> *How much severer punishment do you think he will deserve who has trampled under foot the Son of God, and has regarded as unclean the blood of the covenant by which he was sanctified, and has insulted the Spirit of grace?* (Hebrews 10:29 NASB95)

To reject, alter, or depart from the truths of God is to reject, alter, and depart from the ministry of the Spirit because it is His ministry to woo us to, and to keep us in, the things of God. It takes a willful, rebellious heart to reject God, and it is that hardness of heart that both grieves and insults God because such a heart assumes it knows better than He does and can do without Him. Yet we also know that God is long-suffering and merciful—and, for that, all of us can be thankful!

JAMES

The Oil of Wisdom

There are at least five men named James listed in the New Testament: two were disciples of Jesus, and one was His half-brother. This epistle is generally accepted to have been scribed by Jesus's half-brother, who led the church in Jerusalem. He was likely converted only through a post-resurrection appearance of Jesus. (See 1 Corinthians 15:3–7.)

Sometimes called "the Proverbs of the New Testament," this epistle is practical and discusses ethics, with the Holy Spirit teaching about genuine demonstrations of faith and godly living.

HE WANTS US!

> *Or do you suppose that the Scripture is speaking to no purpose that says, The Spirit Whom He has caused to dwell in us yearns over us and He yearns for the Spirit [to be welcome] with a jealous love?*
>
> (James 4:5 AMPC)

The fact that the Spirit has such strong desire speaks again of His personality and therefore His personhood.

The jealousy of God cannot be understood from our human perspective of "I want you, so no one else can have you" but from the heavenly Father's perspective of "I want you, so no one else can harm you"! God cannot ultimately share us with anything or anyone else because there is nothing or no one else that matches Him in love. This does not mean that we must forgo having human relationships, including those of marriage and family. But God deserves our highest love and devotion. If we were shared between God and something else, God's pure love would be mingled with the impure. God's jealousy for us, unlike human jealousy, is not that we be kept to Him for His benefit but that we be kept to Him for our benefit. God's jealousy is one of wanting life for us so that we might not see death.

God sees His relationship with us as a marriage. (See, for example, Hosea 2:19–20; Isaiah 62:4; Ephesians 5:25, 27.) As in any marriage, the individuals involved should rightly expect exclusivity. God does not intend an "open marriage"—either with us...or for any of us!

THE OIL OF THE SPIRIT

> *Is anyone among you sick? Then he must call for the elders of the church and they are to pray over him, anointing him with oil in the name of the Lord; and the prayer offered in faith will restore the one who is sick, and the Lord will raise him up, and if he has committed sins, they will be forgiven him. Therefore, confess your sins to one another, and pray for one another so that you may be healed. The effective prayer of a righteous man can accomplish much.* (James 5:14–16 NASB95)

The Spirit moves in healing in a multiplicity of ways—and each one of those ways is designed to meet seeking individuals at their level of faith and need. The anointing oil is not a magical, mystical substance but a tangible reminder of the Spirit's anointing. The anointing oil is a point of contact that marks when those seeking healing may release their faith. It can be a tangible substance signifying when a believer can exercise faith that healing and blessings from God have been received. The power of God, as always, is released when faith is applied. The anointing oil is also a point of contact between the minister and the recipient—one to release the anointing, and the other to receive it.

Those whom I have seen healed under my ministry through this method have always benefited from it the most when I took time to instruct them beforehand about the significance of the oil.

1 PETER

Made Alive

The church is not supposed to fit in with the world. The church is supposed to *shine* in the world. Peter wrote this epistle to remind believers shunned by the world that theirs was a heavenly inheritance, not just an earthly one. (See 1 Peter 1:3–5.)

THE SPIRIT OF CHRIST

> *...seeking to know what person or time the Spirit of Christ within them was indicating as He predicted the sufferings of Christ and the glories to follow.* (1 Peter 1:11 NASB95)

The Old Testament prophets operated under *"the Spirit of Christ"*; that is why they were able to testify beforehand about Jesus. Prophesying *always* involves someone either testifying about things or events before they occur or proclaiming current truth under the unction of the anointing. Both Old and New Testaments function in this way with regard to prophecy. The Spirit of Christ can traverse both time and space. This means that the Holy Spirit knows things—from the past, the present, and the future—and can reveal them. It also means that the Holy Spirit can reveal what happened or is happening in one location to someone in another location. The Spirit of Christ is the Spirit of prophecy—this was the case in the Old Testament, and it is the case in the church today!

THE REWARDS OF THE SPIRIT

> *For Christ also died for sins once for all, the just for the unjust, so that He might bring us to God, having been put to death in the flesh, but made alive in the spirit* [or Spirit[13]]. (1 Peter 3:18 NASB95)

The Holy Spirit is a life-giving Spirit, so that what is "*put to death in the flesh*" is always made alive by Him!

Although this verse speaks specifically about the physical body of Jesus, the principle also applies to any of our desires or dreams that would hinder us in the plans of God for our life. The way we put our flesh-inspired desires to death is by choosing to seek God's kingdom, His ways, before we seek our own. (See Matthew 6:33.)

Succumbing to temptation usually occurs when we want the right things but in the wrong way. It is usually not the general outcomes themselves, but rather the ways in which our natural selves seek to acquire them, that God does not want for us. For example, the high of being intoxicated that results from drug or alcohol abuse harms people, but it is really a sense of freedom and weightlessness that they are seeking. Such freedom and lightness are available to us in our position in Christ when we drink freely from the river of the Spirit as the disciples did in the upper room on the day of Pentecost. God is not opposed to our having a sense of freedom and feeling uninhibited! Similarly, God is not opposed to our needs being met but is opposed to our using thievery and deceit in acquiring resources. God's remedy is not to take away our desire for more but for us to see that through the laws of seedtime and harvest (see, for example, Genesis 8:22; Luke 6:38), we can have surplus in all areas of life. When we "put to death" natural, soulish ideas and choose God's way, the Holy Spirit breathes life into us, and we are made alive in and by the Spirit.

---

13. 1 Peter 3:18 NASB95, footnote a.

As always, it takes the Spirit for us to obey the plans and ways of God. (See, for example, 1 Peter 1:2, 22.) The Spirit empowers us to obey the ways of the Spirit. In our obedience to the ways of the Spirit, we get to partake of the rewards of the Spirit, which are an earthly foretaste of the coming kingdom. (See, for example, 1 Peter 4:14.) When we choose to put to death the desires of the fleshly nature, we open the way for the life of the Spirit to be made alive and available through us.

I have found that this process can apply to simple things like yielding to the Spirit in the operation of the gifts of the Spirit. I am learning to do this and am getting better at it, but I remember when I first started operating in the word of knowledge and the word of wisdom. (See 1 Corinthians 12:8.) For me, these manifestations usually involve hearing or seeing something in the Spirit about a person or a situation. I found that to speak out what I was sensing did not just take a step of faith, but it also involved a dying to my ego for fear of being wrong! No one wants to appear wrong and be embarrassed. But when I chose to put aside my personal ego in obedience to the leading of the Spirit, I found that not only were others blessed, but I also grew in my experience of walking with the Spirit.

2 PETER

Divine Power for Life

Toward the end of his life, Peter wrote this epistle to warn believers against false teachers and apostasy. Peter emphasized adherence to apostolic teaching in contrast to the false teachers' adherence to ideas and philosophies that would ultimately be the root of Gnostic heresy. (See the next study on the books of 1, 2, and 3 John for an explanation of the Gnostics.)

The teachings of the original apostles enabled believers to develop steadfastness in their faith as they grew in their knowledge of the Lord. The apostles' constant theme was the believers' need to cultivate maturity in the things of God. The heretical teachers had a fascination with fanciful, ear-tickling theories that did nothing toward developing one's relationship with Jesus.

HIS DIVINE POWER

> *Grace and peace be multiplied to you in the knowledge of God and of Jesus our Lord; seeing that His divine power has granted to us*

> *everything pertaining to life and godliness, through the true knowledge of Him who called us by His own glory and excellence.*
>
> (2 Peter 1:2–3 NASB95)

The Holy Spirit is the *"divine power"* that gives us all things from God. He does this by illuminating our heart and mind to the knowledge of God. This is how the Holy Spirit multiplies grace and peace to us—by giving us a right knowledge of God. The more we know of God, the more of His grace and peace is made available to us! We know Him *only* as the Spirit shows Him to us through His Word. This is why Peter goes on to say the following.

MOVED BY THE HOLY SPIRIT

> *But know this first of all, that no prophecy of Scripture is a matter of one's own interpretation, for no prophecy was ever made by an act of human will, but men moved by the Holy Spirit spoke from God.*
>
> (2 Peter 1:20–21 NASB95)

A move away from Scripture is a move toward heresy. The Word of God is not to be deciphered through *"one's own interpretation,"* meaning that it takes Scripture to comprehend Scripture. The Bible is its own best commentary. Since the whole Bible was written by the inspiration of the Spirit, there will be no misunderstandings and contradictions when we look to the whole counsel of God. (See Acts 20:27.) Prophecy not being a matter of one's own interpretation also means that we do not interpret Scripture based on a personal prophecy, vision, or dream, but we let the Word determine and interpret the words, visions, and dreams we receive. Our worldview should not determine how we understand the Word of God; rather, the Word of God, because it is inspired by the Spirit of God and is God Himself speaking, must determine our worldview.

The human authors of the Bible were *"moved by the Holy Spirit."* The Greek word translated as *"moved," pheromenoi* (*Strong's*, 5342), implies being carried or borne along like a passenger on a ship. The approximately forty human authors of the Bible were controlled by the Divine Author, the Holy Spirit, yet were consciously involved, yielding to Him in the process. They did not write in a state of ecstasy—they wrote in a state of wakeful obedience!

1 JOHN, 2 JOHN, AND 3 JOHN

Taught and Empowered, Abiding and Indwelling

Like in Peter's epistles that come before these three books, and in Jude's epistle to follow, one of John's concerns in these letters was the heretical apostasy of Gnosticism that was starting to rear its ugly head in the early church.

The term *Gnostics* comes from the Greek word *gnosis*, meaning "knowledge." Gnostics believed that enlightenment and salvation were the result of mystical revelations made available to a select few. Like Peter, John responded strongly against the idea that private revelation should surpass established apostolic teaching. Later, second-century Gnostics would also come to believe that the material body was in essence evil and that only spirit was good.

In this epistle, John expertly presented a threefold aspect to the Holy Spirit's ministry:

1. THE HOLY SPIRIT TEACHES AND EMPOWERS

> *But you have an anointing from the Holy One, and all of you know the truth.* (1 John 2:20 NIV)

> *You, dear children, are from God and have overcome them, because the one who is in you is greater than the one who is in the world.*
> (1 John 4:4 NIV)

Contrasting the Spirit's anointing with Gnostic mysticism, John clearly points to the Holy Spirit as the Source of knowledge and knowing. The anointing, an aspect of the Spirit's presence, is what reveals the reality of God and all subsequent truth to us. This means that things of a divine nature are not revealed to us through mystical means but by the Holy Spirit's ministry of teaching and revealing. Believers look within, to the indwelling Spirit's presence, instead of without for guidance from God.

This contrast between the Spirit's revelation within the believer and Gnosticism is further highlighted where John states that the Spirit who is in us is *"greater than the one who is in the world."* Through the Holy Spirit, believers have access to both knowledge and power surpassing anything the world or the kingdom of darkness can offer!

2. THE HOLY SPIRIT ABIDES IN BELIEVERS

> *The one who keeps His commandments abides in Him, and He in him. We know by this that He abides in us, by the Spirit whom He has given us.* (1 John 3:24 NASB95)

> *By this we know that we abide in Him and He in us, because He has given us of His Spirit.* (1 John 4:13 NASB95)

The Spirit's abiding in us is God's stamp that we are His. This doesn't mean we will feel Him all the time, because we are not to be sense-led, nor is the Spirit of God obliged to cater to our emotions. However, it does mean that His presence is available to us because He is in us. We take that promise as we do everything else with God: by faith in His Word.

As believers, we abide in God by keeping His commands, His Word. I have noticed that even when believers miss it and don't keep God's Word, they have a "knowing" inside them that they have settled for less. That should be a sign that they actually are believers. If they were not believers, they would not be concerned about it! Believers know when they do wrong because they are alive to God, have the Spirit living inside them, and know right from wrong. Again, that is one of the signs that we have the seal of the Spirit. So, the Spirit is both a sign and a seal to the believer.

3. THE HOLY SPIRIT TESTIFIES OF JESUS

> *By this you know the Spirit of God: every spirit that confesses that Jesus Christ has come in the flesh is from God.* (1 John 4:2 NASB95, ESV)

> *This is the One who came by water and blood, Jesus Christ; not with the water only, but with the water and with the blood. It is the Spirit who testifies, because the Spirit is the truth. For there are three that testify: the Spirit and the water and the blood; and the three are in agreement.* (1 John 5:6–8 NASB95)

Not only can we know that we have the seal of the Spirit in us, keeping us in the ways of God, but John goes on to inform us that we have a continual Testifier in our life, affirming that Jesus is the One True Way. When the Spirit speaks, He will not deny Christ in personhood, word, or deed. Any prophecy, dream, vision, or prophet that says otherwise can immediately be identified as false.

I have always thought that our acknowledging Jesus as Lord requires a continual Testifier because the circumstances of life and the enemy continually try to get us to deny His lordship. In testifying that Jesus is Lord, the Spirit also testifies that Jesus is Healer when a negative doctor's report comes in. When you receive a report that is contrary to what the Word promises you of "life, and life more abundantly" (see John 10:10 NKJV), remember to let the Spirit testify to you of all that Jesus can do to change that report!

In 2 and 3 John, the apostle continues to urge believers to follow God's commandments and walk in the truth. And he emphasizes, "*Beloved, I pray that you may prosper in all things and be in health, just as your soul prospers*" (3 John 2 NKJV). To relegate this statement to some casual greeting from John to Gaius, the original recipient of the letter, as some have suggested, would be to degrade at least this portion of the Holy Scriptures to mere human civility. But since that was not the case, this was therefore a Spirit-inspired record that God wants us to prosper, to do well, in all areas of life and to have health, all in proportion to our soul prospering.

JUDE

Built Up

Jude is identified as the *"brother of James"* (Jude 1:1, various translations), linking him to both James the leader of the church in Jerusalem and Jesus, since James was the Lord's half-brother.

Written with a sense of urgency, the book of Jude sounds an alert, warning against false teachers.

WHO ARE FALSE TEACHERS?

> *These are the ones who are [agitators] causing divisions—worldly-minded [secular, unspiritual, carnal, merely sensual—unsaved], devoid of the Spirit.* (Jude 1:19 AMP)

Jude classifies false teachers in a three-step process:

First, false teachers are *"merely sensual,"* meaning they teach and live from the human sense realm instead of from the Word-ruled Spirit realm.

Second, false teachers cause divisions because they seek to separate various believers from the rest of the body of Christ through their false teaching, turning them away from the orthodoxy of true apostolic teaching and toward alternate versions of Jesus and His teachings.

Third, false teachers are simply those who are *"devoid of"* the Spirit. Being devoid of the Spirit is what opens false teachers up to the previous two characteristics: living sensually and causing division.

Another way to look at it is that believers have the Spirit, while false teachers do not!

THE SPIRIT BUILDS US UP

> *But you, dear friends, must build each other up in your most holy faith, pray in the power of the Holy Spirit....* (Jude 1:20 NLT)

It should surprise none of us that being built up in the faith is tied to prayer. But it is not just regular praying from our minds that builds us up—it is praying in the Holy Spirit! Remember that praying in the Spirit involves more than just speaking and praying in tongues. Praying in the Spirit is praying from the realm of the Spirit. This means that we are transported from this natural, physical realm and made more aware of being in the Spirit than we are of being in the physical world. In this higher realm in the Spirit, we can speak God's words, praying either in tongues or in our natural language. Just as we can normally speak in our natural language or in tongues at will, anytime, we can do the same when we are in the Spirit. Being in the Spirit should not just be thought of as being in an ecstatic state but rather as being in a place where our mind is stilled, and we are aware of God's presence more than we are of our surroundings. One of the fastest ways to get in the Spirit is to start out by praying or singing in tongues because this immediately connects us to the Spirit and stills our mind, allowing for an easier awareness of the Spirit realm.

I will add that it is only by praying in the Spirit that we are built up in our faith. Praying soul-led prayers does not build our spirit-man. It takes our spirit-man praying by the Holy Spirit, in the Spirit, to build us up. As I wrote earlier, Paul prayed much in tongues and was the recipient of revelation that we are still feeding off today in his epistles!

REVELATION

What the Spirit Is Saying

What God starts with mankind in Genesis, He concludes in Revelation. Revelation is the grand finale of God's master plan for the purpose and redemption of humanity! Yet Revelation is not just a book of endings; it is really a book of new beginnings.

Exiled by the evil emperor Domitian, John, the author of this book, received this revelation on the small, desolate island of Patmos. John was the last of the original apostles; he survived the exile and returned to Ephesus after Domitian's death.

The word *revelation* comes from the Greek word *apocalyptus*, meaning "to unveil and make clear," which is the exact opposite of what many believers think of this book! As with everything else concerning God, it is vital that we not let culture and society determine our view of the Word but rather let the Spirit, through the Word, speak and clarify it. One reason the enemy wants us to stay away from the book of Revelation is that this is the *only* book in Scripture that directly promises a blessing to those who read it. (See Revelation 1:3.)

Some people have mistaken the title of this book to be "Revelations"—plural—when it is really the book of *Revelation*—singular. This book is *not* a revelation about the Antichrist, the mark of the beast, the tribulation, or the one-world government. This is a book about the revelation of Jesus Christ in all His majesty and glory. (See Revelation 1:1.) Like everything else about us, life looks brighter when we filter it through the lens of Jesus!

This book's central message is *"Hallelujah! For the Lord our God, the Almighty, reigns"* (Revelation 19:6 NASB95). Revelation is a book of final victory over all the works of the enemy and the restoration of all that has been lost since the garden of Eden.

Since the Holy Spirit is God Himself, He possesses all the characteristics of divinity: He is omniscient, or all-knowing; omnipotent, or all-powerful; and omnipresent, or ever present, everywhere, all the time. There never has been—nor will there ever be—a season of time without the Holy Spirit's presence on the earth.

This may be clearly seen throughout Revelation. John did not just experience a spectacular encounter of seeing in the Spirit realm by the power of the Holy Spirit; the prophetic visions that he saw unfolding all dramatically demonstrated that the Holy Spirit's activity was to be continually manifest among mankind. Every miracle, every advance of the kingdom of God, and the ultimate defeat of death and Satan are all demonstrations of the Spirit's activity in the natural and spiritual realms.

THE SEVEN SPIRITS OF GOD

Unique to Revelation, the Holy Spirit is described four times as *"the seven Spirits"* or *"the Seven Spirits of God"* (Revelation 1:4; 3:1; 4:5; 5:6, various translations). Some Bible versions translate this term as the *"sevenfold Spirit of God."* Isaiah had described seven aspects of the Spirit (see Isaiah 11:2), but it is in Revelation that they are identified collectively as the seven Spirits of God. This alone shows the multifaceted ministry of the Spirit! Of course, the number seven is biblically associated with completeness and, in particular, when referencing God, perfection. So, the phrase "seven Spirits of God" speaks to us of the Spirit's divine perfection in form and manifestation.

The seven Spirits are described as being "before God's throne" (see Revelation 1:4; 4:5), while also being "seven eyes of the Lamb" (see Revelation 5:6). This shows us the comprehensive cohesiveness of the Trinity. The Father, the Son, and the Holy Spirit are one in essence, three in person. And we see this divine unity in glorious symphony in the book of Revelation!

HEAR WHAT HE SAYS

Revelation 2 and 3 contain seven letters, or epistles, of Jesus to seven churches. In each letter, He demonstrates that He intimately knows the actual goings-on of each church. Looking beyond the challenges they face and the facades they maintain, He commends and chastises them accordingly. It always sobers me when I read these chapters. Jesus knows us, the church, our motives and actions—in detail! He actually walks among us in our communities and in our gatherings. Not only does this sober me, but it has also caused me to pause on many an occasion to prayerfully ponder my thoughts and actions in life and ministry. Jesus is not in a faraway place. He is with us in the here and now!

Each of these seven letters contains the command, *"He who has an ear, let him hear what the Spirit says to the churches"* (Revelation 2:7, 11, 17, 29; 3:6, 13, 22, various translations). Not only are we believers to hear and obey the Word, but we are also to hear and obey the Spirit. To accurately hear the Word, we must hear the Spirit, because it is the Spirit who amplifies and clarifies the Word to us.

It is important for us to hear what the Spirit is saying to the church at large, but it is especially important for each local congregation to hear what the Spirit is saying to them individually. Each local church, planted and raised up by God, has a specific purpose and flow in the Spirit. Each local congregation has a specific supply for the larger body of Christ. Some local churches are raised up to bring a supply of worship, others are raised up to bring a supply of teaching, and still others are raised up to supply people and resources to fulfill a missions mandate. All churches should have all these elements as part of their local church culture, but there will be certain areas in which each congregation is stronger and more active. This is the principle of every joint supplying what is needed. (See Ephesians 4:16.)

No one church should aim to be like any other church because each has a specific purpose. Churches find their purpose like individuals do: by prayer and seeking the Lord...by hearing what the Spirit is saying!

AN EAR FOR HIM

Speaking of hearing, every instance in the Old Testament and the Gospels where we are told to listen, we are told to use both our ears. For example, we read in Matthew 11:15 (various translations), *"He who has ears to hear, let him hear."* In Jeremiah 5:21 (NASB95), the people were chastised in this way: *"Now hear this, O foolish and senseless people, who have eyes but do not see; who have ears but do not hear."* However, in each of the seven letters in Revelation 2 and 3, we are told, *"He who has* ***an ear****, let him hear what the Spirit says to the churches."*

In these times in which we live, it is no longer feasible for us to just lie back and casually listen to God. Because of the intensity of the seasons of God, we have to lean close, press in, and listen with our hearing ear, just as we do when we are in a deep conversation with someone, and they are about to tell us a particularly interesting bit of information.

We need to press in to the Spirit to hear what He has to say to us about the times in which we live!

THE TESTIMONY OF JESUS

For the testimony of Jesus is the spirit of prophecy.
(Revelation 19:10, various translations)

The spirit of prophecy is a function of the Holy Spirit. Prophecy is one of the Spirit's means of communicating and bringing revelation to us and through us. True prophecy *always* testifies of Jesus and the complete work of the cross. Visions, dreams, and visitations from God or divinely sent angelic beings are all forms of prophecy, and they should all point us to Jesus.

I rejoice that we live in a time when there is an abundance of spiritual manifestations and communications from the Spirit. I truly believe it is God's plan that spiritual gifts be manifested in and through the life of the believer and in the local church. However, I am sometimes disturbed and dismayed by what I hear some people claim to be messages or experiences from the Spirit that are clearly not—they are lacking both in scriptural soundness and in discipleship formation. Spiritual experiences are not for the purpose of tickling our ears but to bring us to Jesus and to develop us as disciples!

Since all true forms of prophecy are from the Holy Spirit, they will carry an element of holiness and reverence. As emphasized throughout this book, the Spirit is not just the Spirit...He is the *Holy* Spirit!

The book of Revelation speaks of a time when there will be much spiritual deception and confusion. It is vital that we believers recognize the gold of the Spirit over the brass of the world and the enemy.

AN INVITATION

> *The Spirit and the bride say, "Come." And let the one who hears say, "Come." And let the one who is thirsty come; let the one who wishes take the water of life without cost.* (Revelation 22:17 NASB95)

The Spirit, through the church, is continually beckoning all people to come into the Father's embrace! This has been the Spirit's call since the Old Testament, and it has continued all the way through the New Testament. The Spirit in Revelation presents this call once again at the closing of the age. The Spirit issues the call, and it is the body of Christ that amplifies it so that everyone can hear this invitation.

I see this as a twofold invitation: First, it is a call to Calvary, where mankind can find salvation. Second, it is a call to the upper room, to receive an indwelling empowerment of the Spirit.

This lovingly urgent invitation requires a response from us. When we say yes to God, all of heaven's resources become available to us. We are called to be sons and daughters of the Most High. This is a call that both you and I must respond to!

ABOUT THE AUTHOR

Dr. James Tan is a visionary leader who declares the goodness of God and the reality of the Spirit internationally to a new generation of believers. Called to pioneer and establish a standard of both the Word and the Spirit, he ministers scriptural insights while making room for demonstrations of the Holy Spirit to bless and empower believers. Teaching cross-culturally and across denominational lines, James is a voice and a mentor to a growing number of churches and ministries around the world. He is the author of *Releasing the Anointing: Walking in the Flow and Power of the Holy Spirit* and *Releasing the Miraculous: Walking in All Nine Gifts of the Holy Spirit*.